In the Name of God

Blackwell Public Philosophy
Edited by Michael Boylan, Marymount University

In a world of 24-hour news cycles and increasingly specialized knowledge, the Blackwell Public Philosophy series takes seriously the idea that there is a need and demand for engaging and thoughtful discussion of topics of broad public importance. Philosophy itself is historically grounded in the public square, bringing people together to try to understand the various issues that shape their lives and give them meaning. This "love of wisdom" – the essence of philosophy – lies at the heart of the series. Written in an accessible, jargon-free manner by internationally renowned authors, each book is an invitation to the world beyond newsflashes and soundbites and into public wisdom.

For further information about individual titles in the series, supplementary material, and regular updates, visit www.wiley.com/go/bpp

In the Name of God

The Evolutionary Origins of Religious Ethics and Violence

John Teehan

A John Wiley & Sons, Ltd., Publication

Blackwell Publishing was acquired by John Wiley & Sons in February 2007. Blackwell's publishing program has been merged with Wiley's global Scientific, Technical, and Medical business to form Wiley-Blackwell.

Registered Office
John Wiley & Sons Ltd, The Atrium, Southern Gate, Chichester, West Sussex, PO19 8SQ, United Kingdom

Editorial Offices
350 Main Street, Malden, MA 02148-5020, USA
9600 Garsington Road, Oxford, OX4 2DQ, UK
The Atrium, Southern Gate, Chichester, West Sussex, PO19 8SQ, UK

For details of our global editorial offices, for customer services, and for information about how to apply for permission to reuse the copyright material in this book please see our website at www.wiley.com/wiley-blackwell.

Library of Congress Cataloging-in-Publication Data

Teehan, John.
 In the name of God : the evolutionary origins of religious ethics and violence / John Teehan.
     p. cm. – (Blackwell public philosophy series)
   Includes bibliographical references and index.
   ISBN 978-1-4051-8382-6 (hardcover : alk. paper) – ISBN 978-1-4051-8381-9 (pbk. : alk. paper)   1. Religious ethics.   2. Violence–Religious aspects.   3. Psychology, Religious.   4. Evolutionary psychology.   5. Cognitive psychology.   I. Title.
   BJ1188.T44 2010
   205.01′9–dc22

                                                                           2009041467

A catalogue record for this book is available from the British Library.

Set in 10/12pt Sabon by Toppan Best-set Premedia Limited
Printed in Singapore by Ho Printing Singapore Pte Ltd

1   2010

To Patricia,
who makes everything I do possible

and

To Megan and Daniel,
who make everything I do worthwhile

CONTENTS

ACKNOWLEDGMENTS

This work is the end result of years of writing and speaking on these topics. Some of the basic ideas were first published as "The Evolution of Religious Ethics" in *Free Inquiry* 25, no. 4 (June/July 2005), and then were expanded upon in "The Evolutionary Basis of Religious Ethics" in *Zygon: Journal of Religion and Science* 41/3 (September 2006): 747–774. Comments and suggestions provided during the peer review process certainly contributed to refining those earlier musings.

Also important to the development of my thinking on these issues was the feedback I received at the numerous conferences where different stages of the book took shape. Conversations with Robert Hinde at the Religion, Cognitive Psychology and Evolutionary Psychology Conference, sponsored by the New England Institute, were not only enjoyable but shaped some of the discussions in Chapter 6. The Moral Brain: Evolutionary and Neuro-scientific Perspectives Conference, at Ghent University, Belgium, directed by Johan Braeckman and Jan Verplaetse, was a wonderful opportunity to explore the possible impact of neuroscience on religious psychology, and conversations with Adrian Raine, William Casebeer and Randolph Nesse all raised questions that spurred me to further refine my thinking.

I also benefited greatly from an academic leave from Hofstra University which allowed me to spend a semester studying the Law and the Hebrew Bible, with Danna Nolan Fewell at Drew University. That course of study, along with Danna's aid in negotiating the voluminous literature on the topic, and her comments on the material that became Chapter 3, allowed me to wade more confidently into the world of Ancient Judaism, and limited whatever missteps I may have taken.

During the writing of the book I received more support than I can acknowledge. Arthur Dobrin was a constant source of encouragement throughout the long gestation period of this work. Stephanie Cobb not only provided an insightful review of my writing on Christianity, but was an invaluable source of support throughout the final stages of the project. I need to thank Stan Nevins for starting me on the philosophical path that brought me here. I also owe a debt of gratitude to Patrick Alexander, Balbinder Bhogal, Ann Burlein, Julie Byrne, Steven Clarke, Hank Davis, Chris DiCarlo, Warren Frisina, Terry Godlove, Deena Grant, Stewart Guthrie, Joseph Henrich, James Levy, Linda Longmire, Pete Richerson, William Rottschaefer, Azim Shariff, David Livingstone Smith, and Tim Smith, for their comments on various sections, chapters, and ideas in this work; an additional thanks to Stewart Guthrie for his help in working through some of the issues in Chapter 2. The flaws that remain in this book are of course mine, but they would have been embarrassingly greater without these contributions.

I also benefited from the comments provided by various readers at Wiley-Blackwell, and I greatly appreciate the editorial support and advice that Jeff Dean provided along each stage of development; this helped me turn an undisciplined manuscript into a book.

I also owe more thanks than I can express to my wife, Patricia, without whose support, encouragement, and great patience, this book would not have been written.

INTRODUCTION: EVOLUTION AND MIND

In the distant future I see open fields for far more important researches. Psychology will be based on a new foundation, that of the necessary acquirement of each mental power and capacity by gradation. Light will be thrown on the origin of man and his history. (Charles Darwin, 1859)

Charles Darwin showed great restraint in extending the process of natural selection to the human animal. He clearly saw there was nothing to prevent an application of the evolutionary process to the history of human beings, but Darwin was a cautious man and not prone to making claims that outran the available evidence. Still, he could see that his theory had the potential to reform the human sciences radically. What makes the above quotation from *On the Origin of Species* so prescient is that in 1859 psychology had just taken its first steps toward becoming an empirical discipline. It was then barely distinguishable from philosophic speculation on the mind, on the one hand, and the crude, initial research into brain physiology, on the other. Yet Darwin foresaw the possibility of approaching the study of the human mind from a whole new perspective. Rather than treat the mind as some sort of disembodied "thinking thing," as Descartes termed it, that transcended the natural world, Darwin recognized a much more intimate integration of mental powers and the brain. By situating the mind in nature it too could be conceived of as a product of natural selection.

This approach to psychology was immediately tantalizing to nineteenth-century pioneers of the new discipline. However, the move toward first Freudian and then behaviorist psychological paradigms forestalled the full application of the Darwinian method to the human mind – even though major figures in both of these traditions saw themselves as developing a naturalistic theory of mind that had some connection to evolution, at least as they understood evolution. There were other efforts to bring psychology in line with evolutionary theory, but it really was not until the 1970s, with the publication of E. O. Wilson's seminal work, *Sociobiology: A New Synthesis*, that the application of Darwinian processes to animal behavior, including the human animal, became a full-fledged research project. Wilson's work set off almost as much controversy as did Darwin's, as people responded to what they perceived to be the biological determinism inherent in the approach.

We need not rehearse the various stages of this controversy – a controversy that still rages in one form or another. What we are interested in here is that one result of the efforts to refine and improve the theoretical approach set out in Wilson's work was the emergence of a new discipline: evolutionary psychology. Here, at last, we find Darwin's prediction coming to fruition.

The foundational premise of evolutionary psychology is that behavior, belief, emotions, thinking, and feeling are all functions of a fully embodied brain. As the brain is a physical organ, it, like all other physical organs, has an evolutionary history. The brain that we have today is the product of evolutionary processes that shaped this organ in response to environmental selection pressures. Evolution, as we know, does not work by making dramatic, wholesale changes in organs or organisms. It works in slow, piecemeal fashion, shaping the physical structure on a strictly "as needed" and "as far as the materials already available will allow" basis. Given this view of brain evolution we can expect the brain to be a composite organ, whose constituent parts and powers arose in response to problems that needed to be addressed in order for humans to survive and reproduce successfully. If this is accurate, then the brain we work with today is a collection of task-oriented, problem-solving mental tools – tools, however, that were designed to respond to an ancient environment. Evolutionary psychologists believe that this evolutionary history has left its marks on our contemporary behavioral and cognitive patterns. Therefore, to understand how the mind works today we need to try to understand what tasks it needed to solve in order to allow our ancestors to survive.

This view of human nature runs directly at odds with two theories that continue to exert influence on psychology. One is the "rational actor model," in which humans are conceptualized to be motivated by a rational maximization of their own interests. As you might imagine, this is a model favored by many economists. The other view conceives of the human mind as a "blank slate," waiting for experience to write upon it. In this view, the mind is a general purpose intellectual device that is maximally flexible in response to the directions of culture. Both of these views are undermined by evolutionary psychology, which holds that the mind is populated by a number of cognitive and emotional predispositions that channel the input from the environment into identifiable cognitive and behavioral patterns,

patterns that are now being revealed by the cognitive sciences. These evolved patterns do demonstrate a kind of rationality – if we understand them as ultimately responses to evolutionary challenges – but this is not the same thing as acting rationally, as might be predicted by the rational actor model. We will have ample opportunity to demonstrate that an evolutionary approach to human behavior is a better explanation and predictor of that behavior than a rational model, as there is a growing body of literature, much of it conducted by economists, to support this claim.

More controversial, and continually contentious, is the proposition that the human mind comes prepackaged, as it were, with a series of mental tools. These mental tools are expressed differently in different environments, but by their very existence they overthrow the blank slate view of human nature. Now, part of the controversy stems from a healthy debate over just what the evidence can support. That there is such a debate, and that it is often heated, is to be expected in response to such a relatively new discipline, and one that treads on so much turf claimed by other disciplines. However, it is undeniable that part of the heat in this debate is generated by the fact that this view of human nature – the very idea that there might be a human nature – smacks up against some strongly held political, moral, religious, and ideological positions.

I will admit up front that I find the evidence and the arguments in favor of an evolutionary psychology completely persuasive. If we want to develop a truly scientific study of the mind, and of human behavior, then we must start with the premise that these can be studied naturalistically. If we work with that premise, known as methodological naturalism, then we must apply the best theory we have for explaining the living world, and that is evolutionary biology. Now, as many will be eager to point out, methodological naturalism does not entail metaphysical naturalism. Methodological naturalism says that science must take as its proper domain only those objects that can be studied through empirical means – that is, objects that are part of the natural, physical universe. Therefore, if we are to develop a scientific psychology we must seek to understand the mind as part of the natural, physical universe. Metaphysical naturalism says that the only things that exist are things that are part of the natural, physical universe. In that case there can be nothing more to the mind than what can be understood in physical terms. This metaphysics also rules out religious concepts such as an immaterial soul and gods.

Obviously, making a distinction between the two is important, particularly in a work about religion. When it is said that methodological naturalism does not entail metaphysical naturalism, this means that just because science can work only with natural objects it does not follow that there are no non-natural, or supernatural, entities. There may in fact be non-natural realities that are beyond the scope of science. I accept this distinction without any qualms. Nothing I say in the following chapters should be taken to entail that there is no God. But the methodological approach I employ requires that we bracket any commitment to the existence of such a being. I believe this is also required of a scientific approach. We should apply the methods of science as rigorously and extensively as we can. Once this is accomplished, then it is fitting to ask how the findings of science can be reconciled (or not) with belief in God. I agree that no matter how effective science may be in explaining the universe naturalistically, it does not logically exclude the possibility of a non-natural realm and/or supernatural entities. However, I do believe that the findings of the sciences – physical, social, and historical – can impose constraints on what we may claim about such non-natural possibilities.

The thesis this book intends to develop and defend is that evolution has designed the human mind in such a way that we possess a set of mental tools that shape our moralities and our religions. More specifically, I contend that religious moral traditions are cultural expressions of underlying cognitive and emotional pre-dispositions that are the products of evolutionary processes. They evolved because they helped us in our struggle to survive and reproduce. In effect, we all possess common moral and religious cognitive frameworks that give rise to identifiable patterns in our moral religious traditions. This thesis does not deny the great cultural diversity in both morality and religion found throughout the world, and throughout history, nor does it deny the possibility for true moral innovation. However, it does imply that the power of culture to shape human behavior, while impressive, is limited – and in fact, as we shall see, there is good evidence to support the claim that the human ability to create culture is itself a result of evolved mental tools. It also implies that effecting a lasting moral innovation is harder than we imagine.

I believe that the project of uncovering the evolved psychology beneath religious morality is not merely an academic project, because religion is not merely an academic subject. Religion is one of the most powerful forces in human history, and its power makes itself known in ways both dramatic and intimate in our world today; unfortunately, the impact of religion is often divisive and violent. If we want to truly understand religion's ability to influence human events, we need to grasp its psychological bases, and to take a scientific approach to religious psychology means using our best theories of how the mind works.

Chapter 1 sets out the bases of our evolved moral psychology. In it I try to describe how evolution has shaped the cognitive and emotional predispositions that give rise to morality. I do not claim to be doing anything original in this chapter, and those well versed in the literature may want to skim through it. But what I am attempting in Chapter 1 is not simply to provide an introduction to the uninitiated (although I am trying to do that) but also to pull together some of the best and most recent research from evolutionary psychology, cognitive psychology, behavioral economics, and neuroscience – disciplines all grounded in an evolutionary context, and which together constitute cognitive science – and organize it in a way that presents a cognitive framework for human morality. While this discussion is far from exhaustive, it is rather detailed. I beg the reader's patience, but the topic is complex and I believe we need a solid foundation in moral psychology in order to proceed with our study.

With that moral framework established, in Chapter 2 I turn to the evolutionary bases of religious belief. I am fully aware that talk of a scientific theory of religion will raise suspicion in scores of religious studies professionals that I am going to move forward with a conception of religion lacking in nuance and sophistication. I am certainly going to try to avoid that. However, within the discipline of religious studies the very term "religion" is passionately contested. An important aspect of this contestation is the insistence that "religion" is itself a relatively recent concept, and one shaped by Western sensibilities and experiences. To apply this term to the experiences of people not part of that modern, Western worldview is a problematic move, even more so when we try to apply it to ancient peoples. What complicates things even more is that even within a Western perspective "religion" denotes such a wide range of experiences, practices, beliefs, and traditions that we must be very careful not to reduce the richness of religion by privileging any one aspect of it. Furthermore, even within a religious tradition, how that tradition will be understood and lived by its various adherents is so varied that it is not possible to identify a core set of elements that constitutes any particular religion. In other words, there is no essence to a particular religious tradition that allows us to say that, for example, "this" is real or true Christianity.

I recognize the worth of all these points. Discussions of religion – in public debates and even in books by respected intellectuals and supposed religious authorities – often work with a simplified or overly generalized conception of religion, and this is an obstacle to a clear understanding of the nature and workings of religion. In my discussion of religion I hope to clarify and qualify what I am referring to with enough nuance to do justice to the topic. I do not expect this to satisfy everyone. But I believe that an attitude of intellectual generosity is required of readers on any complicated topic – and by this I mean we must be careful not to read too much of our own theoretical presuppositions into the work in front of us. This does not mean we should not bring a theoretically informed reading to the text, but rather we should be careful of conjuring windmills to battle. Whether or not what I refer to with the term "religion" or "religious" matches your understanding of the term, what is really at stake is not how we use terms but the phenomena at hand.

For example, I focus largely on religious texts and I work with the premise that these texts are accorded a moral authority that shapes behavior. Now, this is obviously not true for all believers, nor is it an equally relevant claim for all religious traditions, but it is true that the texts have been accorded moral authority and have been used to shape behavior, and that they continue to do so. This is the point that is important for my purposes. I make no larger claims about the centrality of the texts to behavior or of belief to religion. The fact that religious beliefs play a role in shaping behavior, for at least some people, and that religious texts shape belief, for at least some people, is I believe a sufficiently significant fact in its own right to justify a serious evaluation.

So, in Chapter 2 I bring together some of the cutting-edge research on religion coming out of the cognitive sciences. My focus is on the evolution of cognitive predispositions that give rise to belief in gods and to beliefs about gods. As with Chapter 1 the contribution of this chapter is not to present any original findings but to organize the fascinating work being done on this subject into a serviceable model of the cognitive framework for god-beliefs. The significant event for the purposes of this book is that the framework for our morality and the framework for god-beliefs, under certain conditions, become entwined, so to speak, and give rise to belief in gods as moral agents – parties interested in the moral affairs of humans – who can assume the roles of moral legislator and moral enforcer. This underlies the development of religious moral traditions.

Having set out the framework for religious moral traditions, I then set out to detect the elements of these evolved cognitive frameworks within diverse religious traditions. In Chapter 3 I test this thesis by applying an evolutionary analysis to Judaism, specifically, to Judaic ethics as expressed in the Mosaic Law. I first explore the character of Yahweh, as portrayed in the Hebrew Bible, to see how this portrayal fits the evolved framework for god-beliefs, and then I examine how the moral law of Yahweh follows the contours set out by our evolved moral psychology.

In Chapter 4 I engage in the same exercise but look at Christianity. Here the focus is the character of Christ, as a divine being whose portrayal fits within the framework for god-beliefs, and the moral teachings of Christ, as set out in the Gospels and elaborated on in the letters of Paul. Christianity is an important test case because it has been claimed that Christian ethics are an explicit repudiation of the type of ethics that flows from evolutionary sources. An evolved morality makes reciprocation a key moral motivation and focuses special moral concern on those in one's community; Christ advocated an ethics in which one is to do good without thought of reward, and which extends to the whole human race. Such an ethics, it is held, could not have evolved. So, the key challenge in Chapter 4 is to demonstrate how even Christ's teachings fit within an evolutionary framework.

In Chapter 5 I turn to the grave problem of religious violence. This is a deeply troubling phenomenon for us all, but it is a particularly difficult one for believers to have to face. Religion is often presented as a force for good in the world, and yet it is too often implicated in some of the greatest evils of which humans are capable. A popular, and understandable, strategy for reconciling these facts is to exonerate religion by distancing it from the violence done in its name, to shift the focus to the individuals who abuse religion by twisting its good teachings to their own corrupt ends. I argue that this move is unwarranted. As we develop an insight into our evolved religious moral psychology, we will see that the same processes that generate the pro-social, constructive morality found in religion also generate prejudice and violence. It is not a question of whether religion, or any particular religion, is peace-loving or violent; they are both, inherently. The issue then is to understand the conditions that trigger one or the other response. I seek to explicate this position by again reading the religious texts of Judaism and Christianity from an evolutionary perspective.

I conclude this chapter applying the insights we have gained into religious violence to a case study: the 9/11 terrorist attacks and the response to them. The purpose of this exercise is to argue that the evolved psychology that gave rise to religious texts is not something we outgrow. We can see it at work in the moral mindset of the major players involved in 9/11, both the terrorists and the President. To make this case I first spend some time showing how our evolved moral and religious frameworks structure Islam, as well as Judaism and Christianity. This unfortunately is a comparatively brief and concise evaluation, given limitations in time, and the author's expertise, but sufficient, I believe, to make the case that the thesis of this book is applicable to all three monotheistic traditions. (Whether it is applicable to non-Western, religious traditions must be left an open question, although my sense is that it is, although the details of the analysis would likely be quite different.)

In the sixth and final chapter I try to elucidate some of the lessons to be gained from the evolutionary analysis of religion, ethics, and violence. I consider what this analysis says about the nature and authority of religious morality, as well as what it says about the possibility of doing without religion. I conclude by trying to draw out some practical, albeit general proposals about how we might use an evolutionary understanding of religion to respond to the dangers of religious violence, and what might be the prospects for developing a moral system that accesses the best that religions can offer, while avoiding the worst.

Before proceeding I want to make one more point about the project I am engaged in, that is, reading religious texts, in this case the Bible, from an evolutionary perspective. An evolutionary reading of these texts does not necessarily conflict with the readings of other hermeneutical approaches; in fact it often is consistent with other approaches, although at other times it may suggest a very different understanding. But even in those instances of compatibility, an evolutionary perspective can make a contribution by uncovering the psychological processes that generate particular social and behavioral patterns that find expression in religious texts and that shape the production of the texts we have. What I am presenting, but not claiming to originate, is a new method of Biblical criticism that employs the methods and conclusions of the cognitive sciences, a cognitive-critical method for textual analysis that may be considered an extension of the historical-critical methodologies.

The developing cognitive sciences, grounded in sound evolutionary thinking, are opening up a new phase in our study of religion. I believe the frameworks set out in this book allow us to gain insight into the workings of the religious mind and offer a fresh perspective on religious texts that may allow us to better understand the complexities and contradictions we find throughout these texts. It is my hope that this new perspective on religion may be translated into a more effective response to the roles religion plays in the world today.

1 | THE EVOLUTION OF MORALITY

Many lands saw Zarathustra, and many peoples: thus he discovered the good and bad of many peoples. No greater power did Zarathustra find on earth than good and bad. No people could live without first valuing; if a people will maintain itself, however, it must not value as its neighbour valueth. (Friedrich Nietzsche[1])

Setting the Task

Evolution via natural selection is a fairly simple, straightforward process. You may be forgiven if you find this strange given all the fireworks surrounding public discussions of evolution, as well as the confused caricatures offered by its foes.[2] But, in fact, it is a fairly simple, straightforward process. Ernst Mayer commented that Darwin's theory of natural selection is the conclusion of "one long argument," as Darwin himself put it, and is based on three uncontroversial principles – inheritance, variation, and competition – that are simple to state and comprehend:[3]

Inheritance: Offspring tend to inherit the characteristics of their parents.
Variation: Offspring will also vary from their parents and from their siblings. In addition, individuals from different families and different species also vary.
Competition: Life is a competition for limited resources in which it is not possible for all individuals to succeed. Not all individuals can reproduce and have offspring who themselves successfully reproduce.

From these simple observations Darwin deduced the principle of natural selection: *variations* that provide an advantage in the *competition* for resources tend to be passed on (*inheritance*) to the next generation.

The corollary to this is that those variations that are not advantageous may not be passed on. "Advantageous" is a relative term. In evolution, a trait provides an advantage if it contributes to an individual surviving to the age of reproduction and reproducing successfully. Success is measured in terms of differential reproduction: which variation(s) allows an individual to out-reproduce its competitors. In the next generation the genes of the successful reproducers will be better represented than those of less successful reproducers. This accumulation of this differential reproductive success, carried out generation after generation, is evolution.

The strength of Darwin's theory is not simply the overwhelming evidence that supports it, evidence supplied by diverse fields such as genetics, microbiology, anthropology, ethology, botany, and paleontology, but also the undeniable logic of the argument. Daniel Dennett argues that what Darwin discovered is the algorithm of natural history. As Dennett puts it, "An algorithm is a certain sort of formal process that can be counted on – logically – to yield a certain sort of result whenever it is 'run' or instantiated."[4] Given that there is differential reproduction (not all individuals will be equally fecund) *and* that certain traits contribute to successful reproduction, *and* that parents pass their traits to their offspring, it follows *necessarily* that those traits will be better represented in the next generation. That Darwin saw this when no one else had is the basis of his genius.

What is not quite so obvious is just how much can be explained by this process of natural selection. What we know, and Darwin did not, is that inheritance works by passing genes from one generation to the next. Genes underlie traits that lead to successful reproduction and get passed on to the next generation. Evolutionary change is driven by differential representation of genes in the gene pool, and here we can begin to see the challenge to an evolutionary account of morality. What makes for a successful gene? In strict evolutionary terms a successful gene is one that gets more copies of itself into the next generation – that's it. Richard Dawkins sets it out as follows:

> Genes are competing directly with their alleles for survival, since their alleles in the gene pool are rivals for their slot on the chromosomes of future generations. Any gene that behaves in such a way as to increase its own survival chances in the gene pool at the expense of its alleles will, by definition, tautologously, tend to survive. The gene is the basic unit of selfishness.[5]

Before proceeding we need to be clear on the use of language when discussing genes and evolution. Using metaphors is almost unavoidable when discussing these issues (or almost any issue, really), particularly if we want to avoid overly technical and tedious qualifications every time the issues come up. Let it be stated here: Genes do not behave selfishly, or morally, or in any other way. Genes encode the directions for the production of proteins, which are the material for the construction of phenotypic structures, such as bodies and brains, which do all the behaving. In more technical language, to say that a gene is "selfish" is to say that it leads to conditions that tend to make its own reproduction more likely than that of an alternative gene.[6]

Here is the problem for an evolutionary account of morality: If successful genes are "selfish" genes, then it seems to follow that these genes will lead to organisms and traits that are also "selfish." After all, it is the behavior of the organism that determines whether its genes succeed. Organisms should behave in ways that promote their own reproductive success – and this is what we find throughout the living world. However, in certain species this "selfishness" is tempered by cooperative behavior, and cooperation needs to be explained. Some cooperative behavior can be explained as mutualism. For example, you and I join together to hunt an animal neither of us could kill alone. We share the risks and then we share the meat. Neither of us is really making a sacrifice for the other, and we can explain this strictly in terms of self-interest. But not all cooperation is like this; take, for example, fighting off a predator. If a dangerous animal attacks us we will be better able to defeat it if we join together and share the risks. I, however, would be better off allowing you to fight the animal by yourself and assume all the risks, while I run for safety. But perhaps I am not fast enough to get away and my only chance is to stay and fight, so I join forces with you. In that case, why would you stay and assume the risks instead of running for safety? Remember the old joke about two friends confronted by a bear in the woods. One turns to the other and asks, "What should we do?" The other says, "Run." The first friend then asks, "Do you think we can outrun the bear?" To which his friend replies, "I don't need to outrun the bear, I only have to outrun you!" It seems evolution would favor genes that support the "run" strategy rather than the "cooperate" strategy.

Even in situations where mutual advantage seems to justify cooperation, things are not as clear as they first appear. Say you and I have hunted successfully for food. Why should I share the meat rather than take it all for myself? Again, I may not be strong enough to overpower you and so it may be safer for me to share; but then why would you share the meat with me? If one of us is strong enough to take all the meat, sharing seems to be a selfless act inconsistent with "selfish" genes. Evolution should favor genes that lead to abilities that allow one to take all the food, rather than to a willingness to share. This has some dire implications. As Thomas Hobbes reasoned, if I am rationally self-interested I will never share when I can take it all, and neither will you. This means it will never make sense to enter into a cooperative venture unless I am confident that I can exploit your trust; and since you are equally rationally self-interested, and will recognize the same logic, you will never trust me, and so cooperation can never get off the ground.[7]

This is captured nicely in the famous Prisoner's Dilemma game. There are many variations, but the basic scenario runs something like this: Brian and Joe are arrested for committing a crime. The police do not have enough evidence to put either away on the most serious charge, which would carry, say, a five-year sentence, but could put both away for one year on a lesser charge. So they separately offer the two a deal: If they each testify against the other they will reduce the penalty to three years. However, if one testifies against the other who refuses to confess, then that person gets to go free, while the one who keeps quiet gets the full five years in prison. Both know the other has been made the same offer, but they cannot communicate with each other.

The best outcome for Brian and Joe as partners is for them to cooperate and both keep quiet; but the best outcome individually is for them to take the deal and testify against their partner, that is, to defect from their partnership. For Brian knows that if he talks while Joe keeps quiet (the cooperation option), then he (Brian) gets to go home, but if he decides to cooperate with Joe, and Joe does not reciprocate, then he is in deep trouble and is looking at five years in jail. So, regardless of what his partner does, Brian's best outcome is to not cooperate, and evolution should favor creatures that make the decision that best serves their self-interest.

However, despite considerable barriers, we know that cooperation does occur; humans have always lived in groups, and are descended from ape-like ancestors that also lived in groups. Group living requires cooperation and so we must have devised strategies to get around these selfish barriers. In fact, the large-scale cooperation characteristic of human societies may be our defining human trait. Theorist Martin Nowak points out, "From hunter-gatherer societies to nation-states, cooperation is the decisive organizing principle of human society. No other life form on Earth is engaged in the same complex games of cooperation and defection."[8] The challenge is to discover how such strategies evolved.

The Prisoner's Dilemma game has generated a great deal of experimental work.[9] A significant insight into developing an account of how a cooperative strategy might evolve is the recognition that in nature such cooperative dilemmas are often not one-shot deals, particularly for social creatures. Individuals often have repeated opportunities for cooperative interactions, with the possibility of having future interactions with the same partners. In iterated Prisoner's Dilemma games, cooperation can develop because the costs and benefits of cooperation are averaged over repeated events. In this scenario the long-term benefits of cooperation can outweigh the potential immediate costs. There is much discussion on how cooperation in the Prisoner's Dilemma may evolve, that is, which strategy poses the winning formula. For now, let's grant the possibility that repeated opportunities to interact with the same pool of individuals may allow cooperation to develop as a long-term rationally self-interested strategy, and so be consistent with the evolution of "selfish" genes. But this does not capture the extent of the human tendency to cooperate. There is a wealth of experimental data that indicate that humans are predisposed to cooperate and share resources with others, even when there is no possibility of meeting that individual again. To get a sense of this we need to introduce the Ultimatum game.

In the Ultimatum game two subjects have to make individual decisions on the division of a sum of money. One individual, Sue, is first given a sum, for example, $100, and is instructed to divide the money between herself and a second individual, Pat, who Sue knows will be given the option of accepting or rejecting the offer. If Pat accepts the offer, both individuals receive the sums proposed by Sue. If Pat rejects the offer, neither one gets anything. This is a one-shot interaction, there is only one round of play and the subjects do not know each other. What should they do? If both are rationally self-interested individuals, then Sue should offer Pat a small cut of the money and Pat should accept it. Even if Sue offers only $1, Pat should accept because the options are to accept and get $1 or reject and get nothing. If Sue believes Pat is rationally self-interested, then she should never offer anything above $1 because to do so would unnecessarily reduce her own benefits in order to benefit another. This is just what should happen if we are Hobbesian individuals, but in fact it is not what happens. The experimental data show that individuals regularly reject low offers.

Studies show that "a robust result in this experiment is that proposals giving the responder shares below 25% of the available money are rejected with a very high probability"[10] – suggesting that responders "do not behave to maximize self-interest" but instead reject what they consider to be unfair offers. Furthermore, the proposers seem to recognize this, as the most common proposal in these games is close to 50/50.[11] Joseph Henrich and colleagues conducted a cross-cultural study of this effect. They had participants from fifteen diverse cultures from Africa, Asia, Oceania, rural America, South America, and that most peculiar population, U.S. college freshmen, play the Ultimatum game. While they found "substantial differences across populations" they also discovered "a universal pattern, with an increasing proportion of individuals from every society choosing to punish [i.e. reject offers] as offers approach zero."[12]

In one sense, the Ultimatum game is not testing the willingness to cooperate as much as the willingness to punish those who do not cooperate. But this willingness to engage in "costly punishment" also needs to be explained as it meets evolutionary challenges as well as cooperation does.[13] In each case the individual makes a choice that is costly in terms of resources. In cooperation, I invest my resources in another's well-being; in punishment,

I commit resources to punish, thereby incurring a cost. From a rationally self-interested position, to punish someone who has treated me unfairly is simply to further waste my resources.

These studies are all addressing the problem of *altruism*, defined as "behavior that benefits another organism – while being apparently detrimental to the organism performing the behavior," with benefits and costs determined by the effects on an individual's reproductive fitness.[14] The problem is to understand how behavior that lowers an agent's fitness in order to raise the fitness of another can arise from a process driven by so-called selfish genes. As Dawkins has put it, "at the level of the gene, altruism must be bad and selfishness good."[15]

The Ultimatum game suggests one way to promote altruistic or cooperative behavior: Punish those who do not cooperate. As noted, the typical offer in an Ultimatum game is nearly an even split. Why would this be? To return to our scenario, Sue realizes that if she offers Pat too little, Pat may reject the offer and Sue will end up with nothing. In effect, Sue recognizes Pat's ability to punish Sue's greediness and so offers a fairer distribution of the goods. A variant of the Ultimatum game, known as the Dictator game, supports this interpretation. The Dictator game works the same as the Ultimatum game, except the second subject cannot reject the offer (the Ultimatum game: Take it or leave it; the Dictator game: Take it!). As we might expect, "the average amount given to the responders in the dictator game is much lower than that in the ultimatum game."[16] The role of punishment in promoting cooperation turns out to be of great significance, and I return to this topic later.

However, as we have said, punishment just repackages the problem of altruism. Punishment may turn out to be vital to large-scale cooperation, but punishing someone comes at a cost, which may or may not be paid back. As the Ultimatum game shows, there is a robust human tendency to punish unfair behavior, even when there is no possibility of being paid back. This is referred to in the literature as "altruistic punishing."[17] The problem remains: How can this be made consistent with rational self-interest? And if evolution works to maximize the reproductive interests of individuals, should it not lead to behavior that maximizes rational self-interest? To borrow a formulation from Marc Hauser,[18] should it not lead to *Hobbesian* creatures?

The answer to this last question is an unequivocal *no*! To see why, we must recognize that "rational self-interest" is not the same as "maximizing reproductive interests" or even "maximizing self-interest." Our look at the Prisoner's Dilemma showed that the rationally self-interested move – defect from cooperative behavior – if acted on by both "rational" individuals leads to a worse outcome for both. In a one-shot Prisoner's Dilemma game defecting may be the best choice, but the lives of social beings consist of repeated interactions, and over repeated interactions cooperation can pay off. Evolution does not shape behavior that leads to the best result in a specific interaction; it shapes behavior that tends to lead to the best reproductive payoff, in general and in the long-run, and so cooperative behavior can be selected. Still, how cooperative behavior gets off and running to such a degree that it can become an object of natural selection remains to be seen.

A clue to the unraveling of this puzzle is revealed by the Ultimatum game. The rational thing for the responder to do is to accept any offer at all – but the responder is not reading this situation in terms of rational self-interest. He or she is reading it in terms of morality: The money was given to us; for you to take more than 50% of that money is unfair and I won't accept such treatment. Also, a proposer who offers anything near 50% similarly recognizes that this is not simply a matter of rational self-interest but is, at least for the responder, a moral situation – and morality is much more than rational calculations of self-interest. To uncover the evolutionary roots of human morality we need a foray into the contemporary scientific study of morality.

The Moral Brain

In discussing the evolution of morality we must have some conception of what we mean by *morality*. This is a complicated issue and we could spend a book discussing it. Fortunately, such an involved treatment is not necessary to the discussion at hand. Here we are concerned with judgments of right and wrong, good and bad, as these terms are used to judge interpersonal relations. Now this hardly scratches the surface of the philosophical issues involved in morality but may serve our purposes nonetheless.[19]

Philosophers, theologians, and poets have long wrestled with the nature of human morality. A perennial and central question is the relative roles of reason and emotion in moral decision making. Hauser has usefully characterized this debate as one between two conceptions of human nature: humans as *Kantian Creatures* or as *Humean Creatures*. Kantian Creatures, made in the image of Immanuel Kant's moral philosophy, perceive an event and make "moral judgments based on conscious reasoning from relevant principles."[20] Humean Creatures, on the other hand, judge as David Hume argued people judge: "with an innate moral sense. ... Emotions ignite moral judgments. Reason follows in the wake of this dynamic."[21] Hauser eventually rejects both of these models, as neither is consistent with what we are learning about how the human mind actually goes about making moral judgments. He proposes an alternative – what he calls a *Rawlsian Creature*

– but we are not yet in a position to evaluate his candidate. First we need to see just what cognitive science is revealing about human morality.

For many moral thinkers, both professional and lay, reason is intimately tied up with moral judgment. We are told to "think before we act," to control our passions with our reason, to do what we know is right, not what we want to do. Kantian philosophers charge us to act only on universal principles derived from reason, uncontaminated by emotion; Utilitarians instruct us to calculate the costs and benefits before acting; theologians present God's Law as the ruling principle of moral life. Unfortunately for the rationalist approach, contemporary research into moral psychology seriously challenges such rules.

An emerging consensus of the cognitive scientific study of morality is that moral judgments are most often the result of intuitive, emotionally based reactions to social interactions that are then given *post hoc* rational justifications. This does not deny reason has a role in moral judgment but does argue that the typical role of reason – in the sense of conscious, reflective thought – is to provide justification for an intuitively pre-determined moral judgment. In terms of a causal role in moral judgment reason comes in to sort through dilemmas caused by conflicting intuitions.[22]

A series of clever experiments, conducted by Joshua Greene and his associates, open a window into the way the brain processes various moral dilemmas. Greene and his colleagues presented dilemmas to subjects who were being scanned by functional magnetic resonance imaging (fMRI). Using this scanner, researchers study brain responses while subjects are engaged in any number of activities, and can determine which areas of the brain are more significantly involved in those activities. Greene distinguished the dilemmas into two categories: "personal-moral" and "impersonal-moral." Personal-moral dilemmas meet three specific criteria: They involve the likelihood of serious harm; that harm befalls a particular person or set of persons; and that harm is not the result of deflecting an existing danger. An example would be to directly cause the death of one person to save the lives of many others. Impersonal dilemmas do not meet these criteria. An impersonal dilemma would be one where you had to choose between saving one person (and letting three people die) or saving three people (and letting one person die). In both examples at least one person is going to die based on your decision, but people treat personal-moral dilemmas differently from impersonal ones.[23]

The fMRI scans revealed what Greene suspected: Different brain areas are engaged by the different dilemmas. The personal-moral dilemmas engage areas of the brain correlated with emotion, while these areas are less engaged by impersonal scenarios. In those scenarios, areas more traditionally associated with cognition predominate.[24] With this distinction in hand Greene and coworkers also analyzed subjects' reaction times (i.e., how long it took people to come to their decisions) in a set of personal-moral dilemmas and a set of impersonal-moral dilemmas and found some important differences. In impersonal scenarios there is no significant difference in average reaction time between people who say it is appropriate to harm one in order to save three and those who say this is not appropriate. However, there is a difference in the personal-moral scenarios. In these cases those who vote to harm one to save three take significantly longer to reach that decision than those who reject this option.

Greene proposes that the reaction lag is caused by a conflict between an emotional response to the situation and cognitive calculation. Those who say it is appropriate to cause one death in to save three seem to be reasoning according to utilitarian principles of producing the least harm. In impersonal dilemmas that response comes very quickly, but in the personal dilemma it takes longer to do that same calculation.[25] Greene's interpretation, supported by the neurological evidence, is that in judging whether to cause an innocent person's death people have a quick, intuitive, negative response. Those who say it is the right decision also have this response but override it with a cognitive evaluation. The engagement of affective brain systems interferes with cognitive calculations, slowing down the judgment.[26]

These studies point to a "synthetic view of moral judgment that acknowledges the crucial role played by both emotion and 'cognition.'"[27] It is not the case that moral evaluations are merely emotional reactions. Reason is involved in moral evaluation, but in a particular situation, that is, when there is a conflict between competing intuitions. For example, in personal-moral dilemmas there is a conflict between an intuitive negative-emotional response to taking an innocent life and an intuitive calculation that it is better to lose one life than three. Not everyone presented with this choice suffers such conflict, but those who choose the option of intervening – that is, those who override their emotional intuition that this is wrong – do. However, it is important to note that this conflict is not worked out consciously. Even the conflicted responders answered, on average, in a matter of seconds. Deliberative reasoning comes into play after the fact and is used to justify the decision already made.

It is possible, however, to slow down our moral judging to allow time for reflective consideration, and brain scans indicate that in some of the slowest responders, areas of the brain associated with deliberation were engaged.[28] But numerous studies of formal and informal reasoning indicate that this is comparatively rare.[29] Greene and Haidt sum this view up with a wonderful quote from William James: "A great many people think they are thinking when they are merely rearranging their prejudices."[30]

It gets worse for reason once we move from moral evaluation to moral conduct. Studies demonstrate that the ability to recognize and apply moral principles to social and moral dilemmas is distinct from the ability to act on moral principles. The ability to understand – on an intellectual level – what constitutes morally appropriate behavior can be very high and yet not result in better behavior. As a colleague once commented to me, "a person can score at a level six on moral development [i.e., the highest level on Kohlberg's moral scale] and still be a bastard!"

Antonio Damasio brought this to prominent public attention with his discussion of the famous head-injury patient Phineas Gage and Damasio's own patient Elliot.[31] These individuals suffered brain damage that left their intellectual skills intact but disrupted their ability to follow appropriate moral standards. Both suffered damage to the same general area of the brain: the medial pre-frontal cortex, an area that mediates the integration of cognitive and affective systems. Deprived of emotional coloring their intellectual grasp of morality was left impotent. Numerous neuroscientific studies of anti-social behavior have discovered correlations between certain types of criminal behavior and deficits in areas of the brain involved in regulating emotional impulses.[32]

All of this seems to tilt the scale toward the Humean Creature; Hume's quip, "Reason is, and ought only to be the slave of the passions, and can never pretend to any other office than to serve and obey them,"[33] presciently captures the state of affairs. Hauser believes this is not quite right.[34] The synthetic view argues for an integration of cognitive and affective systems. Without the input of affective systems moral judgments lack the motivational power to make such judgments effective, but without the mediating function of cognition these emotion-laden reactions may be directed down morally inappropriate paths. It is worth quoting at length Greene's assessment of the current state of a cognitive scientific view of morality:

> While many big questions remain unanswered, it is clear from these studies that there is no "moral center" in the brain, no "morality module." Moreover, moral judgment does not appear to be a function of "higher cognition," with a few emotional perturbations thrown in. Nor do moral judgments appear to be driven entirely by emotional responses. Rather, moral judgments appear to be produced by a complex network of brain areas subserving both emotional and "cognitive" processes.[35]

When we speak of *emotional* and *cognitive* responses we are, of course, employing convenient labels that do not correspond neatly to what is happening in the brain. Any moral judgment is going to be a complex product of various brain systems, none of which can be identified as purely cognitive or purely emotional. What we label "emotional reaction" or "rational conclusion" is our conscious perception of the output of these interacting brain systems. The output that we perceive as emotion or reason is produced through innate mental processes working below the horizon of conscious awareness. This leads us to Hauser's vote for the Rawlsian Creature as the best metaphor for our moral minds.

A Rawlsian Creature, Hauser says, is "equipped with machinery to deliver moral verdicts based on unconscious and inaccessible principles. This is a creature with moral instincts."[36] He adds that "at the core of the Rawlsian creature is an appraisal mechanism that extracts the relevant properties from an event. These properties are represented by physical actions together with their causes and consequences."[37] The Humean Creature perceives an event, which provokes an emotional reaction, which leads to a moral judgment. The Kantian Creature perceives an event, applies the appropriate moral rule, and issues a moral judgment. The Rawlsian Creature perceives an event, analyzes its causes and consequences, and comes to a judgment. This judgment then provokes an emotional reaction and/or rational justification.[38] This is the picture of moral judgment painted by neuroscience and cognitive psychology. In the face of a moral dilemma, humans make quick, intuitive responses that they perceive as emotional or, less often, rational judgments, but such perceptions are actually the product of the judgment, not the cause of it. The judgment is caused by the workings of neurally based cognitive/affective systems. This is the "analysis" of the Rawlsian Creature.

According to Hauser, underlying this analysis is a "moral grammar," which he takes from the moral philosophy of John Rawls. Rawls presents a model for understanding our innate moral sense analogous to Chomsky's notion of a biologically based language faculty. That faculty is comprised of a set of innate universal principles that underlie all human languages and led to a variety of languages in response to various cultural inputs. This faculty allows children to rapidly acquire language, far in excess of the actual linguistic input they receive from their environments. Rawls suggested that some such faculty underlies our moral judgments[39] and Hauser sees this as a way to explain the often quick, intuitive moral judgments so characteristic of humans – that is, there is an innate moral grammar that underlies our ability to make moral judgments, and this is a biologically based, universally shared, human trait, that when exposed to varying cultural inputs generates the various moral systems humans have developed.

This model allows us to understand, for example, why a responder in the Ultimatum game will, contrary to rational self-interest, reject what she perceives to be an unfair offer. The responder is not making a rationally self-interested assessment. The responder is analyzing the actions of the proposer according to innate principles that involve emotional as well as cognitive brain systems. This produces a negatively valenced emotional reaction which the responder labels "unfair."

Hauser, Haidt, and Greene all argue that these affectively valenced, innate intuitions that constitute our moral grammar are themselves the products of human evolution.[40] We need to explore this evolved moral grammar to uncover the various cognitive/emotional predispositions of which it is comprised. These mental tools are evolutionary responses to the particular environmental pressures exerted on our ancestors as they struggled to reconcile the often conflicting objectives of individual reproductive success and the social demands of group living. Given that different social environments pose different problems, and so exert different selective pressures, we can expect to find a complex layering of these moral predispositions. I will begin with the most basic levels and work from there.

Before I begin, however, it is important to keep in mind just what is involved in discussing the evolution of human behavior. Darwinian processes select for traits based on their contribution to genetic success. But much more is involved in genetic success than the biological acts that result in reproduction. Successful reproduction requires success in reaching the age of reproduction and finding a suitable mate. This, of course, requires success at a large variety of tasks. It means one has been healthy and strong enough to reach sexual maturity, that one has developed the skills to meet the challenges along the way, that one was able to acquire and maintain adequate resources, that one has the qualities necessary to attract a mate, and for humans, it means that one was able to negotiate the social fields in which all these other endeavors take place. Failure at any one of these tasks can be sufficient to prevent one from reproducing and passing on one's genes.

And for humans, the demands do not stop there: In many species once the creatures have cleared all the hurdles in order to reproduce sexually, they are finished (sometimes, literally). Humans, due to the extended period of infantile dependency, need to make significant post-coital investments. It matters little that you were able to reproduce if that offspring dies before it reaches maturity and continues the process. Reproductive success requires that individuals continue to meet all the above mentioned challenges, *and* provide adequately for their children, so they can then be successful in meeting those same challenges. Failure anywhere along this sequence can result in an evolutionary dead end. Therefore, any trait that contributes to any of these tasks is a proper target for natural selection, and for humans this includes those skills that enable us to negotiate complex relationships successfully.

Keeping this in mind will help us to avoid an all too common yet badly misconceived critique of evolutionary thinking. This critique goes like this: If evolution is concerned only with reproducing genes, then how can we speak of the evolution of a trait if it does not lead to having more babies?

For example, how can it be claimed that the trait of honesty is a result of evolution since it seems that dishonesty can often contribute to reproductive success (e.g., "I love only you," "I'll love you forever," "There will never be anyone for me but you")? However, by taking into consideration this broader, and more realistic, account of what goes into reproductive success we can recognize many traits that may not lead to an increase in sexual encounters, per se, but which are absolutely vital to the various tasks one must master in order to enhance reproductive fitness. With this in mind we can turn to the evolution of our moral psychology.

The First Layer: Kin Selection

The first step in solving the problem of altruism is the process known as *kin selection*, which was rigorously established by William Hamilton in 1964. As we know, evolutionary theory holds that traits that increase reproductive success (i.e., fitness) will be selected for, and the genes underlying those traits passed on. Reproductive success is measured strictly in the number of genes passed from one generation to the next. The obvious method of getting those genes into the next generation is through children. Sacrificing for your children makes sense because you are protecting your genetic investment. People who do not care for children will not have many descendants. This type of self-sacrifice is really long-term self-interest and poses no problem for evolution. Hamilton realized, however, that child-bearing is not the only way to get copies of an individual's genes into the next generation.

My child carries copies of 50% of my genes, but my full siblings also carry copies of 50% of my genes, and so their children, my nieces and nephews, carry copies of 25% of my genes, and so on through the various degrees of familial relationships. Since a gene's success is measured solely by how many copies of itself get into the next generation, it is wholly irrelevant whether the vehicle for that transmission is my child, my sister, or my cousin. By virtue of genetic relatedness I have a stake in their reproductive success. To sacrifice my immediate interests in order to benefit my kin is also consistent with long-term self-interest. This broader conception of genetic self-interest is termed by Hamilton *inclusive fitness*.[41]

Inclusive fitness via kin selection provides an evolutionary explanation for some very familiar human traits. The all-too-human tendency to show preference for family members, whether in making sacrifices or distributing rewards, is an apparently universal human trait. The power of parental love, too, is a characteristic that transcends cultures, and even species. We do not need kin selection to establish these facts, or perhaps even to explain them. It does, however, provide an explanation that grounds these phenomena in Darwinian mechanisms. Individuals who behave in ways that enhance the reproductive success of kin, particularly close kin, enhance the reproductive success of individuals who possess copies of many of their own genes. In doing so they behave in a way that contributes to passing on those genes involved in the development of those very behaviors.[42] Those genes, and consequently those kin-altruistic tendencies, will be better represented in the next generation. Genes that contribute to behaviors more narrowly focused on self-preservation at the expense of offspring and close kin will tend to send fewer copies of themselves into the future. As this process plays itself out, generation after generation, we have the evolution of a deep-seated tendency to care and sacrifice for family. There is no occult force at work moving humans morally forward. This is simply the Darwinian algorithm at work.

There is, however, an important proviso to bear in mind: Kin selection contributes to the development of altruistic tendencies that, however powerful, are limited in scope. I remember a schoolteacher of mine asking how it was that someone, such as a Nazi camp guard or a mob hit man, could spend his days heartlessly killing and then come home to be tender with his family. Kin selection offers an answer. Kin selection is the most primitive layer of our moral psychology. Peter Singer speaks of expanding circles of moral concern[43] with the self as the center. In evolutionary terms the concerns of the self-focused individual are those basic to survival: security, accumulation of resources, access to sexual mates. Kin selection expands our understanding of fitness. It is the first step of the selfish gene outside the circle of self-preservation.

However, in doing so it creates a new boundary – that between kin and non-kin – and this boundary represents the extension of moral concern. The Nazi who, without the slightest pang of conscience, exterminated Jews as a matter of course, could still be gentle and loving to his family because in going home he crossed the line back into a world of moral significance. Kin selection equips us with emotional regard for family; it does not extend emotional regard to non-kin, who are therefore outside the boundaries of moral consideration.

If we return to the level of genes we can see why this is so. If an individual sacrifices resources that it might need for its own survival in order to care for its offspring, in genetic terms that individual is making an investment that will pay off when the offspring, who carries copies of 50% of its genes, reproduces and sends copies of those genes into the next generation. If I sacrifice for a cousin, who carries copies of 25% of my genes, that sacrifice is rewarded if it helps my cousin send copies of the genes we share into the next generation. However, if I sacrifice for a stranger – that is, if I act in a way that reduces my ability to send copies of my genes into the future in order to benefit someone genetically unrelated – I have wasted my resources, in evolutionary terms. In this scenario, fewer of my genes and more of the stranger's genes will be represented in future generations. Genes that lead to behaviors that result in fewer copies of themselves moving forward soon die out.

So, kin selection starts us on our way to a more fully human morality. To see just how far it gets us we need to consider how it works. We have been discussing how it works at the level of genes, but we do not live at the level of genes. We live in a world of organisms whose genes lay hidden deep within the structures of their cells. Kin selection works by preferentially aiding genetic relatives, but how do we determine who is kin when individuals do not wear their genetic code on their sleeves (no scarlet K, as it were)?

Evolution works with generalities, probabilities, tendencies. Natural selection is not a process that guarantees the best possible result or the perfect design. The outcomes of natural selection are the best-possible-given-the-material-at-hand-and-the-constraints-imposed-by-environmental-conditions. A successful design or behavioral strategy is not necessarily the best of all possible options; it is just better than the alternatives available in a particular ecological niche. Dennett labels this approach "satisficing," which he calls "the basic structure of all real decision-making, moral, prudential, economic, or even evolutionary."[44] As we examine kin selection we can see this is how evolution works. Sacrificing for kin reaps evolutionary rewards, sacrificing for non-kin reaps evolutionary costs. Other than the case of one's own children,[45] how is an individual to make the decision of when and for whom to sacrifice when genetic-relatedness is not an observable property? Evolution works by equipping us with cognitive predispositions that adopt a satisficing approach. That is, there are strategies that if followed will *tend to maximize* our behavior (i.e., lead to a better ratio of kin sacrifices versus non-kin sacrifices). While we may not be able to observe genetic-relatedness there are signs that may provide reliable clues.

In looking for such clues, we must place them in the context of our evolutionary past, what theorists call the *environment of evolutionary adaptedness* (EEA). Our EEA was one in which humans lived in small groups of hunter-gatherers. Certain traits in those situations could function as "kinship estimators," that is, cognitive structures "specialized to take certain cues as input that were reliably correlated with genetic relatedness ancestrally."[46] One such cue would have been co-habitation. Individuals who live with you, and have lived with you since you were young, are more likely to be related than new group members or strangers. This was even more likely to have been true in a small hunter-gatherer group. Behaving altruistically toward such individuals was a satisficing strategy; not a perfect strategy, but one that in the long run was more likely than not to enhance an individual's inclusive fitness.[47]

Note that when we talk about a "cue to kinship" we are not talking about something that a person would consciously use as part of a rational calculation. It works by triggering an evolutionarily ingrained response, which is part of our moral grammar. We must keep this in mind as we continue to investigate the evolution of morality in order to avoid some obvious, but ultimately pointless, objections. These psychological processes work beneath the level of consciousness.

So, this is one satisficing strategy for estimating probability of kinship – satisficing because those who co-habitate may, in fact, not be genetic relatives. There is of course another strategy, and that is resemblance. One of the consequences of genotypic similarity is phenotypic similarity. People who are related tend to look like one another in certain general ways; there are family resemblances that can serve as cues to kinship. Researchers studying the strategy of phenotype matching have provided experimental data supporting the thesis that facial resemblance can function as a kinship cue and enhance cooperation between individuals.[48]

So kin selection provides a primal layer for cooperation between relatives, but due to the satisficing nature of natural selection it actually allows kin altruism a slightly larger scope. These two cues (not necessarily exhaustive) provide cognitive strategies, ingrained rules-of-thumb, for deciding when and with whom to act altruistically:

- Act altruistically toward those who are familiar to you from an early age (which may extend altruism to familiar, but unrelated individuals)
- Act altruistically toward those who look like your people (since physical resemblance is a reasonable, though imperfect, cue to genetic relatedness).

As we see how kin selection works at the level of the organism, we find room to expand the circle a bit more. It is not only genetic relatives who can be the beneficiaries of our kin altruism; the satisficing nature of natural selection creates a somewhat porous boundary through which some non-relatives may slip.[49]

We must take heed, however, that there is correlate to these strategies:

- Be cautious with strangers and people who do not look like your people (for they are unlikely to be genetically related and so any sacrifice for such an individual would reduce your own inclusive fitness).

The flip side of kin selection is xenophobia.

Despite its extension of moral boundaries it should be clear that kin selection, potent though it may be, is severely limited in scope. It does not extend morality in any significant way to non-relatives. Yet we see around us examples of such altruism. Indeed, if human society were ever to develop beyond small family-group structures, another evolutionary means to altruism was needed.

The Second Layer: Reciprocal Altruism

Reciprocal altruism is a model for cooperation developed by Robert Trivers.[50] In simplest terms, it is an "I'll rub your back, so that you'll rub mine" strategy. In short, cooperative behavior can pay off. My sacrificing some time and effort to help you now pays off when you help me later, and so functions as an investment in my long-term fitness. Trivers sets out three conditions under which the natural selection of reciprocal altruism is favored: There must be repeated opportunities for altruism, there must be repeated interactions between potential altruists, and potential altruists must be able to offer comparable benefits to each other, at comparable costs.[51] Humans meet these three conditions, but we are not the only species that does. Patterns of reciprocal altruism have been documented among vervet monkeys and vampire bats,[52] tree swallows, sticklebacks, dolphins, gorillas, and chimpanzees.[53] Trivers discusses a form of reciprocal altruism, known as symbiotic cleaning, practiced by dozens of fish and shrimp.[54]

Despite the great diversity of creatures that exhibit reciprocal altruism, it is in the larger scheme a relatively rare phenomenon. In many species it takes the form of a narrowly circumscribed set of behaviors, and many of the examples often cited as evidence of reciprocal altruism have come under criticism for being made too hasty. Whatever the final verdict on these examples turns out to be, it is clear that to the degree that reciprocal altruism functions in the non-human animal world, it is limited to simple behaviors. For more complex and varied patterns of reciprocation we must turn to primates, particularly gorillas, chimps, and, of course, humans.[55] For such complex patterns to emerge a developed cerebral cortex is required.[56]

Reciprocal altruism, however limited, does allow for the extension of altruism beyond kin and provides another evolutionary mechanism for the rise of cooperative behavior. Sacrificing some of my resources in order to benefit a non-relative can make sense because my sacrifice for you results in your sacrificing some of your resources to me when I am in need. It too is an investment from which I can draw future dividends, not in terms of genetic fitness, but in terms of resources. Those resources, however, contribute to my overall pursuit of inclusive fitness. For example, my sharing food with you today leaves me with less right now, but as long as I have enough for my kin I suffer no direct harm. The cost I incur by sharing is that I will not have as much left over for tomorrow. The benefit I gain is by the debt you incur to me. You now owe me. You pay this debt by sharing food when I am hungry, or by providing some other service.[57] We both benefit by being willing to accept costs in return for benefits we could not get on our own. Given the precariousness of human existence during our evolutionary history a strategy that promoted a system of mutual assistance would have had a great selective advantage. The Hobbesian obstacle to the origin of cooperation and trust is avoided by the fact that reciprocal altruism develops in small groups in which kin selection has already laid the grounds for cooperative behavior. These are cooperative interactions not based on random encounters but directed toward particular individuals, in this case, group members.[58] This is an important lesson in understanding the evolution of cooperation: One layer of our evolved psychology can contribute to the development of another layer.

As we expand the circle of altruism to include non-kin we come to include a greater set of familiar examples of human behavior. Preferential treatment of family is a common human trait, but so too is cooperation with non-kin. The model of reciprocal altruism does not uncover something new as much as explain, in evolutionary terms, the origin of something we encounter daily. However, as it stands, it does not seem to explain enough. Human cooperation and willingness to aid a stranger are not limited to cases where reciprocation is expected or even possible. For example, you are walking home one day and you notice an elderly person fall while crossing the street; you instinctively move to help the person to his feet and escort him safely to the curb. You clearly do not expect reciprocation in such a case. Even more challenging are those examples of a person who sacrifices his or her life for non-kin. Consider the soldier throwing himself on a grenade to save his fellows – how can an action that leads to the death of the person performing the act be explained by a Darwinian process driven by reproductive success? Cases such as these seem to strain the logic of reciprocal altruism – and experimental work supports such skepticism. While it is generally accepted that reciprocal altruism plays a role in explaining human cooperation, it plays a minor role due to its limited extension.[59] Models of reciprocal altruism show that it breaks down quickly as social groups grow in size, with some studies suggesting that groups with many more than ten members undermine reciprocity.[60] This raises a serious challenge to evolutionary accounts of morality since humans have mastered cooperation in much larger groups; and while self-sacrificial behavior for strangers is statistically rare, it is far too common to be written off as an aberration.

The extent of human cooperation cannot be explained by reciprocal altruism, even though this mechanism continues to play a role in the psychology of cooperation. "Help those who have helped you or who may be able to help you in return" is an important part of our innate moral grammar, and it moves cooperative behavior beyond the circle of kin, but not nearly far enough. Human cooperation often extends beyond situations in which it is reasonable to expect reciprocation; a tendency some researchers have termed *strong reciprocity*.[61] That such a predisposition is part of our evolved psychology is not seriously debated; *how* such a predisposition evolved is. These debates and the research that informs them continue to be vigorous, and they constitute one of the richest areas of research into human cooperation. No single model can claim consensus – and researchers concede that no single process can explain human sociality – but the various approaches are settling on a few prominent processes.[62] This is the position I am developing in this chapter: Processes such as kin selection and reciprocal altruism are initial layers of a sophisticated system of human sociality. To explain strong reciprocity, which allows the development of large scale cooperative institutions, we need to add further layers. The debates tend to center on the extent to which one or another process provides a sufficient, and empirically defensible, explanation. I touch on some of these issues in what follows but my main concern is with uncovering the constituents of our evolved moral grammar, and from that perspective these several key processes all play a role.

A Third Layer: Indirect Reciprocity

Reciprocity does not only work in a direct manner, such that if A benefits B, then B repays A. Such a limited model does not capture the potential complexity of reciprocal exchanges, which can occur directly between two people but may also involve more complex interactions. This broader conception is termed *indirect reciprocity*. In this expanded view, developed by Richard Alexander in his classic work, *The Biology of Moral Systems*, the debt from an altruistic act is not necessarily paid to the altruist, and is not necessarily paid by the recipient of the altruistic act. Alexander sets out three major forms such reciprocity may take: (1) the reputation for being a cooperator may encourage others to cooperate with such an individual; (2) an altruistic individual may be rewarded, either materially or in terms of status enhancement, by society for his or her contributions; and (3) an altruist may improve the fitness of him- or herself and family by increasing the fitness of the community.[63] Let's take a look at each of these.

Reputation: By performing altruistic actions, whether by sacrificing for another or by being a reliable cooperator, I send a message to other members of my group that I am willing to act this way toward non-kin. This is valuable information. It should be obvious just how important it is to be careful in choosing when and with whom to act altruistically. It is not possible to know with certainty, in advance, whether or not someone will actually reciprocate. If I act altruistically to you and you fail to reciprocate, then I have wasted resources. A person who consistently makes such bad choices will severely hamper his or her inclusive fitness (just as a financial investor who never gains a return on his or her money will soon face financial disaster). If, however, I know that you have a history of cooperating and reciprocating when you have been benefited, then I have a reason to believe that cooperating with you is a safe investment. So, even if I help someone who does not reciprocate, this action, if publicly known, can add to my social reputation. The return on my investment comes then not in terms of direct reciprocation but in terms of increased cooperative interactions with other members of the group, which increase the total benefits I may reap. Hence the importance of reputation: The greater my reputation, the greater my potential return – and there is empirical data to support this.[64] As Alexander puts it, "In complex social systems with much reciprocity, being judged as attractive for reciprocal interactions may become an essential ingredient for success."[65] People are not only concerned with what others are doing, they are also concerned with what others are thinking about them – and this has left its mark on our psyches. For example, one study found that when experiments on altruism allow altruistic behavior to contribute to a subject's reputation, 74% of participants donate resources compared with 37% in situations with no reputation effects.[66]

Another study using the Dictator game provides further evidence that behavior can be shaped by our concern over social feedback. In a variation on this game, experimenters set two conditions: one in which the recipients of the money were able to send anonymous, written messages to the dictator, one in which no communication was allowed. The study revealed that the amount of money dictators shared with recipients was 40% higher in the communication condition.[67] We are so attuned to how our behavior is perceived by others that even in an artificial situation of complete anonymity we can be moved to act contrary to our own immediate self-interest. In fact, we do not even need real humans to stimulate this concern – studies show that even the presence of images that resemble eyes can increase our giving behavior.[68]

Our mental repertoire not only comes with tools that track what others may be thinking about us, we are also quite attuned to others and have tools for detecting and remembering what others do,[69] particularly when they cheat – that is, fail to reciprocate or cooperate. Evolutionary psychologists have suggested that part of our mental tool kit is a *cheater detection module* that is sensitized to cues of defection from cooperation,[70] and studies provide experimental support for this. In one cleverly designed project the researchers took snapshots of participants in a one-shot Prisoner's Dilemma game at the moment they were making their decisions to cheat or cooperate. They presented these photos to subjects who believed they were involved in an experiment on perception and who were told nothing about the conditions under which the photos were taken. Their results showed that pictures of individuals who cheated in the Prisoner's Dilemma game attracted significantly more attention than cooperators. They concluded that this was provoked by subtle facial cues exhibited by cheaters and the mind's selective attention to such cues.[71] In a separate study these researchers presented the same pictures to a different set of subjects and asked them to predict which individuals were likely to be cooperative (again, the subjects had no information about the nature of the photos). Subjects accurately labeled the actual cheaters as potential cheaters, and at a significant level. To control for possible undetected biases toward particular facial features the researchers took snapshots of their Prisoner's Dilemma participants prior to their playing the game. They presented these "neutral" pictures to a group of subjects and asked them to predict who would be cooperative. In this case photos of individuals who would later cheat were no more likely to be labeled as potential cheaters than those who would later cooperate. The subjects were cueing in on some subtle facial signals of cheating rather than responding to some standard facial features.[72]

The ability to detect cheats also brings with it the importance of masking cheating. Andrew Whiten and Richard Byrne argue that this set off an evolutionary arms race between the ability to deceive and ability to detect deception that has shaped, in profound ways, human intelligence.[73] This task – distinguishing potential cheaters from potential cooperators – plays a crucial role in shaping our moral systems.

Social Reward: Social living requires that members of society be willing to put the good of the group ahead of their own self-interest, at least sometimes. All societies find ways of rewarding those who contribute to the social good, and punish those who do not do their part. Alexander mentions two forms of social payback – material rewards and status enhancement – and there are numerous examples of both in contemporary society. In modern society we pay individuals to take on the roles of social benefactors; they are, for example, our soldiers, police, and firefighters. Not only do we pay these people to be ready to sacrifice for the common good, we laud them when they do so. Think of the social status afforded, appropriately, to rescue workers after 9/11.

Social status gained by undertaking risks for society is a resource that may contribute to inclusive fitness. Here, reputation again comes into play. High social status adds to a person's reputation of being in a position to offer aid and cooperation, and we have seen how this pays off, but it also identifies one as having certain other qualities. It says that an individual has the skills and traits to stand apart from other members of the group. In the example of rescue workers, it signals personal bravery and strength, as well as a willingness to face grave dangers. Someone with such traits not only is a valuable social resource, but also is not a person to be taken lightly. While it is important to have the reputation of being a cooperator, it is just as important to discourage others from trying to take advantage of one's cooperation. A person of high social status signals that he or she has social skills and qualities that go beyond the average group member. Such an individual is not someone one would want to cheat (since he or she likely has the ability to retaliate against cheating). An individual who, because of high social status, can discourage cheating stands to gain the benefits that come with the reputation of being a social benefactor, while minimizing losses. Because such a person will accrue a net increase in the resources required to enhance their inclusive fitness, the traits that lead to a readiness to face hardships for the group may be selected for by Darwinian processes.[74]

Communal Fitness: It is also possible that a sacrifice on my part may not be paid back to me or to my family and yet still contributes to my inclusive fitness. Since we pursue our good within a social environment, the success of our group may impact significantly on any individual's chances of success. If my group is invaded and conquered by a neighboring group, then my reproductive fitness may come to an abrupt end.[75] Sacrificing my life in the fight to save my group may be a necessary part of enhancing my inclusive fitness. Even if I die, and even if society does not compensate my family for my sacrifice, fighting and dying may be the only way my kin have a chance to survive and pass on some copies of my genes. This is not restricted to fighting for my group. Any investment of resources I make in the group may indirectly increase my fitness by creating a more secure and effective social environment for me and/or my family. If we think of how extensive is the list of tasks we must tackle to be reproductively successful, and the extensive time span during which we pursue these tasks, and keep in mind that all of this occurs within a social environment, we can recognize how much a stable and prosperous society contributes to an individual's inclusive fitness. So, even when there is no overt reciprocation of my social contributions, benefits may still accrue that make the investment a wise one.

Indirect reciprocity (IR) constitutes a set of processes through which altruistic behavior can result in a net benefit to an individual's inclusive fitness, and does so within Darwinian parameters. It is an important aspect of an evolutionary account of human morality and a key layer of our innate moral grammar. It is, however, not without its problems. There is a healthy debate, as you must expect by this point, over the extent of its efficacy, although scholars generally concede the capability of IR to establish social cooperation and so create a more secure community.[76] The mechanisms involved in IR expand the circle of moral significance to encompass both kin and non-kin, at least those who are members of my group. More challenging doubts arise about the power of these mechanisms as group size increases.

This is the key problem in explaining the large-scale cooperation characteristic of humans. The mechanisms we have been considering are most effective in smaller social groups. As population size increases so do the opportunities to cheat (to fail to reciprocate an act of altruism) or to free ride (to enjoy the benefits of social cooperation without contributing) and we need to understand why this is so.

Despite the contribution of cooperative behavior to an individual's success the basic evolutionary logic of promoting one's own inclusive fitness continues to impact on human behavior. In that ruthless logic, each time I sacrifice resources, whether in the form of time, energy, goods, or risks taken, I diminish my own fitness and enhance that of a competitor. Individuals who make a habit of this tend not to be favored by evolution. Mechanisms for indirect reciprocity provide avenues that allow long-term self-interest to lead to socially cooperative behavior. There is, of course, the crucial proviso: Such processes work only if people do in fact reciprocate. However, there is a great temptation not to reciprocate, since if you have already benefited from someone's cooperation any reciprocation on your part would just be an unnecessary cost – and the temptation grows as group size increases. The larger the group, the more individuals there are to interact with and to keep track of, and consequently the easier it is to cheat and get away with it. Also, the larger and more complex a society, the more indirect are the costs and benefits of altruism. One may contribute to the general fund and never realize who is cooperating and who is cheating. This too lowers the cost of cheating and consequently raises the cost of cooperating. Moral systems weaken as societies become larger and more anonymous. As early hunter-gatherer societies began to grow in size they were met by the *problem of extension* – how to extend the circle of moral significance to encompass and support a larger group with cognitive/emotional tools designed for a much tighter circle.[77]

Indirect reciprocity can address this problem but it needs help from other tools to continue to function. One key tool is the cognitive/emotional predisposition to punish those who do not contribute appropriately to social cooperation. Our comparison of Ultimatum and Dictator games revealed that generosity is significantly higher in Ultimatum games in which greediness can be punished. The recipient in that game can impose a cost on the donor by rejecting the offer and thereby deprive the donor of any benefit. Donors in Dictator games have nothing to fear by being greedy and so are less generous. But we also have evidence that in Dictator games that include feedback to the donor, generosity increases. This can be understood as a punishment effect. To be known to be greedy can reduce one's reputation and social standing, and since reputation is a resource that impacts on fitness, damage to one's reputation counts as a cost. The fear that one's poor behavior may be made public – a form of punishment – can increase cooperative behavior.

The logic behind this is apparent. The obstacle to cooperation is the possibility that one is wasting resources. From self-interested calculation I should cooperate only when it results in a net increase to my fitness. That calculation must take into account not only possible benefits of cooperating, but also potential costs of not cooperating. Punishment attaches costs to the strategies of cheating and free-riding that make those strategies less promising to the self-interested calculator. Furthermore, by raising the cost of non-cooperation punishment makes cooperation less risky. A wealth of studies conclude that for cooperation to develop on the larger scale required by complex societies, systems of punishment are required.[78]

As important as punishment is, it too raises problems because the act of punishment imposes a cost on those who do the punishing. This is known as *altruistic punishment*, and comes with the same problems associated with cooperation. It also brings with it a variation of the free-rider problem: a person who contributes to collective action but does not contribute to punishment of free-riders. These individuals benefit from the punishment without contributing anything to the cost of punishment. Despite these challenges, there are indications that punishment may not be too hard to get off the ground. Experimental evidence shows that even a small number of punishers can stabilize cooperation in large groups.[79] Also, human tool-making skills may have contributed to making punishment less costly[80] (i.e., if punishing you requires that I personally beat you up, that can be quite costly; it is less so if I may shoot you with an arrow when you are not looking). Furthermore, the willingness to punish can add to an individual's reputation for being a cooperator and this can then reap the benefits that go with such a reputation, offsetting to some degree the costs of punishing.[81] As important as these matters are we must direct our attention beyond the mind and consider one more layer of our moral psychology: the impact of culture.

A Fourth Layer: Cultural Group Selection

Evaluating the role of culture in shaping human behavior can be a contentious activity. Even though any minimally informed view of human behavior recognizes that both biology and culture – both nature and nurture – make contributions, the battles have shifted to just how much a role each plays. Evolutionists are too often presented as biological extremists pushing an agenda of genetic determinism. This is a caricature. There is no professional (at least none I have ever met, heard, or read about) working in the fields of evolutionary study today – biology, anthropology, psychology, or philosophy – who espouses biological determinism or who denies that culture plays a formative role in shaping human behavior. Today, one of the most serious objections to evolutionary studies comes not from the extreme religious right (that is just the most politically potent objection) but from culture advocates within the academy. Now, however, is not the time to take up this cause,[82] but let me just point out a serious flaw in such objections: Positing a cultural explanation for a behavior or institution does not exclude a biological explanation, and this is because culture itself has evolutionary origins.

Scholars debate whether any other species can be said to possess a culture. Interesting arguments have been put forward to answer this in the affirmative – at least the rudiments of culture can be found in non-human species, particularly among the higher primates.[83] But what is not debatable is that no species on the planet comes close to the variety, complexity, and diversity of human culture. It is as close to a defining trait of our species as can be found. When we find a universal species trait, and one that is unique to that species, we need to look for biological roots and an evolutionary explanation. Human culture is not an alternative paradigm to evolution; it is part of the evolutionary account of human behavior. Appropriately, this area is generating theoretical and empirical work, with some of the most significant being done by Peter Richerson and Robert Boyd.

Richerson and Boyd present a summary of their years of research into evolution and culture in their recent book, *Not by Genes Alone: How Culture Transformed Human Evolution*. In it they define culture as "information capable of affecting individuals' behavior that they acquire from other members of their species through teaching, imitation, and other forms of social transmission," with "information" being broadly understood as "any kind of mental state, conscious or not, that is acquired or modified by social learning and affects behavior."[84] Culture is the product of information sharing between members of a species and the transmission of that information across generations. This is possible because humans have evolved the cognitive equipment to process, store, and transmit information, as well as the motivational systems that guide us to attend selectively to certain stimuli. It is also made possible by, and in turn facilitates, complex social arrangements – all of which are themselves the products of our particular evolutionary history. It is worth quoting Richerson and Boyd at length here:

> Culture is an evolving product of populations of human brains, brains that have been shaped by natural selection to learn and manage culture. Culture-making brains are the product of more than two million years of more or

less gradual increases in brain size and cultural complexity. During this period, culture must have increased the reproductive success of our ancestors; otherwise, the features of our brains that make culture possible would not have evolved.[85]

Once the cognitive equipment that allows for culture evolves, we have a new path for human development, but this is not inconsistent with an evolutionary account of that development,[86] nor does it mean we leave biology behind. One consequence of culture is that behaviors that are inconsistent with evolutionary goals can arise – that is, culture, which is an evolutionary adaptation, can lead to behaviors that are evolutionarily maladaptive (e.g., the institutional celibacy of Catholic priests).[87] But culture does not eliminate the biological layering of our evolved psychology – these intuitions and predispositions remain part of our make-up and can continue to have an impact on behavior (e.g., the sex-abuse scandal involving Catholic priests). E. O. Wilson has commented that "biology holds culture on a leash." I believe this is an apt metaphor for the relationship between culture and biology. This is sometimes read to imply biological determinism, although this is certainly not how Wilson meant it, nor is it what I mean by endorsing it. A leash does imply constraint, but there are many different kinds of leashes. A dog leash made of metal chain sets an absolute limit to where the dog can go. But this is not the leash joining culture to biology. When I use this metaphor I imagine a leash made of a flexible material that can extend quite significantly, allowing the dog the freedom to explore and roam, even in places its owner does not want it to go – but ultimately there is a limit to how far the dog may go. This is how I understand the relationship between culture and biology. The evolution of mental tools that allow for culture to develop have given humans the flexibility and behavioral plasticity to explore a wide variety of cultural niches without, however, negating the pull of the other layers of our evolved psychology.

Just how far that leash allows us to move away from our biology is an open question. Can we break the leash of biology? In one very clear sense the answer is an unambiguous *no*. We are biological creatures, and however far we strive to move away from our evolved heritage we will do so as biological creatures, with all the limitations entailed by our physical nature, including the limitations of our physical brains. However, if we see the leash of biology as having many strands, each contributing some of the pull of biology, it is an open question whether culture can move us so far from our evolutionary roots that we snap part of the leash. The point that I want to make here is that in introducing culture into the evolutionary picture of human psychology, I see it not in opposition to our evolved psychology but as another layer of that psychology.[88]

This cultural layer of our moral grammar is based on what Richerson and Boyd term "biased transmissions." Culture is all about the transmission of information. This information, however, is not picked up in a random fashion; certain modes of transmission earn a preferential bias. There can be several modes of biased transmission but here I focus on two particularly important ones: *frequency-based bias* and *prestige-based bias*.[89] Frequency-based bias leads us to selectively favor behaviors that are common in our social environment. If people in my group regularly eat a certain plant, then that is sound evidence that the plant is edible; if people in my group avoid or are aggressive toward certain individuals, then that is a good sign for me to also be wary of them. The human tendency to conform, so often bemoaned (and often for good reasons) is actually an important cognitive adaptation that allows members of a social species to benefit from the accumulated information of the group, rather than being forced to rely on a costly trial-and-error process.[90]

That a behavior is commonly practiced is evidence that it is *generally* successful, but of course there will always be people who are more successful than others at various tasks. Some people will be healthier, wealthier, or wiser than the average group member. This signals that these individuals have special skills or information that enabled them to excel beyond their peers. Such individuals stand out as valuable models for imitation. Paying particular attention to the behavior of successful people is an effective learning strategy. This is prestige-based bias – we are particularly attuned to the actions of individuals who have attained positions of prestige in our group (a tendency not uncommon in contemporary society).

Richerson and Boyd believe that culture plays a significant role in facilitating the large-scale cooperation we are trying to explain. They argue, and many others agree, that once it gets started culture not only expresses our evolved psychology but allows groups to themselves become units of selection in the evolutionary process. Groups that hit on practices that trigger our evolved tendencies toward pro-social behaviors (what they call "tribal social instincts") are poised to develop into cohesive, stable societies. Cooperation contributes to success, and successful practices get preferentially transmitted via prestige-based biases; this increases their frequency, which makes them targets for frequency-biased transmission as well, further expanding the scope of cooperative practices, and so further increasing the prosperity of the group. In an environment with several groups competing for resources these successful cultural practices give a society a competitive advantage in the struggle for cultural survival.[91] This is not genetic group selection but rather *cultural group selection*. It is "analogous to genetic group selection but acts on cultural rather than genetic differences between groups."[92]

I believe there is much merit to this view of human evolution; the basic logic of cultural group selection, as I have just outlined it, is unassailable. The question that remains is one of mechanism, or the relative importance of various mechanisms. Cultural group selection is at times presented by some as an alternative to indirect reciprocity, while others are reticent to admit into human psychology anything that smacks of genetic group selection.[93] In any case, cultural group selection still depends on earlier evolutionary developments to work, so we do not need to resolve the dispute here. More germane to our discussion is that Richerson and Boyd take a position similar to the one set out in this chapter, that is: These earlier developments are the more basic cognitive/emotional tools produced by evolution. We can now add frequency and prestige biased transmissions to our tool kit for constructing moral systems, as we turn to emotions.

A Fifth Layer: The Moral Emotions

The metaphor of cognitive layering is really not apt when talking about the emotions. As Hauser argues, the emotions are the products of prior cognitive processes that evaluate the situations we find ourselves in. Yet this in no way minimizes the power of the emotions. Indeed, as Haidt points out, it is the emotional dog that wags the rational tail – at least, often wags the tail. It is emotions that typically motivate behavior. So, in one sense the emotions are the end results of the various processes we have been considering. Reproductive fitness generates sexual attraction and romantic love; inclusive fitness generates feelings of care and concern for our children; reciprocity generates feelings of guilt and shame; cultural group selection generates feelings of fellowship and loyalty; and so on – but it is the power of the emotions that drives humans to act, and often to act contrary to their rationally calculated self-interest. In this sense, it is our emotions, particularly our moral emotions (e.g., guilt, shame, resentment, outrage, loyalty, love, sympathy) that allow the processes we have been considering to do their work.

An adequate discussion of the moral emotions is too large a task to be attempted here. Instead I want to focus on how the emotions come into play in terms of social cooperation. How do emotions help us to deal with the danger of cheats, defectors, and free riders? How do they support cooperative behavior and discourage narrow self-interest?

The issue we need to consider is the problem of *commitment*. Imagine that your neighbor does not have enough food to feed his or her family, while you have more than enough. If you share your excess you assist your neighbor today and set up a situation in which your neighbor will be obliged to return a favor in the future. This makes sound sense if you can count on your neighbor to reciprocate. But how do you know whether you can in fact count on him? From your neighbor's perspective, the way to maximize self-interest is to accept your donation now but refuse to reciprocate in the future. This way he gets your extra food and keeps his own resources for his family. However, your neighbor knows that you recognize the danger of being cheated and so realizes that you will not share your food unless he can communicate a credible commitment to reciprocate. Robert H. Frank, author of a seminal work on this topic, writes that "the commitment problem ... arises when it is in a person's interest to make a binding commitment to behave in a way that will later seem contrary to self-interest."[94]

The challenge is to make a commitment that is credible. It is easy enough to promise to pay someone back, and just as easy to break that promise. What creates the conditions that allow such promises to be believed? In general, there has to be a cost associated with backing out of a commitment that outweighs the benefits that could be gained, and there are several ways this can occur; punishment was one effective strategy we considered. Emotions provide a powerful means of signaling commitment and, indeed, support the strategy of punishment. Let's look at commitment.

Randolph M. Nesse, an evolutionary psychiatrist and a leading figure in commitment studies, sets out two categories of commitments. There are *secured commitments* in which "once such a commitment is made, its fulfillment becomes in the actor's interest."[95] These, in effect, are guaranteed by laws and social sanctions – punishment figures in significantly here. In such cases commitments are credible because each party is confident that external sanctions will compel the other to fulfill the contract. The fulfillment of *unsecured commitments* is not motivated by extrinsic concerns. Nesse notes two main types of unsecured commitments, which he calls *reputational* and *emotional commitments*.[96]

A *reputational commitment* is secured by your interest in maintaining your reputation. We have already seen how important reputation is in encouraging people to cooperate with you, and in discouraging them from cheating you. A good reputation can be a major resource in pursuing inclusive fitness and so it is in our interest to maintain our reputations. So, a person who puts his or her good reputation on the line is a person capable of making credible commitments. And since a person who cannot make credible commitments loses out on the benefits of social cooperation, concern for reputation and willingness to defend it, even at great personal cost, are aspects of our evolved psychology.

Emotional commitments may be the most ubiquitous mode of commitment. Research into the evolutionary function of emotions presents perhaps the most fascinating and potentially significant insight into human behavior to come out of evolutionary psychology.[97] According to Nesse, "emotions are ... shaped by natural selection to adjust the physiological, psychological, and behavioral parameters of the organism ... to respond adaptively to the threats and opportunities" in the environment.[98] For example, take the emotional response of panic. Nesse writes that "imminent danger of attack elicits panic," which is "a coordinated pattern of physiological, psychological, and behavioral alteration" and which prepares the individual to respond to the threat.[99] It is an emotional reaction that enables an organism to act in a way that has a positive impact on fitness. Nesse discusses a series of other emotions shaped by evolutionary processes either as adaptive responses, such as fear and anxiety, or as responses to cues correlated with reproductive success, such as happiness and sadness.[100]

Emotions enable us to respond to the commitment problem. Frank claims that "certain emotions act as commitment devices"[101] that help us to make credible, though unsecured commitments. An emotional commitment is one which is secured by a "complex psychological reward mechanism"[102] in which certain emotional costs and benefits are associated with keeping/breaking commitments. There are, in effect, "moral sentiments" such as "anger, contempt, disgust, envy, greed, shame, and guilt," which function to regulate behavior.[103] These emotional reactions move us to act in ways that from a purely rational calculation may appear foolish (which is why emotions have been labeled "irrational"). Frank asks us to imagine a situation in which a good friend loses a wallet with $1,000 in it that, unbeknownst to your friend, you later find. In this situation you can keep the money without your friend ever finding out. What do you do? We hope that there are at least some situations in which you would return the money. But why? From a purely rational calculation you have nothing to lose and $1,000 to gain by keeping the money and keeping your mouth shut – why would you possibly consider returning the money? Because to keep the money would make you feel guilty and ashamed of yourself.[104]

The bonds formed by friendship go beyond rational calculation of self-interest. They are grounded in emotional commitments that lead us to act in ways not necessarily consistent with our own immediate profiting. And it is not merely friends that evoke these feelings. We noted that participants in a Dictator game share a much greater portion of the money when there is the possibility of feedback from anonymous strangers. The authors of that study propose that sentiments of guilt and shame supply the impetus to increased generosity.[105]

Of course, these acts of emotional commitment are inconsistent with self-interest only in the narrowest sense of that term. There are benefits that can be gained only by being able to make emotional commitments. Friendship is one prime example. To believe that a person is willing to support you only if they believe they can get something out of you in return is to believe that that person is no friend. Another important example is marriage, or what Frank calls the "marriage problem."

From a purely rational calculation, making a life-long commitment to one person does not make sense. Marriage certainly provides a wealth of emotional and physical payoffs, as well as contributing to reproductive success, but it is also a costly investment of resources. In the course of an extended relationship we can imagine that numerous opportunities may arise when either partner would be wise, in terms of rational calculation, to break his or her vow; when, for example, a more attractive or successful potential mate comes along. Based solely on a rational calculation of costs and benefits, a person should be wary of entering into a marriage and should be ready to leave when a more profitable situation arises. How do we get around this problem?

One way is to turn marriage into a secured commitment. Pre-nuptial agreements, marriage licenses, and divorce laws are all methods of securing the commitment to marriage. However, much of the reward of marriage comes from subjective conditions between partners. If you believe that your partner is committed to you only because of, or even partly because of, material concerns ("Of course I'll always be yours, it would be too expensive not to be"), you are unlikely to reap deep emotional satisfaction from that knowledge; and of course there is always the possibility that the calculation will one day tilt toward leaving. The commitment required to solve the "marriage problem" is secured by emotions. Frank writes, "The best insurance against a change in future material incentives is a strong bond of love. ... a deep bond of affection will render this change in incentives irrelevant, which opens the door for current investments in the relationship that might otherwise be too risky.[106] Our "irrational" emotions allow us to form committed relationships that provide rewards not attainable via rational calculation.

Emotions motivate us not only to fulfill our promises. They also allow us to make credible threats to those who defect from their commitment to us. Your belief that I am willing to punish you for cheating me serves as a motivation for you to keep your promise. But a problem lurks here, also. While it is in my interest to threaten you for cheating me, it is not always in my interest to actually punish all cases of cheating. Punishment, as we saw, comes with costs, too. I may be annoyed that you let your dog use my lawn as a toilet and threaten to sue you if it happens again, but the costs of going to court, paying a lawyer, losing time at work to testify, and so on are much greater than any price I would have to pay to repair my lawn. So, such a threat is not credible on rational grounds. However, a threat backed up by an emotional commitment has greater bite. If you know me to be deeply, emotionally, upset by your dog's actions you have reason to fear that I might act irrationally and fulfill my threat. Irrational, emotional reactions to being cheated function to secure commitments to retaliate and allow us to make credible threats. Nesse tells us that anger "signals that a defection has been detected and will not be tolerated. Its most basic function is to protect against exploitation." He continues, "This helps to explain why the angry person is unpredictable and irrational. If anger is to be effective, the target of the anger must believe that the angry person may act in ways that have substantial costs"[107] (this factor later plays a role in our discussion of moral gods).

This need to make credible threats is, of course, often socially disruptive, but it is an important part of maintaining social cohesion in that it raises the cost of cheating, which in turn makes cooperative action and interpersonal commitments less risky. Emotional reactions to defection also play a significant role in the effectiveness of moral systems. Trivers writes that "much of human aggression has moral overtones. Injustice, unfairness, and lack of reciprocity often motivate human aggression and indignation."[108] These moral sentiments motivate people to punish those who break the rules and threaten the systems of reciprocity and commitment that constitute the moral bonds of society. Punishment is a crucial aspect of any moral system and emotions make the threat of punishment credible, despite its cost. Individuals with strong moral-emotional responses are the individuals willing to engage in altruistic punishment so important to large scale cooperation.[109] The desire to punish, or a "punitive sentiment," seems to be part of our emotional make-up.[110]

In summary, emotions allow us to make credible commitments. Whether due to the bonds of affection that lead us to want to benefit others, the desire to avoid the shame and guilt associated with cheating, the sense of outrage at being cheated, or the desire to protect our reputations, emotions motivate us to act in ways not necessarily dictated by rational self-interest. In return, however, the ability to make such credible commitments allows us to gain rewards not available to those who act simply from rational self-interest. As Nesse puts it, "the rational pursuit of self-interest is sometimes an inferior strategy."[111] The capacity to make credible emotional commitments leads to systems of interpersonal relationships and cooperation between non-kin that contribute to long-term inclusive fitness. Because of these benefits to inclusive fitness, natural selection could "shape mental mechanisms that induce individuals to follow rules, even when not in their interests," and this allows "genuine moral capacities a place in human nature."[112] We need no transcendent source to explain the nobler aspects of human nature:[113] love, friendship, marital bonds, self-sacrifice for the group, moral pride, and indignation can all be built upon purely naturalistic foundations.

Understanding the role of emotions allows us to avoid another common, though misplaced criticism. We must recognize the distinction between ultimate causes and proximate causes. Proximate causes are the present conditions that lead to a behavior. These are the underlying emotional/affective springs to action. Ultimate causes are those conditions that result in our having the set of emotional/affective predispositions we do;

such causes are often best explained in terms of evolutionary processes. Take, for example, parental investment in children.

Humans have evolved to feel love and pride in their children (proximate causes of parental investment) because in the course of our evolutionary history those emotions were effective causes of behavior that increased genetic fitness (ultimate cause of parental investment). Evolution explains the development of the emotional response, the emotional response explains the behavior. However, because evolution is a satisficing process, humans are endowed with these emotional responses even though they may not always lead to reproductive success. Parents are not necessarily, or even likely to be, calculating the probable return in genetic replication on their investment of time and energy. As evolution favors behaviors that have a higher *probability* of enhancing reproductive fitness than competing behaviors, it follows that in certain cases that behavior will not enhance reproductive fitness. It is crucial to keep this lesson in mind because it helps to address a number of proposed counter-examples (such as sacrificing for a complete stranger, with no expectation of reciprocation) that only appear to weaken the argument for an evolutionary account.

Conclusion: From Moral Grammar to Moral Systems

The goal of this first chapter was to present an overview of the current state of moral psychology, as understood from an evolutionary perspective. The picture emerging is that moral decision-making is a largely intuitive process that occurs quickly and below the surface of conscious awareness. Social situations that demand a response are evaluated according to a set of innate principles; these principles constitute our innate moral grammar and are the products of human evolution. They were developed through natural selection to solve the demands faced by individuals pursuing their reproductive fitness in a social environment. Among the elements of our moral grammar are kin selection, reciprocal altruism, indirect reciprocity (including concern for reputation and cheater detection devices), frequency-biased transmission, and prestige-biased transmission. This moral grammar generates judgments that are emotionally valenced, giving them great power in shaping human interactions, and it is expressed in a culture's moral systems.

Moral systems are essential to a culture. If a society is to function at a level beyond the clan it must develop a system to effectively encourage and reward cooperation, and to discourage and punish defectors and cheats. This is what moral systems are designed to do: to establish a code of behavior that promotes and rewards behavior necessary to cohesive social functioning, while condemning and punishing behavior contrary to cohesive social functioning (so important are social norms that the mind appears to process normative information differently from non-normative information[114]). A crucial implication of this view of moral psychology is that the boundaries of the group mark the boundaries of moral concern.

Moral systems are effective not because of any transcendent moral quality possessed by humans but because these systems are expressions of our evolved moral psychology. To the extent that a moral code taps into this evolved moral sense it gains great intuitive and emotional appeal. It can move people to act because it triggers the cognitive and emotional predispositions that generate behavior. Consequently, as we analyze any moral tradition we should be able to uncover embedded in that tradition the various layers of our moral psychology we have identified.[115]

One of the most common, ancient, and powerful cultural institutions for the promotion of group cohesion is, of course, religion. It is the central thesis of this book that religions can be explained as cultural institutions that regulate individual behaviors in a pro-social manner by triggering evolved cognitive/emotional mechanisms. An evolutionary model of moral psychology allows us insight into the power that religions wield, for good and for woe, to shape human behavior, even in a post-modern, industrialized world very different from that inhabited by our earliest religious ancestors.

Before we turn to an evolutionary analysis of specific religious moral traditions we first need to see how humans came to interpret the world in ways that set the ground for religions to develop, and what it is about religions that make them such effective vehicles for extending our evolved moral sense.

2 | THE EVOLUTION OF MORAL RELIGIONS

Religion is the recognition of all our duties as divine commands.
(Immanuel Kant)

Setting the Task

In his fascinating book, *Guns, Germs, and Steel*, Jared Diamond presents a developmental sequence for the rise of large, densely populated groups, delineated into four stages of social growth.[1] The simplest organization is the *band*, which is a small group, consisting of perhaps a few dozen individuals, related by blood. This is characteristic of the hunter-gatherer period of human evolution, and was the model of human society for the major portion of our history. Next comes the *tribe*, consisting of hundreds of individuals organized into clans based on kinship. Both of these groupings tend to be egalitarian in their political structure, with "informal" methods for conflict resolution. Although Diamond does not describe it as thus, these informal means of conflict resolution can be understood to function according to the logic of evolutionary morality set out in the previous chapter.

Things began to change, however, as humans moved into the next stage of *chiefdom*. Chiefdoms number in the thousands, are comprised of numerous villages, and extend beyond relations based on kinship. A *state* is the final developmental phase, with tens of thousands of individuals grouped into large settlements such as cities, with multiple levels of bureaucracy and highly formalized social organization.[2]

With the shift from tribe to chiefdom we begin to see a more centralized, less egalitarian form of social control and conflict resolution. Seats of authority become established and codes of social behavior are formalized. This is necessary, Diamond writes, because with populations beyond a few hundred individuals "the difficult issue of conflict resolution between strangers becomes increasingly acute."[3] Put more bluntly, "With the rise of chiefdoms around 7,500 years ago, people had to learn, for the first time in history, how to encounter strangers regularly without attempting to kill them."[4]

This is what I have termed the problem of extension. The evolution of our basic moral tools took place largely in hunter-gatherer bands. Indirect reciprocity provides a way of extending moral concern beyond kin and close neighbors, but this strains under the pressure of increasing population density and the consequent social anonymity it allows. Evolved moral mechanisms for social cohesion and conflict resolution that may have functioned effectively even at the tribal level needed to be supplemented by other means. As Diamond points out, part of the solution was to centralize the power to resolve conflicts into the hands of an authority and to formalize social regulations and methods of control.[5] Another part of the solution came from a change in religion:

> Bands and tribes already had supernatural beliefs. ... But the supernatural beliefs of bands and tribes did not serve to justify central authority, justify transfers of wealth, or maintain peace between unrelated individuals. When supernatural beliefs gained those functions and became institutionalized, they were thereby transformed into what we term a religion.[6]

Diamond proposes that socially available religious beliefs were developed into more organized and formalized systems and used to bolster social cohesion as social pressures threatened to overwhelm our ingrained moral mechanisms. In other words, religion helped to solve the problem of extension.

It is not startling news to claim that religion plays a role in fostering pro-social, moral behavior. What Diamond contributes is the suggestion that religion takes on this role at a certain point in social development, that this moral/social function of religion is a response to changing social conditions. While he is correct that religion needed to change to accommodate the strains on social cohesion that came with larger, more complex societies, it would be a mistake to believe that morality and religion were first yoked together at such a late stage. The connection is much older than Diamond suggests, and much deeper than suspected by some of religion's critics – although the nature of the connection may not be what is expected by some of religion's advocates.

That religion and belief in god often serve a moral function in society goes without question. We need to ask, What is it about religion and religious belief that makes them so well suited to serve this function? To answer this we need to investigate the cognitive/emotional underpinnings of religious belief in order to see *how* religion came to support and extend morality; we must not remain content with a mere description of that function. However, before we turn to that difficult topic, we must get a grasp on something far more mysterious and hidden: the origins of religious belief itself (since religious belief must first exist in order to be called into the service of society[7]); this is where evolutionary accounts of religion come into play.

The Evolution of the Religious Mind

To discuss the evolution of religion is to walk into a minefield, and not simply because of religious sensitivities. One perennial problem is the question of definition. What constitutes a religion? How do we differentiate religion from magic or superstition? The debate over the proper definition of religion has the appearance of an intractable problem, with no proposed solution able to avoid controversy. However, this is not an issue we need to get into here. In our consideration of the evolution of religion we are interested in a mind-set that interprets the world in ways that contribute to the development of systems we would today categorize as religious – and the beliefs, doctrines, practices, rituals, and traditions I will be discussing clearly fall into this category.

The other significant problem we face is that we are again engaged in a project of intellectual archaeology, attempting to uncover the origins of phenomena that have left no physical traces. For certainly the religious mind-set must predate, in order to be able to account for, the creation of religious objects and rituals. When we consider the earliest physical or cultural evidence of religion we have already passed the point of religious origins.

Despite these formidable challenges, the attempt to explain the origin of religion in empirical terms dates back at least to David Hume's *The Natural History of Religion* (1757) and was a popular project throughout the nineteenth century. Without disparaging or discounting any of the contributions of those early investigators, I believe it is only within the past few decades that we have developed the tools that can give us a fair chance of setting out a scientific account of religious origins. In fact, I believe we are living in the midst of perhaps the greatest period of intellectual discovery in the history of religious studies. Scholars from the fields of evolutionary biology, cognitive psychology, anthropology, philosophy, and the neurosciences are forging a cognitive science of religion that promises to shed new light on the nature of religion.

There have been several major works published recently on this topic, along with a burgeoning body of research being published in journals all across the academic landscape. While these treatments of the evolution of religion are not completely consistent with one another (which is appropriate, as it is a new and developing field), there are general points of agreement that allow us to sketch a consistent model.

Given the wide-ranging and amorphous nature of the category *religion* we need to focus our discussion, and in terms of our ultimate goal of understanding religious ethics the most appropriate focus is on the *gods*. Scott Atran writes, "Supernatural agency is the most culturally recurrent, cognitively relevant, and evolutionarily compelling concept in religion."[8] Supernatural agents – whether gods, spirits, ancestors, or ghosts – play a prominent role in religions the world over, and have done so throughout history. This is a core element of many cognitive accounts of religion. Religion, whatever else it may be about, is about supernatural agents.[9] I will clarify just what constitutes a *supernatural agent* later, but for now our concern will be on how it was that such a concept came to be an almost universal aspect of humanity's mind-set.

Explaining belief in gods is a complex task. I believe it makes most sense to approach it by distinguishing various cognitive strategies that together generate belief in gods. In his seminal work, *Faces in the Clouds: A New Theory of Religion*, Stewart Guthrie set out a compelling account of the evolution of the most basic cognitive strategy underlying god-beliefs.

Guthrie's explanation is grounded in an evolutionary logic, with a focus on perception's contribution to survival. Whatever strategies or behaviors a creature develops in order to make its way in the world will be based on what it perceives about its environment. Our perceptual equipment, therefore, evolved to be sensitive to those environmental stimuli that had an impact on our quest for survival; our senses do not merely register whatever there is to perceive, but rather what it is important to perceive. For example, there is more to the spectrum of light than our naked eyes can see, and there are sounds and smells that other creatures perceive that go undetected by us. While we might be tempted to think it would be an advantage to have a more extensive perceptual field, selective perception allows us to focus our attention on what is most relevant to dealing successfully with our environment. Imagine the chaos if our eyes could perceive not only ultraviolet and infrared light, but x-rays and other forms of radiation. We might imagine some situations in which such sight would be useful, but it is unlikely that such occasions arose often in the lives of our pre-human ancestors. Our faculties of sight and sense were shaped to be selective to the stimuli most relevant to survival in the environment of evolutionary adaptedness (EEA). So perception must be understood not as a passive mirroring of reality,[10] but as goal-directed.

Our perception is selective not only in what we can perceive, but in how we actually perceive things. As Guthrie puts it, "perception is interpretation."[11] To make this clear consider the experience of walking through a forest. Such an environment provides an overwhelming amount of sensory information, visual, aural, tactile, olfactory. As we walk, our senses are bombarded with colors, shapes, movements, sounds, smells, but we do not perceive this as a "buzzing, booming, confusion." We integrate these perceptions into recognizable units: that patch of brown and green shapes ahead is a tree, that patch of black slithering through a patch of green and hissing is a snake in the grass, and so on. Individuals with minds unable to perform this interpretive perception end up walking into trees and being bitten by snakes. Such individuals are unlikely to be passing their genes on to future generations.

Being able to interpret perceptual cues in our environment accurately is an essential survival task – what is food and what is not; what is prey and what is predator – and so this ability has been subjected to the pressures of natural selection. However, it is not always possible to interpret the available stimuli clearly, or at least not before it is too late. Is that big, roundish patch of black up ahead a boulder or a bear? Is that rustling in the brush just the wind or a hidden predator waiting to pounce? Our ancestors faced such situations of under-determined stimuli on a regular basis, and one wrong interpretation could spell disaster. What type of strategy would we expect natural selection to favor here?

Guthrie argues that the mind uses two main criteria in interpreting under-determined perceptions: coherence and significance.[12] Under the criterion of coherence the mind settles on the interpretation that best fits with pre-existing knowledge of the world. For example, the roundish black object up ahead may trigger the interpretation of "boulder" or "bear" because both objects roughly match my perception, and both are known to be found in the woods (I am less likely to think "Volkswagen"). In terms of significance, the interpretation that generates the most important information will be favored over less useful interpretations. Although interpreting the rustling in the brush as the wind is a coherent interpretation, it does not provide as much significant information as interpreting it as, say, a hidden predator. I may or may not care which way the wind blows, but I am always interested in knowing where danger lurks. So, while both interpretations are equally coherent, and the rustling of leaves is often caused by the wind, clearly the safest strategy is to "Think predator," or as Guthrie puts it, "to discover as much significance as possible by interpreting things and events with the most significant model."[13]

The evolutionary benefits to such a strategy are obvious. If I over-interpret the stimuli, that is, if I choose the more significant model, that is, predator, I will take action to avoid the situation. If I am correct and there was a predator waiting to pounce, I have saved myself from a mortal confrontation; if I am wrong, and it was just the wind, then I have wasted some energy in escaping, and have given myself a fright, but I will otherwise be able to continue on my way. On the other hand, if I use the less significant model, that is, wind, and I am correct, I have saved all the energy I would have expended running away; but if I under-interpret and I am wrong, then I am lunch. So, while there are costs and benefits to both strategies – each will be more successful in certain situations – in evolutionary terms, that is, using a satisficing rule, over-interpreting is clearly the superior strategy. We are all the descendants of people who faced these choices and tended to think "Tiger!"

The strategy to over-interpret under-determined stimuli in terms of the most significant model is a cognitive pre-disposition, ingrained by natural selection. It remains part of our cognitive tool kit as we interact with our environments; it is not an outdated artifact from our past nor is it a rarely used tool. Perceptual uncertainty is common, even though we may often be unaware of it. Guthrie writes,

> Perceptual uncertainty may seem rare, since we seldom doubt for long what we are seeing. Bears and boulders quickly appear distinct. But perceptual uncertainty *is* the common state ... any sensation may be caused by an indefinite number of conditions. Normally, however, we are unaware of the uncertainty because most perception is rapid and unconscious, and suppresses ambiguity. Hence, perception appears definite, even while interpretation fluctuates.[14]

Guthrie provides a wealth of examples to show that this cognitive strategy to over-interpret stimuli remains a common part of our engagement with the world, emphasizing that this is not the result of irrational thought or sloppy, primitive thinking. It is not the mind going wrong, but the mind making a rationally justifiable attempt to bring coherence to experience.[15]

This cognitive strategy explains animism, that is, the tendency to attribute living forces to nature. To see rivers and forests and mountains as alive and exhibiting purposeful action is not the result of primitive irrationalism, it is the result of the mind's natural function to interpret the world in a meaningful way. When met with under-determined stimuli, such as a flooding river, or the rumbling of a mountain (these are under-determined because we do not understand the cause of the flooding or the rumbling), the mind seeks to impose the most significant interpretation. Understanding a phenomenon as alive is more significant than understanding it as merely mechanical – and this is a natural, automatic response. In fact, psychologist Deborah Kelemen and her associates have done some fascinating studies that provide empirical support for the notion that humans, from a very early age, are prone to interpret natural phenomena in terms of purpose and intentions.[16] Children as young as four and five years old not only interpret artifacts, such as chairs, as made "for" something, but they regularly ascribe purpose to natural phenomena as well (e.g., clouds were made "for raining," lions are made "to go into the zoo").[17] This finding is so robust that Kelemen suggests this cognitive strategy – which she terms "promiscuous teleology" – may be our "innate adaptation for biological reasoning."[18]

This strategy, of course, has functional payoffs. If a river is a living thing, then I have a model to use in deciding how to respond to it. If I am wrong and I am in fact offering sacrifices to an inanimate object, then I have wasted some energy and my rituals will be ineffective. But if I treat a living thing as an inanimate object I leave myself vulnerable to its powers. It may be objected that whether I offer sacrifices to a raging river or merely quiver in fear, neither action is going to make a bit of difference to the course of the flood. This is true, but my actions do not merely affect the world around me, they also affect the world inside me, and here there is an important difference between acting, albeit ineffectively, and quivering passively in fear. Action gives us a sense of control, which functions to reduce anxiety.[19] Finding meaning in the world, even when that meaning is threatening, provides psychological benefits to the individual. It reduces the psychic costs of facing the unknown. And the benefits are not simply subjective. Failed action can serve as an impetus to further investigation and experimentation: Why did this action fail? What did I do wrong? Have I misread the nature of the river? Failed action is the spur to future successful action.

So, even when the strategy to over-interpret the world does not directly result in successful action, we see that the strategy can have payoffs. In any case, mistakes are part of the package for any satisficing strategy: "the mistake embodied in animism ... is the price of our need to discover living organisms. It is a cost occasionally incurred by any animal that perceives."[20]

So, animism is one significant model the mind uses to interpret the world, but it is not the most significant one. To see a river as a living, breathing thing gives us certain information about it, but to see it as a living, breathing, angry, vengeful being provides much more, and here we move from animism to anthropomorphism. This tendency to over-interpret stimuli results not only in a world animated by spirits but in a world populated by beings who act, think, and feel in a human-like manner. This is our evolutionary bridge to the gods.

Understanding religion as anthropomorphism is perhaps the oldest explanation of religion. It first surfaces in the written record with the Pre-Socratic philosopher Xenophanes, who noted, "If oxen and horses and lions had hands and were able to draw with their hands and do the same things as men, horses would draw the shapes of gods to look like horses and oxen to look like oxen."[21]

Guthrie provides a useful analysis of the history of "religion as anthropomorphism," which we shall not review here.[22] Suffice it to say that he finds these accounts of varying worth but all are ultimately misguided for they treat anthropomorphism as either "a trivial mistake ... embarrassing ... [or] an aberration."[23] The most common explanation of this embarrassing, aberrant mistake is that anthropomorphism results from trying to see the world in a comforting manner. But in fact anthropomorphized religion is often far from comforting with its notions of vengeful spirits, powerful demons, and wrathful gods.

Guthrie argues that anthropomorphism is neither a trivial mistake nor an embarrassing aberration, but is rather a "plausible, though in hindsight mistaken, interpretation of things and events. It is inevitable in ordinary perception and cognition" and "results from a strategy universal in human perception."[24] Anthropomorphism stems from the strategy to find as much significance in perception as possible, and other humans are the most significant part of our environment. Other humans pose harm as potential predators, as hostile opponents, and as competitors for scarce resources. They also present benefits as potential mates and allies. Therefore, they are a vital aspect of the environment in which we must pursue reproductive success. Being able to detect and anticipate the action of such beings is an essential survival skill, but it is not a simple task. Humans are also not always easily detected. They can employ disguises and hide themselves away; they can act at a distance through tools such as weapons and traps. This means that "one cannot confidently predict human appearance."[25] For the mind to perceive human-like traits only when the perceptual cues are clearly determined (e.g., only when a human is clearly present) is a dangerous strategy. Those ancients who employed such a strategy would have been easy prey to all sorts of deception and subterfuge. Such individuals were unlikely to do well in the competition for resources, or be very successful in reproductive terms.

Therefore, to attribute human characteristics to events and objects not clearly human, or even in the absence of any visible being at all, is not necessarily an example of the mind malfunctioning. Since "virtually no phenomenon can be known with confidence not to be the result of human action,"[26] guessing that humans or human-like qualities are present is a sensible default position in the face of under-determined stimuli. It is better to misinterpret some event as the working of a human agent and be wrong than to misinterpret the action of a human agent as a meaningless event. In evolutionary terms, a strategy of betting on the presence of people is clearly an adaptive response to a world that is (1) filled with hidden dangers and deadly threats and (2) filled with humans.[27]

It is important to again keep in mind that these cognitive pre-dispositions that evolved to help solve fitness challenges in early human history are not left behind or disengaged as history unfolds. It makes no more sense to imagine these cognitive structures are irrelevant today because they evolved to address ancient problems than it would be to imagine that our digestive structures are irrelevant today since they evolved to respond to an ancient diet. Even though human dietary practices have changed drastically over the past 100,000 years, we must today make do with equipment designed in a primitive era. Of course, this can have maladaptive consequences, for example, the human predilection to consume large amounts of sugary foods. This is a major source of health problems in many areas of the modern world. However, this preference for sweets was adaptive in our EEA where the primary source of sugar was ripe fruit, which, while sweet, was rich in vital nutrients and vitamins. An early human with a "sweet tooth" would have had a healthy diet. Today we can indulge our evolved preference for sugar without any nutritional gain, with clearly maladaptive consequences. However, the fact that a trait is no longer adaptive does not mean that evolution will necessarily select against it. This occurs only when that trait begins to decrease reproductive fitness. So, unless the effects of our love of sweets has an impact on reproductive rates (a possibility that must now be considered given the levels of childhood obesity and the health dangers obesity brings) we are stuck with it.[28]

This same logic holds in discussing our evolved cognitive and emotional predispositions. Anthropomorphism does not fade away simply because we have become more sophisticated in our understanding of the world. Increased empirical knowledge does limit the cues that trigger anthropomorphism, but it does not remove the strategy from our mental tool kit.[29] For example, a person who has just moved into a new house and is unaccustomed to the creaks that the house naturally makes is going to be particularly primed to interpret those noises in an anthropomorphic manner. As the person gains more experience with the house those same noises are less likely to trigger that response – this cognitive strategy is context-sensitive – but an unfamiliar noise will bring the anthropomorphic response right back into play. Guthrie provides a wealth of examples that demonstrate that the strategy of betting on a human or human-like presence remains a common response, not only in everyday life but in the arts, sciences, and religion.[30]

The importance of all this for religion should be obvious. Indeed, Guthrie goes so far as to claim that "religion *is* anthropomorphism."[31] It may not be necessary to go that far, but Guthrie makes the case that religion, in both the East and the West, can be understood as "a system of thought and action for interpreting and influencing the world, built on anthropomorphic and animistic premises."[32] I believe that on a general level this is a workable definition of religion, but we need not debate that here, as our prime concern is not with the nature of religion, per se, but with the gods. And in terms of gods we can now see that the evolved strategy to over-interpret under-determined stimuli in anthropomorphic terms (as the model that brings the most coherence and significance to our experience) is the genesis of god-beliefs. As Guthrie puts it, "our perceptual uncertainty and our need to detect human presences wherever they may exist" are the "progenitors" of belief in the gods[33] and lead to a "proclivity for finding disembodied agents everywhere."[34]

This is the basic cognitive layer of god-beliefs, but over-interpreting uncertain stimuli in anthropomorphic terms is not itself belief in gods. When I interpret a glass shattering in the middle of the night as the result of human action I may be anthropomorphizing, but I am not interpreting that agent as a god. More needs to be done to turn this basic cognitive strategy into an actual belief in gods, but Guthrie has uncovered the evolutionary foundations for building such beliefs.

Before proceeding we should note that Guthrie's work has been criticized for being too focused on anthropomorphizing.[35] As Harvey Whitehouse points out, "what arrests attention when there is a rustling in the bushes is not necessarily the inference that a person is present but that an agent (an animal, a human, or perhaps a supernatural being) of some kind may lurk within."[36] This is a point that Guthrie anticipates.[37] What is most significant for us is that the cause of the bushes' rustling may be able to inflict harm on us, that is, it is an agent of some sort. This refines Guthrie's position a bit, without changing at all the evolutionary logic at work.

Justin Barrett has developed Guthrie's position, and has done important work testing it. Barrett refers to the strategy to interpret stimuli in terms of agency as an Agency Detection Device. He finds this a well-established part of our cognitive equipment, but points out that this device "suffers from some hyperactivity, making it prone to find agents around us, including supernatural ones, given fairly modest evidence of their presence."[38] In fact it seems all that is needed to trigger this device is "for the object to move itself (or in some way act) in a way that suggests a goal for its action" – this leads Barrett to refer to this tool as the Hyper-active Agency Detection Device (HADD).[39] He adds that "sometimes HADD's tendency to attach agency to objects contributes to the formation of religious concepts."

The Agency Detection Device is a fundamental concept in the cognitive explanation of religion: The human mind is designed to naturally, and automatically, interpret the world in terms of agents – that is, beings acting with intention.[40] This design is a product of evolution. The tendency to interpret the world in terms of agency constituted an effective strategy in an environment filled with uncertainty and danger and so was favored by natural selection. But, of course, not all agents are gods. How we move from the perception of agency to the formation of god-concepts is our next concern.

Conceptualizing the Almighty

Supernatural agency is the most widespread and significant concept in religion. The most recognizable example of a supernatural agent is a god, but the label applies to spirits, ghosts, ancestors, demons, angels, and a host of other cultural variants. These are examples, but what does it mean to be a supernatural agent? We have seen that to count as an agent an entity must, at minimum, express goal-directed activity. It must act with purpose, intentionality. It is this that renders an entity particularly significant to us, because it is this quality that empowers an entity to do us harm or good. What is it, however, that distinguishes a natural agent from a supernatural agent?

Before continuing we should note an objection. It is pointed out that the very notion of *supernatural* is a Western construct, that many cultures, ancient and contemporary, do not draw the same sharp line between the natural and the supernatural as is common in modern Western religious thought, and so to focus a study of religion on the concept of supernatural is culturally biased. While this objection raises important issues it is not relevant to our present discussion. The concept of the supernatural as we will use it is not a metaphysical concern with a different realm of reality, so familiar to Western forms of religion. "Supernatural" is here being used to refer to different kinds of beings or, rather, different ways of categorizing beings. To see this more clearly we must look at how the mind goes about categorizing the world.

Cognitive scientists see the brain as a complex system composed of specialized tools designed to carry out various tasks. One such tool may be labeled a *Categorizer*. This is a tool that receives "information primarily from our basic senses ... and use[s] that information to determine what sort of thing or things we have perceived."[41] The Hyper-active Agency Detection Device is an example of the categorizer at work. It receives information from the environment and categorizes the stimuli as an agent.

Having detected the presence of an object, the mind makes more discreet classifications and assigns the object into an *ontological category*. Ontological categories are groupings of different kinds of beings or things. For example, some things are inanimate physical objects, some things are self-animating biological objects, some objects talk and laugh. There are various ontological categories into which these things may be slotted, such as *tool*, *animal*, or *person*. This is a very important step. Slotting an object into one or another category is not merely a way to organize the world, it is a way of generating information about those objects, for these ontological categories carry with them a store of information that allows the mind automatically to generate a rich set of detailed inferences.[42] Barrett tells us that by placing an object into an ontological category we trigger other mental tools he calls *describers*, that is, "devices that our minds automatically use for supposing the properties of any given object or thing once it has been identified by a categorizer."[43]

Ontological categories conceptually organize the world and allow us to generate inferences and expectations. From these expectations and inferences we form a strategy for dealing with the things we meet in our environment. Is it the kind of thing that must be avoided? Can it safely be ignored? Can it be eaten? Simply by assigning an object to the correct category we gain access to detailed information about even unfamiliar objects, based upon very limited input. Take for example, an okapi. Now, you may have no idea what an okapi is, but if you are told it can be found at the zoo you are likely to categorize it as *animal*. Given only this limited information, however, you can now generate a rich set of detailed beliefs about this unknown creature: that it breathes air, it eats, it moves of its own power, it seeks to reproduce, it has a habitat, it can be seen and touched, it can be killed, and possibly kill, and so on. Clearly, there is much you will not learn about an okapi simply by categorizing it (e.g., that it looks like a cross between a giraffe and a zebra) but you will gain enough information to generate expectations about this unknown creature and be able to develop some approach to it.

These expectations constitute a kind of intuitive psychology about things in the world. If in observing an okapi you learn that it is an herbivore, this should not surprise you because having a vegetarian diet is a natural variation within the category *animal*; if you learn that the okapi has stripes on its legs, this too should be accepted as a natural feature of members of this category. If, however, I were to tell you that the okapi has legs like a zebra, a head like a giraffe, and sings like Bob Dylan, you are likely to be surprised. This last trait does not fit naturally within the category *animal*. It is a violation of our intuition about what this creature should be like – and note, we will feel this way instinctually, without having ever had any direct experience with an okapi. Singing like Bob Dylan is just not something non-human animals do. A Dylanesque okapi is a *counter-intuitive concept* and it is with such concepts that we can come to understand supernatural agency.

Religious entities, such as gods and ghosts, also can be fit into ontological categories, but are distinguished by involving counter-intuitive traits. Pascal Boyer writes that "religious concepts invariably include information that is counterintuitive relative to the category activated."[44] Such concepts may concern human-like beings that are capable of becoming invisible, non-human animals with human-like cognitive abilities, or natural objects, such as streams or mountains, that stand apart from typical streams and mountains by possessing certain capabilities. Gods, for example, fit into the ontological category of *person*, and this classification generates inferences about such beings based on the expectations captured by this category. Consider the gods of Olympus.

Zeus fits into the ontological category of *person*. This categorization generates certain beliefs, consistent with persons, that we can see exemplified by Zeus. He eats and drinks, he seeks sexual satisfaction, hides his indiscretions from his jealous wife, asserts his power, is offended when insulted, can be deceived, and so on. However, we also learn that Zeus can change form at will, that he never dies, that he controls the forces of nature. These are all violations of the intuitive expectations we have of members of the category *person*, and it is just these counter-intuitive concepts associated with Zeus that distinguish him as a supernatural agent. Gods, ghosts, spirits, and so on are supernatural in that these beings possess traits that go beyond the natural expectations for members of an ontological category (so, our gruff-voiced okapi would also count as a supernatural agent), and it is in this sense that supernatural agency is ubiquitous to religious systems.

This gives us a formula for generating religious concepts. Pascal Boyer, who has done some of the seminal work in this area, writes, "Religious representations are particular combinations of mental representations that satisfy two conditions. First, the religious concepts *violate* certain expectations from ontological categories. Second, they *preserve* other expectations."[45]

It should be clear why religious entities must violate normal expectations. If an ostensible god had only the powers and traits natural to all persons, then that being would not be a god, it would be a human. If a sacred animal or a holy object had all and only the qualities of natural animals and objects, it would not be considered sacred. What distinguishes a holy relic from any other object is not anything about its physical constitution but its possession of special powers, for example, the power to heal. It is the violation of natural categorical expectations that designates an object or agent as supernatural.

What might not be as clear is that our conception of religious entities must also preserve expectations generated by ontological categories. If we keep in mind the evolutionary origins of our mental tools this should become more evident. The function of categorizers and describers, and all the other accoutrements of our mental system, is to provide information that can be used to navigate our environment successfully in pursuit of survival and reproduction. We categorize not in order to have an organized representation of the world but in order to act more effectively in the world. By placing an entity into a category we generate useful information about that object without having to go through trial and error. If our ancestors had to use trial and error each time they came upon an object in the wild each individual encounter would be a new and confusing experience.

However, by being able to categorize an entity as *animal* I generate information, such as, it may be a predator to be avoided, or it may be prey to be hunted. I know this because I know members of the *animal* category are made of flesh and blood, and can be killed and eaten; I also know that members of this category seek to kill and eat other things. Certainly I need to make more refined categorizations (carnivore vs. herbivore; large and sharp-toothed vs. small and flat-toothed, etc.) but by virtue of this mental tool I am able to reduce the amount of trial-and-error experiments and raise the possibility of successful action.

A concept that does not preserve some categorical expectations is useless. It no longer fits into an ontological category and so I have no way of knowing what to do with the entity or how to respond to it. We can certainly dream up some such concept but it will have no practical significance for us.

This sets a limit on god-concepts. As Atran puts it, "Gods and other supernatural beings are systematically unlike us in a few general ways – more powerful, longer lived, more knowledgeable... – and predictably like us in an enormously broader range of usual ways."[46] We see this clearly in the Olympian gods who engage in a wide variety of human activities, of both the virtuous and vicious kind, despite their superpowers. However, we also find this in the god of the monotheistic religions. God loves us, cares for us, is watching us, can be offended, has expectations, can be angered when those expectations are disappointed, and so on. In both popular media and popular imagination God takes on a host of other anthropomorphic characteristics as well, such as gender (God the father), an abode (heaven), even physical characteristics such as a fierce visage, long white beard, and flowing robes. These are all expectations generated by placing God in the ontological category of *person*. If our conception of God did not preserve some of these expectations, then we would have no idea of how to respond to that being. A conception of God as "wholly other" would be useless. How would we know where to start in worshipping such a God? Would such a God want to be worshipped? Would such a God want anything of us at all? "Wanting" is a trait of persons, as is commanding, prohibiting, being offended, having plans and purposes, and so on. Without these categorical traits God would be an insignificant concept.

Of course, theologians spend a great deal of time and energy arguing that these categorical expectations are not true representations of God. They teach that God is spirit and so has no gender nor body, nor does God feel anger or take offense in any way familiar to human experience; that god is omnipresent and so has no physical abode; and so on. People may accept all these teachings as true, and be able to recite them when asked. However, there are limits to theology. Justin Barrett has studied the relationship between theologically correct beliefs and default positions for religious concepts (i.e., those beliefs more consistent with underlying cognitive schema). He found that when asked directly about the nature and abilities of God, believers are able to reflect and provide generally correct theological answers. However, under conditions of having to answer quickly, without time to reflect, these same believers "systematically misremembered God as having human properties in contradiction to ... theological ones."[47] For example, a believer may accept that God is spirit and has no gender, and still pray to the Almighty Father to watch over his children.

D. Jason Slone had provided an extended treatment of this topic in his book entitled, appropriately, *Theological Incorrectness*.[48] In it he exemplifies this concept by considering the reception of Puritanism in colonial America. Puritans preached what Slone calls "a maximally counter-intuitive theological tradition," Calvinism,[49] in which God predetermines the ultimate fate of each individual, leaving the individual powerless to resist. Yet Puritan tradition was "replete with rituals and other activities ... that were felt to be able to engender favorable outcomes in this world" and was characterized by strict laws intended to discourage sinful behavior.[50] These are elements of religions found throughout the world and across cultures – and they make intuitive sense. However, they are not consistent with the belief that what will be has already been determined by an immutable deity and that if one has been pre-destined for damnation, no human incentive will change that. The theological teachings of Calvinism pushed too hard against the cognitive constraints that shape god-beliefs and so eventually yielded to more intuitive religious practices.[51]

Conflicts between reflective beliefs about God – such as those provided by theology and philosophy – and cognitively constrained conceptions of God have played a formative role in the history of religious thought and continue to be a dynamic and often controversial factor in religious belief. This tension between different ways of understanding God will be a significant theme throughout the rest of this book. Much more needs to be said on this topic, but here I can at least stake out the position of cognitive science: The more that reflective beliefs about God move away from cognitively intuitive conceptions, the less influential those beliefs become. As religion scholar Todd Tremlin puts it, "people who present gods as radically different from the category *Person* make them incomprehensible and irrelevant as well."[52]

So, conceptions of supernatural agents assume a particular form in which certain ontological expectations are preserved and some are violated – although there seem to be limits to such violations.[53] These constraints stem largely from the demands made by counter-intuitive concepts on our cognitive tools. As noted, with imagination almost any wildly counter-intuitive notion may be entertained, but will it be believed or passed on? Concepts also face a survival test. Concepts that are not memorable are not readily preserved or transmitted to other minds, and concepts that grossly violate categories are not good candidates for transmission. This is not simply because they are hard to classify (i.e, they do not trigger innate tools for categorizing and describing) but because they lack inferential significance. Such concepts do not generate practical inferences and expectations, and so they are just not important enough to be memorable. Concepts that do pass this survival test preserve enough of the category to generate useful inferences but violate enough to make the concept significant and memorable.[54] There is also research that suggests beliefs with minimally counter-intuitive elements are not only easier to remember but are subject to less recall degradation over time than purely intuitive beliefs.[55] All of this leads Boyer to claim that this "two-fold condition ... is sufficient to account for the recurrent features of supernatural concepts the world over."[56]

In the current parlance of the field these concepts are referred to as minimally counter-intuitive (MCI), although I should note that there is a debate within the field as to whether "counter-intuitive" is an appropriate way to describe supernatural concepts.[57] Guthrie, for example, stresses the naturalness of even some counter-intuitive traits, such as invisibility. As we discussed, detecting agency does not require the physical presence of an agent. The ability of humans to hide, to disguise themselves, to act from a distance with various weapons all goes to argue that an agent need not be visible in order to be present in some way. Guthrie refers to this as "distributed agency."[58] Given this, in what sense is "invisibility" counter-intuitive? That is, how does "invisibility" violate the categorical expectations of *person*? Guthrie concludes that a physical body is not a necessary element of our conceptualization of human-like agents; the one necessary element is a mind, and we need not connect a mind with a body. Some intriguing support for this position comes from psychologist Paul Bloom's work on child development.

In *Descartes' Baby*, Bloom argues that humans are, from early childhood, natural Cartesians. That is, we approach the world as dualists, easily and naturally separating bodies from minds. He writes, "Children are dualists. ... in the sense that they naturally see the world as containing two distinct domains ... what I have described as bodies and souls."[59] This results from humans possessing separate cognitive systems for processing information about physical objects and information about social interactions. Studies with human infants indicate that we come into the world with innate expectations about how physical objects should behave. Child psychologists test these expectations by using "look-time" experiments. Babies, even in infancy, show a well-documented tendency to look longer at novel stimuli. It has also been shown that they look longer when presented with surprising stimuli.

Consider an example: A toy is put on an empty stage in the visual field of a baby. A screen is placed in front of the toy. Then another toy is placed behind the screen – this the baby sees, but unseen by the baby is that the second toy was not placed on the stage, so when the screen is lifted there is only one toy visible. Babies as young as 5 months old stare longer at this stimuli than when two toys are revealed behind the screen, indicating that they expected to see two toys. They also stare longer when the experiment is manipulated so there are three toys behind the screen, instead of the expected two. Bloom reports that this is "a remarkably robust finding, and has been replicated in several laboratories." Similar experiments have shown that babies have expectations of physical objects in terms of cohesion, continuity, solidity, and contact.[60]

As remarkable as these findings are, they are not unique to humans. These experiments, or variants of them, have been done using a variety of non-human animals, with similar results. Bloom notes,

> As best we know, there is nothing special about our species when it comes to knowledge of the physical world. Whenever there has been a careful comparison, it turns out that the same understanding of objects that you find with human babies shows up in other animals, particularly other primates. They seem to think about bodies the same way we do.

"But" – significantly – "the situation is very different with regard to social understanding."[61]

Research shows that before they reach their first birthdays babies are able to attend to the eye gaze of an adult to figure out where the adult is looking; they can follow the pointing of an adult; they can respond to emotional cues; and soon they are able to employ these methods of communication themselves. These are skills that are even beyond the abilities of chimpanzees.[62] That humans share innate expectations about the physical world with non-human animals speaks to a shared evolutionary history; that humans possess unique social abilities speaks to a separate cognitive system, and one that evolved to serve particularly human needs.

These two cognitive systems are adaptations that "give human beings a badly needed head start in dealing with objects and people," but these systems can be decoupled, allowing us to "perceive the world of objects as essentially separate from the world of minds, making it possible for us to envision soulless bodies and bodiless souls."[63] In this sense, conceiving of invisible or disembodied agents is not counter to our intuitive understanding of agency – it is a natural output of the kind of mind we have[64] – and so Guthrie is correct to challenge the appropriateness of "counter-intuitive" as part of the formula for god-concepts.

However, I believe that while this shows that belief in disembodied agents, such as gods, is a natural output of a mind designed to "promiscuously" attribute agency and intentionality to stimuli, none of this denies that gods are conceptualized differently from typical persons. There are certain traits that if exhibited by your neighbor, say, the ability to make herself invisible in the middle of a conversation, would catch your attention and lead you to suspect that there was something unusual about your neighbor. As open-ended as our conception of a human-agent might be, that is just not something we would expect a person to do. In this sense, then, the ability to become invisible, to control the forces of nature, to create *ex nihilo*, and so on, are notions that violate our intuitions about what members of the category *person* are able to do – they are counter-intuitive.[65] Therefore, leaving aside some of the more technical aspects of this debate, we can move forward with an understanding of gods as minimally counter-intuitive concepts, that are natural outputs of our evolved minds.

These MCI concepts, since they are constrained by structures of the brain characteristic of all humans, are not culturally determined but provide a universal template for religious representations; the supernatural beings we meet in various guises in the world's religions are built upon this template. Culture does, of course, play an important role. The variety of supernatural agents is a result of varying environmental and cultural pressures working on these universal templates. To fully understand a religious tradition we need to pay careful attention to the culture in which that tradition developed, just as we need to pay attention to the physical environment in any study of biological evolution.[66] Although these religious concepts are grounded in and constrained by our evolved psychology, culture provides the social environment in which these concepts are expressed. As noted in the last chapter, nothing said here should be taken to imply genetic determinism, or a reduction of religion to biology. We are seeking to uncover the biological bases for religious experience and to understand the psychological conditions that contribute to the development of religious thought.

That said, we must also be careful not to commit the more common mistake of allowing the great diversity of religious forms and ideas to "blind us to the underlying recurrent features" shaped by evolutionary pressures[67] – and as we have noted, and we will see in greater detail, the god of the Bible falls within this domain.

Before moving on, one more potential criticism must be addressed. Although MCI concepts provide the template for religious concepts, not all MCI concepts are religious concepts – but why not? Why is our Dylanesque okapi, which is clearly an MCI concept, not a religious entity? Or as Atran asks, what distinguishes Mickey Mouse from Jesus?[68] How do we distinguish between religious beings and fantasy figures if both fit the template for an MCI concept? In some cases the answer is that we know the fantasy character is a work of fiction because we know the author (although this does not stop Scientologists). Walt Disney created the concept of Mickey Mouse and I created the concept of a Dylanesque okapi. But there is a deeper answer. For a concept to function as a religious belief people must be motivated to believe in that concept, and people are motivated to believe in a concept because the information generated by that concept is relevant to significant life pursuits. Joseph Bulbulia refers to this as a "conviction constraint."[69]

An important part of this motivational component of religion is the emotional power religious concepts often provoke. We will have the opportunity to discuss the connection between religion and emotion at points in the discussions that follow, but suffice it to say that this connection is a significant aspect of religious belief and practice, as is well attested to by a number of researchers. Religious beings can inspire awe,[70] are associated with purity,[71] invoke and relieve dread and anxiety,[72] can serve as attachment figures[73]; and at least one function of religious rituals is to develop emotionally conditioned responses to religious beliefs.[74] My musical okapi may be an entertaining concept but it generates no expectations that affect our lives in any meaningful may, nor is it designed to evoke significant emotional response. Even though it may fit the model for a supernatural being, it is a poor candidate for a religious belief.

So, let us pull together our findings thus far: Evolution has equipped us with a hyper-active agency detection device – that is, an ingrained cognitive strategy to over-interpret under-determined stimuli with the most meaningful model available – that regularly detects the presence of agents, even when no agents are present. These perceptions that are interpreted as agents are processed by various cognitive tools and are conceptualized in a minimally counterintuitive manner. Some of these MCI concepts are memorable because they grab our attention by including surprising information, and because they also provide strategically significant information. These features give such concepts a greater chance of being transmitted from person to person and from generation to generation. God-concepts are particularly well suited for transmission. Gods fit into the important ontological category of *person*. Since persons are the most important feature of a human's environment our minds are sharply attuned to members of this category. Gods are especially attention grabbing for not only do they trigger cognitive and emotional responses that other persons do, they also possess counterintuitive traits, for example, supernatural powers, which make them even more significant than other agents. As Barrett says, "Thus, once introduced into a population, God concepts hold strong promise to spread rapidly and gain tenacious adherents."[75] He later adds that "belief in God may be among the most selectively privileged of religious beliefs."[76]

However, since the cultural conditions may change from generation to generation, these concepts may also change. Some concepts may be revised, expanded, or re-interpreted, while still retaining the structure of MCI concepts; others may be rejected.

The counter-intuitiveness of a concept is not sufficient for a concept to continue to function as a religious belief. The concept must continue to be relevant. As social conditions change some concepts may lose their relevance – that is, the inferences and expectations they generate may no longer be useful, or new versions of the concept may prove more valuable. This allows for development within religious systems. The aim of this chapter is to understand one such development in religious evolution: the rise of moral religions.[77]

The Moral Function of Gods

Scholars point out that religion is much more than morality, and may not always be concerned with morality; the gods are not necessarily represented as moral beings. However, there is an obvious relationship between religion and morality, and under certain conditions the connection between morality and religion becomes particularly significant. In the last chapter we saw that the larger and more complex a society becomes, the greater the temptation to defect from social cooperation, and the greater the chance of doing so successfully. This makes sacrificing for the social good more costly, and even for the socially conscientious, a less rational option. The danger of this spiraling out of control threatens the sustainability of such societies. Religion plays a role in solving the problem of extension for evolutionary mechanisms of morality.

Supernatural agents, as we know, come in many variations. But we also know there are recurrent features behind this diversity, and the most common, if not universal, feature attributed to such beings is a mind.[78] Tremlin points out that even sophisticated theological descriptions of God, ones that "seek to do away with ... unfortunate anthropomorphic ideas," are still constrained by this: "they never abandon the idea that gods have minds."[79]

In dealing with the mind of God, the same cognitive strategies that allow us to understand supernatural agency are at play. That is, we understand the mind of God the way we understand the mind of typical members of the ontological category *person*, but with some minimally counter-intuitive elements thrown in the mix. In dealing with persons (but not just persons) another mental tool is called into action – we employ a *theory of mind* (ToM). We know *persons* are agents, that is, they act with intention. However, we bring a much richer set of intuitions to our beliefs about *persons*: We recognize that not only do they act with intention, but they have reasons for what they are intending to do; they can think about what they are doing, what they want, what they don't want; and they have feelings (happy, sad, angry, scared, etc.). These intuitions provide valuable strategic information in determining how to respond to other agents.

For example, if I see a person eating, I do not merely see this as a random series of actions. My Agency Detection Device is triggered and I intuit that the person is doing these actions to accomplish a goal; but my ToM is also triggered, and I intuit that the person is hungry and is eating to sate that hunger. I can also intuit that if I were to take his lunch away from him he would become angry, and angry agents can act with dangerous intentions. I do not need to ask the person if he would be upset if I took his lunch; and I do not need to conduct an experiment to see what would happen. Our ToM device is, in effect, a mind-reading tool that allows us valuable insight into the thoughts and feelings of others.[80]

Once a supernatural agent is categorized as *person*, our ToM is also engaged and we understand that being – that god – as an intentional agent with a mind; and we conceive of that mind as containing thoughts, plans, intentions, feelings, desires, expectations, and so on. We conceive of the mind of God in much the same way as we conceive of the minds of *persons* – but with some vitally important exceptions.

In our day-to-day interactions with other people it is crucial, you will recall, to distinguish potential cheaters from potential cooperators. To do so requires a wide range of information: the person's reputation, any past dealings with this individual, what the person might have to gain or lose from cheating, their social or familial relationship to us, and so on. Perhaps the most significant type of information concerns the mental states of these other agents: What information do they have? What do they lack? What are their intentions? Humans are very sensitive to a wide array of cues that might provide insight into the minds of other people in order to surmise their intentions. Pascal Boyer argues that the ability to predict the behavior of others is a significant competitive advantage and has led to the evolution of a "hypertrophied social intelligence" in humans.[81] A person who cannot read the facial cues or emotional responses of others and integrate this into his or her decision making is at a terrible disadvantage in social situations. Such an individual is a target for exploitation by more proficient mind readers and is less able to make his or her way in a socially complex world.[82] Natural selection would not have been kind to such people.

A prime function, then, of our social mind is to search for strategic information, that is, information that may be used in guiding future social interactions. We recognize in ourselves a limit to how much information we can gather. No matter how sensitive we might be to other's feelings and responses, no matter how much background information we collect, there are always things beyond our grasp. We can never fully know the mind of another, which is why there is always an element of unpredictability in dealing with people. However, we also recognize this limitation is mutual. Boyer points out that we conceive of humans as "limited access strategic agents."[83] That is, we assume that others do not have access to complete or perfect information relevant to social interactions, and this mutual limitation often plays an important role in our social dealings.

People the world over, however, represent gods as "full access strategic agents."[84] They view their gods or ancestors not necessarily as omniscient but as having access to all information relevant to particular social interactions. They may not know how many grains of sand are on the beach, but they know what you did last night and what you are doing now – and *that* is the truly important information. The gods have access to all that is needed for making a sound judgment in any particular situation. Not all gods may be represented as possessing this quality – it may be possible to deceive some gods – but the ones that are will be of particular significance. As Boyer puts it, "The powerful gods are not necessarily the ones that matter; but the ones that have strategic information always matter."[85]

Here again we have some empirical evidence suggesting that this view of God's mind is a natural output of the kind of minds we have. Justin Barrett and his colleagues used a standard false-belief task to test how young children think of the mind of God.[86] In this experiment a child is shown, say, a box of cereal that has pebbles inside it rather than cereal. The child is then asked a question: If someone came in the room and saw this box of cereal, what would they think is inside it? Children three years old tend to answer "pebbles." This is a well-documented result. Children at this age have a hard time entertaining the notion that someone would believe something that they themselves know to be false. However, by the time they reach five years old, this is no longer a problem, and most children understand that the person will believe there is cereal inside the box. The interesting twist in Barrett's experiment is that he also asked children what they thought God would believe was in the box. In this case all the children tended to answer "pebbles." Even the five-year-olds who had mastered the skill of recognizing false beliefs attributed superior insight to God. Gods are not fooled by superficial appearance the way people are, and humans recognize this at a very early age.[87] This is the mental trait that contributes to a god's standing as an MCI concept, and beings that possess such a trait are in a particularly privileged position to assume a moral role.[88]

We are now ready to bridge the evolution of religion and evolutionary morality: Gods, as "full access strategic agents," occupy a unique role that allows them to detect and punish cheaters and to reward cooperators. In moral religions such gods are conceived of as "interested parties in moral choices."[89] They are concerned with social interactions and they are fully cognizant of the behavior and motives of those involved. The gods know who reciprocates and who cheats, and the gods remember.

Boyer sets out three models or roles for moral gods: god-as-legislator (the gods issue commands and prohibitions), god-as-paragon (god, or some other supernatural agent, serves as a moral role model), and god-as-interested-party (god cares about what we do).[90] While god-as-legislator or god-as-paragon may be theologically privileged in teaching about god, "in people's actual reasoning about particular situations, in the practical business of judging people's behavior and choosing a course of action, the interested party model is largely dominant."[91] As Boyer points out, the problem with the legislator and paragon models is that they are too specific to be of general usefulness. People may know that God has set out the Ten Commandments as his law for moral behavior, but may not be able to list all the commands, or even know just how to apply them to their lives (e.g., just how does the prohibition against "graven images" apply to contemporary forms of entertainment? What constitutes "coveting" in a consumerist society?) And despite the popularity in some quarters of "What Would Jesus Do?" paraphernalia, it is far from clear how the actions of Jesus set out in the gospels provide a guide to dealing with life in the twenty-first century. However, whatever the situation the belief that God is watching and cares about what you do is relevant. In fact, I would argue that god-as-interested-party is not only the dominant model, it is the original model, for if god were not interested in morality why would he bother to legislate commands or exemplify correct behavior? It is the intuition that god cares about right and wrong that makes the other two models plausible.

Now we can draw some connections between several of the lessons we have already learned. Evolution has pre-disposed us to favor kin; to expect reciprocation of altruism and to approve of those who cooperate, while denouncing cheats; and to support those in our group, while showing caution toward others. These evolved moral mechanisms provide the baseline for our expectations about how people will respond to social interactions. These form part of the default expectations and inferences bound up with our conception of people. We conceive of God as a "full access strategic agent," and so we believe that he is aware when people cheat and that he knows when someone makes a great sacrifice. And given that the concept of god triggers the ontological category of *person*, all the relevant expectations about how a person responds to cheats and heroes are also triggered. If God knows about a cheater we cannot help but intuitively believe that he must disapprove of that cheat. The god-as-interested-party model arises automatically once God is conceived as a full access strategic agent. It does not have to be taught, it flows naturally from the way our minds process the relevant information concerning God and morality.

Once the concept of god-as-interested full access strategic agent is developed, it bolsters the social functions of morality. Communal belief in such beings raises the cost of cheating by making detection more probable (God sees all), and punishment more certain (God can do all); this in turn lowers the risk of cooperating and makes it less risky. The strains placed on our evolved moral mechanisms are eased by belief in a god who cares. Religion then becomes the vehicle for the moral code of a society required for that society to continue to function as a coherent unit as it grows in size and complexity.

Some recent research provides data in support of this proposition. In a study of the relationship between population density and religious belief, anthropologists F. L. Roes and M. Raymond found a significant, positive correlation between society size and belief in moralizing gods (i.e., gods supportive of human morality). They suggest that such a belief provides the cohesion that allows societies to grow larger, and so out-compete other groups. This has been followed up by political scientist Dominic Johnson, who in a study of 186 world cultures also found a significant correlation between population size and belief in "high Gods" (i.e., a spiritual being who is believed to have created all reality and/or to be its governor).[92] This is part of a growing body of literature supporting the claim that religion solves the problem of extension.

A major part of religion's ability to shore up a moral psychology designed for much more intimate groups is its role in punishment. In our discussion on the evolution of morality we saw how important punishment, or at least the possibility of punishment, is to promoting cooperation and increasing generosity. Many researchers see punishment as the key to the effectiveness of moral systems, and morally interested, full access strategic agents are well suited to contribute to this moral task. That the gods have the power to dole out punishment is, of course, an obvious fact. What is more significant is that empirical evidence is mounting attesting to the importance of divine moral enforcers.[93]

For example, psychologists Azim Shariff and Ara Norenzayan conducted experiments using the anonymous Dictator game discussed in the previous chapter. Recall that this game tests how people will split a sum of money with another person, with no limits on how greedy or generous they can be. We saw that under anonymous conditions people tend to be quite greedy. In their version of this experiment they had a control group play a standard anonymous Dictator game, but the experimental group was given a priming task before playing the game. In this task the subjects had to unscramble ten five-word sentences. Five of these ten sentences contained religious words, such as *spirit*, *divine*, *God*, or *sacred*. Their results showed significantly greater generosity from the primed group than from the control group, and this was independent of the self-professed religiosity of the participants. In fact, in one set of trials the priming increased generosity even for atheists – that is, individuals who denied believing in God were still more generous when primed by religious words (although this particular result was not consistent across all trials).[94]

In other studies, Jesse Bering found that the behavior of children could be altered simply by telling them that an invisible being, "Princess Alice," was in the room watching them.[95] Another experiment conducted by Bering and colleagues found that cheating levels on an experimental task (one designed to test cheating propensity) were significantly lowered when students were informed that one of the experiment's designers recently passed away and that his ghost had been seen in the testing area.[96] And the belief that supernatural agents are involved in visiting punishment on humans is a cross-culturally robust one. In Johnson's review of the 186 cultures, he reports that all societies attributed illness "to the malicious work of some supernatural agent or other."[97]

The bottom line in terms of this research is that belief in supernatural punishment can decrease cheating and increase cooperation and that this effect is easily triggered and ubiquitous.

This is one moral function of religion, but once this step is taken much more can follow. Consider this: We know it is imperative to discriminate between potential cooperators and cheaters, and as societies become larger and more anonymous, this becomes increasingly difficult. Belief in a moral god addresses this difficulty, but only if such belief is commonly shared. If you do not believe God is watching you, then you have less to fear from cheating, and I have more to lose by cooperating with you. My belief that you will be punished someday for your lack of belief does little to protect me now. This explains why people can be so interested (at times, to the point of obsession) with other people's beliefs. As Boyer puts it, "to assume that there is a fully informed agent around is likely to change my behavior. But then if others assume that there are such agents it will change their behavior too, which is why their representations [of gods] are of great interest to me."[98] If I do not know what you believe how can I trust you to reciprocate my cooperation? We are back to the commitment problem we discussed in Chapter 1. There are various ways to secure a commitment to cooperate or to reciprocate cooperation. Some commitments can be secured by law, but many cannot. Even ones that can be secured by law leave us vulnerable to those willing to risk punishment. Reputational and emotional commitments are also important means of securing commitments, but too many people are willing to sacrifice reputation, and many are quite skilled at faking emotions. Even though humans have developed strategies for assessing an intention to commit, we also possess the ability to deceptively signal such an intention and so we must be wary of the sincerity of any such signals. Given this, evaluating signals of commitment is an important task.

In attempting to determine the sincerity of signals of commitment there is a sound rule to follow: The harder it is to fake a signal to commit to cooperation, the more trustworthy it is. As William Irons notes, "For such signals of commitment to be successful they must be hard to fake. Other things being equal, the costlier the signal the less likely it is to be false."[99] This is known as costly-signal theory. The logic of this theory is obvious and compelling. In determining whether to trust someone and risk engaging in a cooperative venture ("risk" because of the potential to be taken advantage of and to waste resources), we look for clues that may signal that this person is a good risk. These clues may, however, be insincere. It may be in that person's interest to fake a signal to cooperate in order to earn my trust, which they can abuse to their own advantage. However, if the particular signal they use is costly to fake, then I have more reason to treat that signal as sincere (because faking this particular signal will cost the person more than they can hope to get by taking advantage of me).

Here is another vital moral role played by religion. Religious rituals and traditions serve as hard-to-fake signals to commit to cooperative behavior. Indeed, Irons has characterized religion as a "hard-to-fake sign of commitment."[100] He writes,

> Most religions are expressed in elaborate rituals that are costly in time and sometimes in other ways. These rituals also provide extensive opportunities for members of a community to monitor one another's commitments to the community and its moral code thereby facilitating the formation of larger and better-united groups.[101]

Irons points out that religions are typically learned over a long span of time, their traditions are often sufficiently complex to be hard for an outsider to imitate, and their rituals provide opportunities for members to monitor each other for signs of sincerity. This is a costly and time-consuming process. Showing oneself to be a member of a religion by mastering the traditions of that religion signals that one has already made a significant contribution of time and energy to the group, and this signals a willingness to follow the code that governs the group. That is, it signals that one is a reliable partner in social interactions and can be trusted to reciprocate.

This is another area ripe for empirical evaluation, and the person doing some of the most interesting work here is anthropologist Richard Sosis. Sosis invites us to consider religion as a form of communication. Aside from typical means of communication, religions communicate "most effectively and uniquely" through what he calls "the three B's" – behavior (rituals), badges (distinctive markings or garments), and bans (prohibitions or taboos)[102] – and what these three B's communicate is commitment to the group. All three of these religious elements are costly, in terms of resources (rituals require an investment of time, money or other goods, or comfort[103]; prohibitions require forgoing the use of specified resources) and by precluding one from benefiting from other groups (badges mark one as belonging to this group but not that one). By taking on such costs you communicate your investment in the group, and doing so raises your status as a potential partner in social cooperation. The more costly the signal, the more effective it is as a sign of commitment, and the greater the level of social cooperation may be.

This makes sense on a theoretical level, but Sosis is going beyond theory and gathering empirical data. He and his colleagues have been conducting studies of religious and non-religious communes, using both databases and field research. He has found that groups that demand costlier commitments of their members last longer than groups that require low levels of commitment: "Costly constraints have a positive impact on the longevity of religious communes, suggesting that increases in the level of sacrifice imposed on members enhances group commitment."[104] Groups that ask more of their members have greater cohesion and fare better than less demanding groups because (at least in part) the costliness of being part of that group creates a strong, mutual presumption of commitment on the part of the members, thereby facilitating cooperative social action. And this sense of mutual commitment is not merely an intellectual exercise. It is deeply felt as well, as rituals imbue religious beliefs and practices with powerful emotional associations.[105]

This too helps us to understand why members of a religious group are so concerned about the beliefs (Sosis adds *belief* as a fourth B) and behaviors of other people. These beliefs and behaviors are signals of commitment to the group. Failure to adhere to the traditions and beliefs of the group may be a signal that one is a potential defector – someone who can no longer be trusted to be cooperative or to reciprocate acts of altruism. Monitoring the behavior of others in the group is such a serious concern because the danger posed by defectors and cheats (to individuals as well as to the group) is so serious. Defection and cheating threaten to undermine the moral fabric that sustains the group, and since I seek my good as a social being, this moral fabric sustains me as well.

God, as a full-access interested-party, serves as a guarantor for the moral bonds that hold society together and that make cooperative social action possible. Commitment to God signals a commitment to that moral code that God upholds and marks the individual as a trustworthy member of the group. It is on this role of religion – as enabler of effective social existence, as social glue both internally and in the face of external threats – that the cognitive study of religion is in greatest accord, even when offering different explanations of how religion comes to assume this function. William Irons believes that this function is so important that the "core of religion is not belief ... but rather, for the most part, commitment to socially constructive behavior."[106] Scott Atran also recognizes the special role that the gods play in promoting pro-social attitudes: "Supernatural agents contribute to maintaining the cooperative trust of actors ... by sanctifying the actual order of ... social relations as the only morally and cosmically possible one."[107] And David Sloan Wilson, perhaps more so than any other theorist in the evolutionary study of religion, sees the group-level effects of religion as the key to understanding the evolution of both religion and social organization.[108]

Religious signals of commitment perform another crucial role: They define the boundaries of the group. By signaling commitment to the group's religion individuals identify themselves as trustworthy members invested in the group's success. They have tied their fortunes, and their family's fortunes, to this community. Someone who does not signal commitment to the gods of the group is suspect. This person has not signaled that the moral code of the group has been accepted; his or her lack of belief, or lack of mastery of tradition, may signal only a meager investment in the group, if not outright disregard. Such individuals are poor risks for cooperative behavior, for if they are not significantly invested in the group (evidenced by their religious failings), then they have less to lose in defecting from the group. Such individuals are not to be trusted; in fact, they are to be treated as potential threats to the group. Every group, if it is to maintain social cohesion, must identify who is part of the group, and so worthy of the group's trust and resources, and who is not. Religion becomes a powerful tool for drawing this line between in-group and out-group (with significant consequences).

Sosis, again, provides some empirical support for an in-group moral bias in religious moral psychology. Using members of Israeli kibbutzim as subjects, he and colleague Bradley Ruffle ran a cooperation game that paired members of a kibbutz with other kibbutz members and with non-kibbutz members. Sosis argued that the kibbutz provided a valuable test case, as it is "one of the most successful modern collectives" and preaches an ideology of general cooperation with all Israelis, whether members of a kibbutz or not. What they found, however, is that kibbutz members were markedly less generous with non-kibbutz players (i.e., out-group members) than with fellow kibbutz players (in-group), despite cultural traditions that preached against such discrimination. Furthermore, not only did they find an in-group bias, they also found that kibbutz members showed no more generosity to out-group members than did non-kibbutz participants. So not only did kibbutz members show an in-group bias, but it was just as strong as those whose upbringing did not specifically teach them to ignore such distinctions.[109]

While this experiment did not focus on groups defined by different religious beliefs, a religious tradition is certainly part of the group's identity, and so the results are salient to our discussion.[110] Also of importance is the apparent resilience of the in-group/out-group bias in the face of social conditioning to the contrary.

To recap: religious morality provides a vehicle for extending the evolutionary mechanisms for morality, that is, kin selection and reciprocal altruism, via communal belief in supernatural beings, conceived as full-access interested parties. Belief in such beings is a natural outgrowth of cognitive processes that did not evolve for religious purposes but that channel human experiences in such a way as to lead to religious beliefs. Once such beliefs become culturally available they are in a prime position to support and extend our evolved moral psychology, thus making the development of larger and more complex social organizations possible.[111] Also by serving as hard-to-fake-signs of commitment, religions function to identify those committed to the moral code of the group and to discriminate between in-group members (those who have invested in the religion and can be trusted) and out-group members (those who have not invested in the religion and so cannot be trusted). If this is an accurate account of the evolution of religious morality, then it should be possible to detect these evolutionary concerns embedded in religious moral traditions and so ground such ethical systems in an evolutionary matrix.

In the next two chapters we will turn our attention to the moral traditions of Judaism and Christianity, and I will argue that these moral traditions are examples of cultural variations of the evolved template for religious beliefs. Our goal in the upcoming chapters, however, is not to reduce each tenet of Judaism and Christianity to an evolutionary strategy to increase reproduction. This would be a caricature of the work being done by evolutionary theorists and it would ignore the real phenomenon of cultural/moral innovation. The goal instead is to pull out from these traditions the principles of evolutionary morality embedded within them. We will then have the opportunity to step back and evaluate what this project teaches us about these religious traditions and, perhaps, about the prospects for religion and morality in the twenty-first century.

3 | EVOLUTIONARY RELIGIOUS ETHICS: JUDAISM

Some laws, though unwritten, are more firmly established than all written laws. (Seneca the Elder)

Setting the Task

Now we turn to the task of applying the evolutionary model developed in the first two chapters to religious ethical traditions. I will focus the discussion on the Judeo-Christian moral traditions, although I contend it can be just as readily supported by a consideration of Islam, and later in the book we will have a chance to spend some time on that religion. Clearly, this thesis will be more powerfully supported if it can be extended to other religious moral traditions, but that goes beyond the scope of this work. However, even if limited to monotheistic religions, given the role these traditions play in the modern world it will not be an insignificant thesis.

Before turning to our first case study I must set some qualifications about the purpose and proper scope of this discussion. The purpose is to support the thesis that religious ethical traditions are cultural expressions of under-lying evolved cognitive processes. In the first two chapters I set out just what those processes are and how they evolved. The support for my thesis comes from identifying expressions of these processes in religious ethical traditions, in the present case, Judaism.[1] However, it is important to under-stand just what it is we are and are not looking for. The difficulty becomes clear when we consider what we mean in referring to Judaic ethical tradi-tions. Judaism presents a history of such complexity as to bewilder the mind. Stretching back thousands of years into the misty reaches of antiquity there is no non-controversial starting point for a discussion of Judaic ethics. Do we work with the more philosophically sophisticated treatment of the Law that comes out of Rabbinic Judaism? Do we attempt to reconstruct the moral codes of the monarchic period? One obvious option is to focus on the Mosaic Code and the theophany at Sinai, but scholars recognize that even here there are serious questions. The Mosaic Code includes not only the Ten Commandments, but also the Code of the Covenant, the more developed code of ethical prescriptions and penalties that follow immediately after the Decalogue in the book of Exodus, as well as the prescriptions found in Leviticus and the restatement of the Law in Deuteronomy. Scholars even suggest that there are two separate ethical traditions brought together in the compilation of Exodus and that parts of Code of the Covenant, specifically the Mishpatim, represent an older strain of Judaic thought.[2] Recent archaeological studies cast the entire Sinai narrative into grave doubt.[3] Further complicating matters, each of these options can be charged with privileging Palestinian Judaism and ignoring the complexities of Jewish traditions of the Diaspora.

This raises the formidable task of clarifying the historical record of Judaism, a task made all the more challenging by the myriad methodological and disciplinary approaches that are employed in its study. John Rogerson has noted that there has been so much change in the study of the history of Judaism over the past decade that there is no standard textbook on early Israel.[4] One way around these difficulties is to focus on the finished text as we have it today, and this is the approach I adopt here. Even with this approach we cannot ignore the historical context, especially when looking for evidence of evolutionary processes at work, but such considerations will be raised in a limited and careful manner. Despite the limitations I heed here, I do believe that a more comprehensive treatment would be a promising project for one more deeply immersed in the literature on early Israelite history and the writing of the Bible – if, that is, a plausible case for an evolutionary analysis can be made on the present limited grounds.

There is a sound argument for focusing on the finished text rather than the historical process of composition. The finished product is the text that serves as a moral text for both Jewish and Christian communities.[5] Whatever political and historical factors shaped the writing of the Hebrew Scriptures, I contend that the process of formulating and editing the material and traditions into a completed version that could function as a communal text is itself a process constrained and influenced by the evolved psychology of religious and moral cognition. This is the constant. What is variable is the cultural setting that plays the role of environment in providing selection pressure bringing different processes into play to different degrees at different times. If we could reliably reconstruct the history of the Israelites from their origins as a self-identifying community to their development into an established political state, *and* if we had an equally reliable and complete record of the accompanying moral traditions embraced by those communities during their historical development, then we would have the data to truly test the hypothesis of evolutionary religious psychology. But, as with the evolution of species, we need to construct the best picture we can working with an incomplete record, and always be open to revising our conclusions as more evidence becomes available.

While focusing on the finished text simplifies matters, it does not make our job a simple one. The Bible may or may not be a good book, but it is certainly not a coherent one. Even in its completed form it is a jumble of literary genres and styles, and competing theological and political agenda, composed in an age when boundaries between fact and fiction were loosely drawn and widely ignored. Jacques Berlinerblau has wryly defined a Biblical scholar as "a person who has devoted his or her life to reasoning with a madman."[6] I am going to attempt to retain my sanity by once again limiting the extent of the discussion. Rather than consider the breadth of moral concerns throughout the Hebrew Scriptures, I focus primarily on the Decalogue, and to a lesser extent the Covenant Code, as they are presented in Exodus (although when we turn to the issue of religious violence in Chapter 5 I will need to bring in other material).

It might be argued that in limiting the scope of my discussion I am stacking the deck in favor of my thesis by picking out favorable examples and ignoring the tough ones. But my goal is to make the case that an evolutionary approach to understanding the bases of religious ethics is a worthwhile contribution to such studies. By choosing representative moral teachings that exemplify an evolutionary logic I hope to demonstrate the plausibility of this approach and its potential for shedding new light on these issues. Of course, an important aspect of defending an evolutionary approach is to account for those moral precepts that do not immediately fit into this schema, and this is part of the work to be done, but the priority must be on establishing the evolutionary approach as a theoretical tool, before extending its application.

Constructing Yahweh

We have defined *god* as a minimally counter-intuitive concept, that is, a concept that meets many of the expectations of an ontological category – in this case that of *person* – while violating some of those expectations. We pointed out that these violations must be such as to make the concept memorable and must allow us to generate inferences that are significant to the way people live their lives. Also, gods are conceived as full access strategic agents who know all the information relevant to judging any interaction. This enables them to play a moral role in the lives of believers. As far as morality is concerned, there are three such roles: (1) as a paragon of moral behavior, (2) as a legislator of moral rules, (3) as an interested party to moral disputes – or any combination of the three. Before turning to ethics we will first look at how the character of *Yahweh*, as presented in scripture, fits the evolutionary template of god-concepts.

In discussing Yahweh we face the same complexities as when we approach scripture in general. There are many descriptions of Yahweh, stemming from different time periods and expressing different theological and authorial perspectives. We cannot expect to find a single, coherent depiction. But this is not unique to Yahweh. It is commonplace through out religions of the ancient world to find competing and even conflicting stories and representations of various gods and goddesses. This underlines the fact that for the ancients (but not just for them) stories about the gods were designed not to transmit historical fact but to relay messages of moral/social import or to provide a way to understand some aspect of their world. These stories were valued to the degree that they served these functions, not because they agreed with one another or because they painted a coherent picture of the deity. This allowed room for a great deal of flexibility and creativity in developing god-concepts. It also opened the door for widespread syncretism in which god-concepts from different cultures could be borrowed or integrated into the belief system of another culture without causing any religious or intellectual dissonance. It is only with the development of a monotheistic tradition that this practice becomes problematic (which is not to say that the concept of Yahweh does not bear the marks of syncretism, as it clearly does).

The complex, changing, at times inconsistent presentations of Yahweh actually do not impede an evolutionary analysis but are rather just what we should expect if we understand Yahweh as a concept culled from ideas generated by human cognitive processes functioning to make sense of the world (i.e., more primitive god-concepts), which is then formalized in scripture written to serve varying political and theological interests. As we evaluate the claims made about Yahweh from the perspective of evolutionary psychology we will find that these varying representations still cohere as expressions of these psychological processes.

We meet Yahweh at the very beginning of the Bible, and we find in the first two chapters different conceptions of the god; in fact we are given two different names for him – *Elohim* and *Yahweh*. These differences alerted Biblical scholars to the presence of different textual traditions in these stories. The exact explanation for these differences is still open to dispute but there is enough agreement to construct a general purpose explanation. Genesis, chapters one and two, contains two different creation stories. The second account, found in Genesis 2:4–25, is considered the earlier account and was attributed to the author identified as *J* for *Yahwist* (J standing in for Y in German, the language of the Higher Criticism that originated this approach), since this author uses YHWH to identify God. The first account (Gen. 1–2:3) is believed to stem from a much later period

– that is, the Exilic or Post-Exilic (after 587 BCE) – and is attributed to the authorial tradition identified as P for *Priestly*, as these texts place an emphasis on issues of concern to the priestly class and the institutionalizing of Judaism.[7]

More important for our study is how Yahweh is depicted in these two stories. In Genesis 1 we are impressed with the cosmic power of a god who creates order from chaos by the power of his words: "Then God said, 'Let there be light'; and there was light" (Gen. 1:3). We follow the creative acts of God's words through six days, culminating in the creation of humans. Immediately, we are presented with a being that fits into the category of *person*, as he is an agent acting with purpose and verbal intelligence. What leaves a greater impression is the fact that this being has the power to summon the world by the mere expression of his will – clearly a violation of the expectations associated with members of this category, and one that has important implications. A being so powerful in creation can also be powerful in destruction, as the universe seems to owe its existence simply to his will. However, we are also given information that shows Yahweh fulfills many other expectations of *persons*. After each act of creation Yahweh reflects on his work and finds satisfaction: "and God saw that it was good." This judgment, whether one of relief that things came out well, pride in achievement, or moral approval, is consistent with what we know about humans and how we would expect them to respond at the end of a successful project.

That Yahweh fits the category *person* is made more vivid in the creation of humans: "Then God said, 'Let Us make man in Our image, according to Our likeness'. ... So God created man in His own image" (Gen. 1:26–27). Leaving aside that the divine utterance is in the plural, and the question of whether this implies a polytheistic tradition embedded in the Jewish Scripture, what is relevant is that Yahweh *has* an image, and a human one. This anthropomorphic conception of God comes across vividly as we turn to the second account of creation.

Here we read of Yahweh creating Adam, not by simply calling him into existence – that is, "Let there be Adam" – but by taking dust from the earth to form Adam's physical being and then breathing into Adam's nostrils, bringing him to life (Gen. 2:7). These are physical acts involving hands and lungs and a mouth, and actual work in putting the materials together. Then we hear that Yahweh "planted a garden" (Gen. 2:8) and issued directions on how Adam could use that garden, setting a penalty for disobedience (Gen. 2:16–17). Later we find the god "walking in the garden in the cool of the day" (Gen. 3:8). All of this is consistent with what we know about *persons*. It is perfectly reasonable that a person who went to the trouble of planting a garden would want to be sure that garden was cared for and not abused and so might set rules; and he certainly would enjoy the pleasures of the garden himself, and so consequentially these are intuitively acceptable depictions of Yahweh. One might want to ask, of course, if this picture is consistent with an incorporeal, purely spiritual being, but such a question may never occur to a believer reading these passages because these descriptions are natural inferences from the ontological category of *person*. These implicit expectations about *persons* structure our thoughts about God and are as much part of our conception of God as the more dramatic supra-human attributes. They are so natural that we are often oblivious to them and to the problems in consistency that they raise. Theological doctrine to the contrary notwithstanding, in scripture and in the daily reflections of believers, God is conceived in human terms.[8]

Stewart Guthrie has pointed out that the line between human and divine was not always drawn as clearly as we assume it to be today.[9] This comes across in a somewhat startling way if we reflect on Yahweh's reaction to Adam and Eve's disobedient behavior in the garden. Yahweh's initial response, as might be expected of a person, is to become angry and to curse them for this transgression. But then we find Yahweh thinking about the implications of what has just happened:

> Then the Lord God said, "Behold, the man has become like one of us, knowing good and evil; and now, lest he put forth his hand and take also of the tree of life, and eat, and live forever" – therefore the Lord God sent him forth from the garden of Eden. ... and at the east of the garden of Eden he placed the cherubim, and a flaming sword which turned every way, to guard the way to the tree of life. (Gen. 3:22–24)

What comes across from a strictly literal reading of the text is that Yahweh banishes Adam and Eve from paradise *not* because of their sin – that punishment was already set out in earlier verses: for Eve, pain during childbirth and submission to her husband; for Adam, hard toil for his food and ultimately death – but to protect his divine prerogatives.

Having sinned once Adam may sin again and attain immortality. To prevent that, God cast him out and set angels with flaming swords to guard the tree of life. Here is a sovereign jealously defending his domain. What is more striking, however, is how malleable is the line between mortal person and divine supra-person. Adam and Eve have become like gods by acquiring moral awareness. If they were to eat from the tree of life they would, presumably, become gods.

This Genesis story is not the only creation account connecting moral wisdom and immortality as the criteria for godhood. There is a Mesopotamian myth of Adapa,[10] the first man, who is summoned by the high god Anu to answer for a transgression.

Before entering Anu's presence he is advised by the god Ea, who often plays the role of intercessor for humans, to make himself look penitent and is warned not to eat the food offered to him. Anu accepts Adapa's repentance and according to the standards of hospitality offers him fruit to eat.

Adapa, heedful of the advice he was given, politely refuses, unaware that the fruit offers immortality. Only later does he learn what he has passed up. Ea enabled Adapa to gain wisdom by visiting the abode of the gods and living to tell about it, but was careful to not allow Adapa to gain the divine attribute of immortality.

Both of these stories match the understanding of God as a minimally counter-intuitive being. God is like a member of the category *person* in having moral knowledge but unlike a typical member by virtue of immortality. A human who had both would be a god.

These stories tell us not that God is like humans in having moral knowledge but that in possessing moral knowledge humans share in the divine. This is of great significance to the thesis of this book. Here, in one of the first accounts of Yahweh, we are told that an essential part of his divinity is that he possesses knowledge of good and evil. Throughout the Hebrew Bible we are reminded of the moral nature of Yahweh, who is often held up as a paragon of virtue, one of the three moral models for gods to assume. We are told that "the Lord is a God of justice" (Isa. 30:18) and "righteousness and justice are the foundation" of his throne (Ps. 89:14); "the Lord is good, for his steadfast love endures for ever" (Jer. 33:11).

And this is more than devotional rhetoric; we see the evidence of Yahweh's moral nature in his actions. We have already seen Yahweh's capacity for moral outrage in his response to the transgression of Adam and Eve. That moral sensibility is displayed even more emphatically in the story of Noah:

> The Lord saw that the wickedness of man was great in the earth, and that every imagination of the thoughts of his heart was only evil continually. And the Lord was sorry that he had made man on the earth, and it grieved him to his heart. So the Lord said, "I will blot out man whom I have created from the face of the ground." (Gen. 6:5–7)

We know how this ends: Yahweh sends a flood that kills every man, woman, and child on the earth, with the exception of Noah and his family. As an indication of the nature of God, this story does not serve to Yahweh's credit. Evil as man may have been, could it have justified mass murder of the children and infants that perished in the divine punishment? Furthermore, we are told that once the slaughter was over and the waters subsided, Noah offered a sacrifice that pleased God and prompted him to reconsider his acts, which he promised never to do again. The impression we are left with is of God acting impulsively with murderous rage, and then when his anger is sufficiently vented, he calms down and regrets his action, promising to act better in the future. More damning, there is an appalling lack of foresight on the part of Yahweh. This drastic, destructive action was aimed at eliminating evil from the world – wipe out the evildoers and start over from scratch. As such, it was a singularly unsuccessful strategy.

This story raises serious problems as a tale of a moral God who is also proposed to be all-knowing and all-powerful. It follows from those attributes that Yahweh (a) could have discriminated the evil adults from the innocent babes and wrought destruction on the sinful alone, and (b) should have foreseen that the generations following Noah would also sink into sin and evil thoughts and come up with a more effective strategy. Of course, one may argue that this story is to be understood not literally but rather as a cautionary tale of the costs of sin, and from such a perspective such problems do not arise. This point is well taken. However, it is more telling that this tale was accepted as a faithful account of Yahweh's actions in the world (and still is accepted as such in some corners of the world), and understanding it that way is a more immediate expression of religious cognition than any allegorical interpretation.

When we treat this tale not as allegory nor as history but as an expression of religious cognition it becomes easier to make sense of it. As a minimally counter-intuitive member of the ontological category *person*, it makes sense that Yahweh would be grievously offended by the evil acts of his creation, and from a sense of bitter disappointment would want to erase his work and begin anew. It also follows intuitively that a powerful person who was so offended would respond with a display of that power. It is also a common human experience to lash out in hurt and anger only to regret it once the storm of passion has passed, resulting in a remorseful promise never to do it again. This all makes perfect sense because this is how people act, and since beliefs about gods are generated by cognitive processes that treat God as a member of the category *person* they are intuitively acceptable descriptions of Yahweh. The fact that Yahweh's lashing out takes the form of a universal flood is a category violation that distinguishes him as belonging to a special subset of *person*, and makes him a memorable being of great significance to humans – that is, it marks him as a god.

In the flood story we not only learn of Yahweh's power, we are signaled in an unmistakable manner that this god is an interested party in moral matters, a second model for moral gods. His wrath is kindled against humans because of their moral failings; he saves Noah because of his moral righteousness. This aspect of Yahweh is driven home again and again. The Book of Psalms, to look at just a single text, provides numerous testimonies to Yahweh's moral concern. We hear that "the Lord is righteous; he loves righteous deeds" (Ps. 11:7), that "he judges the world with righteousness, he judges the world with equity" (Ps. 9:8), that "his soul hates him who loves violence" (Ps. 11:5), and that "morning by morning [he] will destroy all the wicked in the land, cutting off all the evildoers from the city of the Lord" (Ps. 101:8).

To be an effective player in moral matters it is not enough that God cares. God's interest in moral matters is particularly significant because gods surpass a typical person by having full access to all morally relevant information. We are shown this in the Noah story when God sees that in man "every imagination of the thoughts of his heart was only evil continually." This is not something that a human can know with any certainty. We make inferences to a person's intentions from his or her behavior, but as limited-access strategic agents we cannot see into the heart of a person and read his or her deepest feelings. This is why it is possible for evil people to deceive us. They can hide their sinister hearts behind a show of good intent, but Yahweh cannot be fooled. Even the mighty King David cannot hide his sin from Yahweh, who signals his role as moral enforcer by exposing and punishing even the great ones (2 Sam. 12:1–23): "With him are strength and wisdom; the deceived and the deceiver are his" (Job 12:16).

This conception of Yahweh, as it is developed and presented in the Hebrew scriptures, flows readily from the evolved cognitive channels that generate god-beliefs. Yahweh fulfills many of the expectations of a member of the ontological category *person*, while violating in memorable fashion several of those expectations. These category violations are not only memorable but significant. They generate important information about the deity that is relevant to human existence. Most significant is that this god is a moral being who is interested in the moral doings of his people. Such a concept was of profound importance to a people struggling to maintain social cohesion in the face of the challenges and hardships of an often brutal ancient world. The one moral model we have yet to discuss may be the most important in this regard, and that is god as moral legislator. We turn to this next.

The Ten Commandments:
An Evolutionary Interpretation

Our discussion has highlighted several key components of our evolved moral nature. Kin selection and reciprocal altruism, particularly indirect reciprocity, form core layers of our moral cognition. As such, the concerns and values that flow from them should be evident within the moral traditions we examine. Furthermore, for a moral system to function there must be confidence that an act of altruism will be reciprocated, if not directly then through benefits to the actor's family, through enhancement of reputation within the community, or by strengthening the group (which may in turn benefit the individual and/or kin). Humans, therefore, are very sensitive to signals of commitment to reciprocate and of commitment to punish defectors. An effective means of demonstrating commitment is by engaging in costly signaling. Also, we learned that punishment motivates cooperative behavior and discourages cheating.

As we examine the Decalogue, along with some other elements of the Mosaic Law, we will find all these elements embedded there and given divine sanction. The Law is a vehicle for expressing these evolutionary strategies in a religious idiom, thereby reinforcing and enhancing them in a way that contributes to the development of a cohesive social unit on a scale larger than that of family or clan. We will work our way through the Ten Commandments (as they are presented in Exodus[11]) to uncover signs of our evolved psychology, with occasional tangents into other material when further examples are needed. We begin with the introduction:

"And God spoke all these words (Exod. 20:1)."

This leads us directly into the Ten Commandments and in a powerful, yet concise manner, signals the importance of what is to follow. The moral code that will establish the standard of community behavior is given a divine status. Yahweh assumes the role of legislator of group morality, imbuing the communal code with significance and objectivity that encourages acceptance and justifies the sacrifices imposed by group living.

I) I am the Lord your God, who brought you out of the land of Egypt, out of the house of bondage. You shall have no other gods before me. (Exod. 20:2–3)

This first command establishes the identity and the reputation of Yahweh. By referring to the escape from Egypt Yahweh reminds the people of the wondrous things he has done, that he commands the very forces of nature and he has used that power for their benefit.[12] This is a god who cares about the good of the community and has at his disposal immense power. This command also sets the conditions of the covenant that is being established. God has done a great good for the people and they therefore owe him. This taps into the implicit psychology of reciprocation: Worship no other god, since it is I, Yahweh, and no other god, who did this great deed for you.

This exclusive bond with Yahweh is not simply what morality demands in return for the good received. It calls for commitment to a supreme being who functions as overseer of the community. To be committed to that being and no other signals commitment to the moral code that that god upholds, since being committed to that god is demonstrated by keeping his law and marks an individual as a trustworthy member of the group. Breaking this commandment carries serious social consequences. If one is willing to defect from a contract with such a powerful being, who has done so much for you, how much more ready must you be to defect from commitments to a fellow group member.

This command generates a great deal of discussion over exactly what is implied by the Hebrew phrase *'al-panay*, translated as "before me." Does it imply monotheism or simply the priority of Yahweh over other gods? Biblical scholar Brevard Childs points out that the Hebrew phrase does not imply the exclusive existence of Yahweh but emphasizes instead the exclusive nature of the relationship between Yahweh and Israel.[13] The question of whether early Judaism was originally monotheistic, whether this is a tradition that developed over time, or whether it was the position of a minority camp within Judaism that gained ascendancy during the Post-Exilic period is also an ongoing debate. Although I do not have the credentials to jump into this controversy as a professional in Jewish studies, I must say that the first option – that of Judaism as originally monotheistic – seems the least plausible. Given what we know about early religious systems, what we gather from more contemporary hunter-gatherer societies, and what we can infer from the cognitive study of religion, polytheism seems the default position.[14]

Fortunately, we do not need to resolve the debate in order to appreciate the evolutionary significance of this first command. Whether or not "no other gods before me" accepts the existence of other gods, it clearly marks them off-limits for members of the covenantal community. Even if there are other gods, there is only one legitimate moral code for anyone wishing to be considered a member of that community, and that code is tied to Yahweh.

> II) You shall not make for yourself a graven image, or any likeness of anything that is in heaven above, or that is in the earth beneath, or that is in the water under the earth; you shall not bow down to them or serve them; for I the Lord your God am a jealous God, visiting the iniquity of the fathers upon the children to the third and fourth generations of those that hate me, but showing steadfast love to thousands of those who love me and keep my commandments. (Exod. 20:4–6)

This commandment combines a prohibition with the motivation for respecting that prohibition. The prohibition is a somewhat strange one and there seems to be no scholarly consensus on why it bans graven images in such terms.[15] It has been suggested that this was a way of distinguishing the worship practices of the Israelites from that of the neighboring, and so competing, Canaanite religion. If this is so then the prohibition may have functioned as a signal of communal membership. Whatever the case, the second part of the command, the motivation, clearly speaks to our evolved psychology.

The Israelites are informed, in no uncertain terms, why they need to respect this prohibition: "for I the Lord your God am a jealous God." This is a fascinating admission. What are we to make of a jealous god? From a certain theological perspective this claim seems incongruent with the nature of a supreme being, but we already know how to answer that point. Yahweh is conceptualized as a minimally counter-intuitive being and so will be defined, at least partially, in human terms. This command, following on the heels of the first commandment, has clearly set out an exclusive relationship between God and his people, and it is an intuitive inference that when one's partner is unfaithful a person will be jealous. However, while jealousy is a human characteristic, it is not a particularly positive one. We often think of jealousy as a weakness, a sign of insecurity and possessiveness. People who are secure in themselves and in their relationships are supposed to be beyond the torments of jealousy. And Yahweh is not just any person, he is a god – a supremely powerful being. Should he not be beyond that ugly human emotion? We might think so, until we reflect on the nature of this particular emotional response.

Jealousy, here and elsewhere in the Bible, is a response to unfaithfulness. It is the divine reaction to Israel worshipping other gods, and is often discussed as though Israel were an adulterous wife. The intuitive response to such betrayal is a feeling of jealousy; this is not the sort of thing that can be tolerated or ignored. In evolutionary terms, for a wife to be sexually unfaithful presents the prospect of a man raising a child that is not his own. For someone to invest resources, to make sacrifices for a child carrying someone else's genes – resources that could have and should have gone to one's own offspring – and with no hope of reciprocation, is an evolutionary disaster. The powerful emotions that are triggered in response to even suspected infidelity are evolution's means of discouraging and punishing such defections from the social contract of marriage.[16] Anyone hearing this description of Yahweh would understand his jealousy and, more important, would recognize its ramifications. If we leave Exodus temporarily and turn to the Book of Hosea we can see how explicitly this was spelled out.

In this text Yahweh addresses Israel as a bride, with even a hint of sexuality: "And in that day, says the Lord, you will call me, 'My husband'. ... And I will betroth you to me for ever. ... I will betroth you to me in faithfulness, and you shall know the Lord" ("to know" is often a Biblical euphemism for sexual intimacy) (Hos. 2:16–20). And Israel's supposed idolatry is portrayed as infidelity. Here Yahweh speaks as if to his children about their promiscuous mother:

> Plead with your mother, plead – for she is not my wife, and I am not her husband – that she put away her harlotry from her face, and her adultery from between her breasts; lest I strip her naked and make her as in the day

she was born, and make her like a wilderness, and set her like a parched land, and slay her with thirst. (Hos. 2:2–3)

And just to be sure everyone gets the message: "Upon her children also I will have no pity, because they are children of harlotry. For their mother has played the harlot" (Hos. 2:4–5).[17]

Danna Nolan Fewell poignantly asks us to consider how this divine model of marital behavior has impacted on our sorry history of domestic abuse.[18] It is a question well worth pondering, particularly by those who present the Bible as a moral guide to be read literally. But in describing Yahweh in these terms the Biblical authors are not concerned with establishing an ideal moral norm, they are drawing on their moral psychology, as experienced at their level of social development, to express in terms as forceful and as visceral as possible the strength and passion of Yahweh's commitment to his people, and the consequences of breaking the pact with him.

Indeed, the fact that Yahweh is capable of such emotional extremes is part of what makes him such an effective enforcer of moral norms. If we reflect back on our discussion of the moral emotions this should become clear. For a moral system to work there must be ways of securing commitments to cooperate and to reciprocate. One method is to have a third party with the power to enforce commitments and to punish defections. As we have seen, there is a wealth of research on moral psychology indicating the importance of punishment in motivating social cooperation, and there is a growing body of research in the cognitive science of religion that points to this being a common role of supernatural beings.[19] Gods often assume this role for a community, as Yahweh assumed this role for the ancient Israelites. But for Yahweh to function as a credible enforcer we need to have reasons to believe that (a) he has the power to enforce – and this was signaled by the reminder of what he was able to do to the Egyptians – and (b) he is committed to enforcing the moral rules he sets out. From experience we know that sometimes a person in authority may not be diligent in enforcing the rules. Some people talk tough but are not willing to follow through, others are more willing to let things slide. This makes a person a less credible enforcer and weakens the motivation to keep our commitments. How does Yahweh signal his commitment to enforce the law?

Two means of securing commitments previously discussed were *emotional* and *reputational*. I consider each in turn. Emotional responses can work very effectively to signal willingness to punish behavior. In Chapter 1 we considered that sometimes from a purely rational calculation it is not worthwhile to actually retaliate against a cheat. But the powerful emotions that often accompany a moral complaint – that is, anger and jealousy – signal that a person is not responding from rational calculations and is prepared to retaliate even if it costs them more than ignoring the offense would (think back to the example of the annoying neighbor with the incontinent dog). Let's apply this to the present issue.

The ancient Israelites were surrounded by people who worshipped many gods, and may have themselves engaged in polytheistic practices. This was the norm. People in the ancient world were pragmatic about their religious worship. While most cities and nations had patron gods, there was no reason to risk offending or missing out on the blessings of any god, and it was not unusual for a person to offer sacrifice or prayer to other gods if the occasion called for it. The Romans, that most practical of ancient peoples, even dedicated a shrine to the Unknown Gods, just to be sure they did not miss any.

So we can imagine that it would have been very tempting as an ancient Israelite, in a time of need, to offer up sacrifice to one of the many gods who might be able to provide assistance. Now, I might be quite aware of the prohibition against such behavior yet reason that Yahweh would not get terribly upset over just this one dalliance with a foreign god; that he would not rain destruction down upon me and thereby lose out on all the future worship and sacrifice that I, the repentant sinner, would provide Yahweh over the course of my continued and hopefully long life. If Yahweh were known to be a purely rational agent this might make sense. To destroy a person for one occasion of unfaithfulness would mean losing out on all the future benefits of continuing to have this person worship him. It does not make good business sense.

However, an ancient theo-philanderer would know that Yahweh is not a purely rational agent – he is a jealous god. Jealous agents lash out irrationally, and often violently and impulsively. And not only does Yahweh promise to get me but he promises to visit "the iniquity of the fathers upon the children to the third and fourth generations." So even if I were willing to risk Yahweh's wrath it is not I alone who will suffer but my children as well. Note how this threat effectively taps into our evolved psychology. Yahweh will take his anger out on my genetic legacy, making for naught all that I have sacrificed for my children and raising the specter of reproductive failure. Evolution has made sure that we are very sensitive to such threats.

But what if one were skeptical about Yahweh's claim? What if one were to wonder if this was all divine bluster? People engage in posturing all the time – all bark and no bite. This is where reputation comes in and the Hebrews would be well aware of Yahweh's reputation. First, he has just reminded them of how destructive he can be – "remember the Egyptians" – and then there are all the stories of Yahweh's response to unfaithfulness. If the story of Noah and the universal deluge did not secure Yahweh's reputation as a committed enforcer of moral behavior we are given another vivid example immediately following the revelation of the Ten Commandments: the story of the golden calf. The people, worried that Moses has been gone for so long, have Aaron build a golden calf that can serve as their god – the very sin prohibited by the first two commandments. That this sin occurs here seems an intentional literary choice to demonstrate that Yahweh meant what he said.[20] Yahweh's first instinct is to destroy all the Israelites: to Moses, "I have seen this people, and behold, it is a stiff-necked people; now therefore let me alone, that my wrath may burn hot against them and I may consume them" (Exod. 32:9–10). Moses is able to talk Yahweh out of this by reminding him of his promises to Abraham, Isaac, and Jacob – showing that even in his anger Yahweh is committed to his promises and can be reasoned with on moral grounds. Moses then goes down the mountain and oversees the execution of three thousand sinners, which mollifies Yahweh but does not satisfy him. After telling Moses he may lead the people away from Sinai we hear: "Nevertheless, in the day when I visit, I will visit their sin upon them." This is a chillingly ominous threat, one that we are told was fulfilled: "And the Lord sent a plague upon the people, because they made the calf which Aaron made" (Exod. 32:34–35). This is not a god who makes empty threats.

Rather than being a flaw in the divine nature, Yahweh's jealousy is essential to making him a credible enforcer of the moral code, thereby strengthening the moral bonds of society by making punishment of defection more certain. In fact, being a jealous god is rather distinctive of Yahweh. We do find other examples of divine jealousy in the ancient world, but of a more mundane version (e.g., think of the stories of Hera and Zeus's many mistresses); jealousy because of devotion to another god is unique to Yahweh. Perhaps this is necessary to promote monotheism. If Yahweh were tolerant of the worship of other gods, what reason would people have to devote themselves to him alone? G. Henton Davies has written: "the word [jealous] is used in contexts where the solity ('only-ness'), unity or distinctive character of Israel's God is threatened or compromised. The word is the antidote to idolatry."[21]

Before leaving this commandment, we need to further address the second clause that has Yahweh "visiting the iniquity of the fathers upon the children to the third and fourth generations of those that hate me, but showing steadfast love to thousands of those who love me and keep my commandments." Besides driving home the consequences of sin, this clause also ties the well-being of the community to the behavior of its individuals. My sin not only costs me but has consequences for others. It will reverberate through the generations, threatening the future of the community. On the other hand, we are also reminded of the rewards for faithfulness, rewards that we can expect with confidence as we know that Yahweh is a god who delivers.

III) You shall not take the name of the Lord your God in vain; for the Lord will not hold him guiltless who takes his name in vain. (Exod. 20:7)

The most common interpretation of this command sees it as a prohibition against false swearing, although Childs claims this does not follow from a purely linguistic reading of the text and that the Hebrew implies a broader meaning. But he concedes that from early on it was understood primarily as a command not to invoke God's name in a false promise, or an empty oath.[22]

The function of such a command fits neatly into a system of evolutionary morality. Promise-making and oaths are mechanisms that support reciprocation. They seek to guarantee behavior that allows others to interact with the promise-maker with confidence. It indicates a commitment to follow through on an agreement, to reciprocate for the considerations or favors one seeks to encourage from others. It is reciprocal altruism (either direct or indirect) made explicit. Furthermore, invoking the name of the deity that oversees moral transactions signals several important pieces of information: you accept the same god as I do; you recognize that god's role as moral enforcer; and you invite retribution for failing to reciprocate that outweighs any advantage you might hope to gain by reneging on your word. This is invaluable information for any potential partner trying to gauge whether it is worth the risk to do business with you. In addition to concerns about your reputation (it is costly to be marked a cheater), by invoking God's name you add the reputation of God to the equation. To invoke God's name in an empty oath is a more serious offense than merely cheating. If I cheat you I do you damage, and to the degree that I get away with it I may weaken the moral bonds of society. But falsely swearing by God's name threatens to undermine the very fabric of social morality. If you are willing to cheat me, while swearing to God, then you have completely rejected the code that allows a system of reciprocation to develop. It is an offense not only against me but against society itself. Such offenses cannot be taken lightly by a group, and so it is not surprising that such a prohibition, along with threats of divine retribution, is included in the basic dictates of this religious morality.

Childs points out that this command has also been interpreted as a means of protecting God from abuse. To associate God's name with deception is to abuse it, and to weaken its power to signal commitment to reciprocation. But there is more to it than this. The name of God has a special place in the Jewish religion. It is revealed under sacred conditions and is treated with special reverence, in speaking and in writing. This is a distinctive aspect of Judaism, and with all distinctive aspects of a religion we must suspect it serves as a signal of commitment to the group. The holiness associated with the name of the Jewish God is unique among ancient peoples. To respect the special practices surrounding the name of God signals one takes the behavioral code of the group seriously, and therefore that one is a trustworthy member of the moral community.

> IV) Remember the Sabbath day, to keep it holy. Six days you shall labor, and do all your work; but the seventh day is a sabbath to the Lord your God; in it you shall not do any work, you, or your son, or your daughter, your manservant, or your maidservant, or your cattle, or the sojourner who is within your gates; for in six days the Lord made heaven and earth, the sea, and all that is in them, and rested the seventh day; therefore the Lord blessed the sabbath day and hallowed it. (Exod. 20:8–11)

This law has great significance for the thesis of this book. Childs reports that there is general consensus that the command did not originate with the Sinai tradition but is an earlier tradition being reconfirmed[23] – note the language "remember the Sabbath day." He also discusses possible historical analogues among other Ancient Near Eastern traditions. As interesting as this is, more relevant to the present discussion is the function of this command, and to gain insight into this we must look at the motivation for keeping the command.

Actually, I should say, "motivations," for while the command to remember the Sabbath is straightforward, the reasons for doing so vary throughout its numerous appearances in the Pentateuch. In Exodus 23:12 it seems intended simply as an admonition to rest: "Six days you shall do your work, but on the seventh day you shall rest; that your ox and your ass may have rest, and the son of your bondmaid, and the alien, may be refreshed." In the Exodus Decalogue the Sabbath is connected to God's creative act and his rest from his work: Yahweh "rested the seventh day." Scholars have pointed out that this is clearly intended to connect with the Priestly account of creation in Genesis 1–2:3, emphasizing that the Sabbath tradition influenced the creation account and not the reverse.[24] In Deuteronomy, however, we find a different rationale.

Deuteronomy gives the command a different introduction – "Observe the sabbath day, to keep it holy, as the Lord your God commanded you" (Deut. 5:12) – but lists the same instructions for observation as we find in Exodus (Deut. 5:13–15). It is worth noting that Exodus and Deuteronomy are consistent in who is to rest on the Sabbath, and this extends to omitting the wife. Given how specific the list is – your sons and daughters, your manservant and maidservant, your ox and ass – this omission is all the more glaring and reminds us that this is a law written within a patriarchal society and addressed to men. And not just any men, but men of means, those with the wealth and position to own oxen and asses and slaves.[25]

The significant change in the Deuteronomic version is in the motivation: "You shall remember that you were a servant in the land of Egypt, and the

Lord your God brought you out thence with a mighty hand and an out-stretched arm; therefore the Lord your God commanded you to keep the Sabbath day" (Deut. 5:15). We have seen that a reminder of Yahweh's might and the debt owed to him establish Yahweh's credibility as a morally interested party in the affairs of Israel, and as a mighty enforcer. This should tip us off that this command too serves as a signal of commitment, whatever other function it may have, or originally had. This comes across most clearly in a further expression of the command. In Exodus 31:12–17 we are told:

> And the Lord said to Moses, "Say to the people of Israel, 'You shall keep my sabbaths, for this is a sign between me and you throughout your generations, that you may know that I, the Lord, sanctify you. ... Therefore the people of Israel shall keep the sabbath, observing the sabbath throughout their genera-tions, as a perpetual covenant. It is a sign for ever between me and the people of Israel.

Here it is explicit: observing proper Sabbath restrictions signals allegiance to the covenant that sets the conditions of community membership and moral behavior. To observe these practices is to demonstrate one's commit-ment to that group. The Sabbath is a holy day, distinguished from all others. On this day, whatever differences may exist between members of the com-munity, all are to rest from their labor and remember their unity under a common God and an allegiance to a common code. So significant is this sign of commitment that the penalty for violating the command is death (Exod. 31:15).

Observing the Sabbath was just one of several practices that defined the boundaries of the group for ancient Israelites and signaled commitment to that group. Circumcision and kosher food laws also distinguished Jews among the peoples of the Ancient Mediterranean world.[26] A variety of purposes have been ascribed to these practices, but whatever other functions they may serve, in terms of moral psychology a more basic interpretation is to see them as "hard-to-fake" signals of commitment. Consider for example the intricacies of kosher regulations. These are so complex and so specific that they are virtually impossible to fulfill without a deep and long-term immersion in the group. There is no obvious reason, to take one example, to not eat dairy and meat during the same meal. The casual observer might not even notice such a pattern if not alerted to it. Such practices are difficult for an outsider, looking to infiltrate and take advan-tage of the benefits of altruism within the group, to fake successfully. It is by being raised in a Jewish household, and one that keeps Jewish law, that one becomes adept at such practices, and so showing one's mastery of these practices is an effective signal that one has already invested significant time and energy to being a member of the community. Such a person is less likely to defect from the group and is therefore a more trustworthy partner in social cooperation.

Circumcision also functions as such a signal. It is a physical sign that one has, since birth, been a member of the community. In Genesis we read of the function of circumcision:

> And God said unto Abraham, "....This is my covenant, which you shall keep, between me and you and your descendants after you; Every man among you shall be circumcised. You shall be circumcised the flesh of your foreskins, and it shall be a sign of the covenant between me and you. ... Any uncircumcised male who is not circumcised in the flesh of his foreskin shall be cut off from his people." (Gen. 17:9–14)

Circumcision was not unique to Israelites in the ancient world, though rare enough that the Romans saw it as a Jewish practice. What does appear to have been unique was its role as a sign of group membership. This signal carved into the flesh of the individual is a costly signal to fake. In fact this became an issue of division in the early Jewish/Christian communities because the costliness to an adult male of adopting this signal was impeding Paul's mission to the Gentiles (see Galatians).

Joseph Blenkinsopp has noted that kosher laws, circumcision, and Sabbath observations, while rooted in early Israelite religion, took on increased importance after the Babylonian exile – which makes sense from so many perspectives, not least of all an evolutionary one. Exiled from their home, integrated into a foreign community, group survival depended all the more urgently on being able to recognize who was and who was not a member. Distinctive practices and rituals became the ties that not only bound the community but that defined a community no longer in its own land, no longer under the control of its own laws. He writes that while the Sabbath practice "is certainly ancient ... it comes into its own as a confessional mark of identity only from the time of the Babylonian exile."[27] And he points out that the Priestly author(s) goes to great lengths to tie these practices to the re-establishment of the temple cult in Israel. The temple becomes the physical center of Judaism in Post-Exilic Israel, and by uniting cultic practices to these signals of commitment the Priestly author(s) define what it is to be part of the community in this new phase of Jewish history.[28]

Reading this commandment as an example of a signal of commitment to the group is in line with scholarly tradition. In fact, much of the analysis I present is consistent with the views of many Biblical scholars, but this does not mean that an evolutionary perspective adds nothing new to our understanding of the Bible. Cognitive science allows us to ground the historical/cultural interpretations, provided by scholars from other disciplines, in the workings of the evolved mind. In our discussion of these Jewish practices, an evolutionary analysis uncovers how intricately connected such signals are to a suite of moral and emotional responses, and explains the vital significance such practices have in establishing the moral boundary of the group and facilitating social cooperation – so significant that they are presented in the language of divine command.

V) Honor your father and your mother, that your days may be long in the land which the Lord your God gives you. (Exod. 20:12)

This command serves as a transition from the earlier commands, which focus on obligations to God, to the remaining commands that focus on obligations to our fellow humans.[29] In itself it does not appear as amenable to an evolutionary analysis as the earlier commands, since evolution is more dependent on how parents treat their children than on how children treat their parents. Yet we may find this command has some resonance with our evolved psychology. Scholars have suggested that this injunction is intended to protect parents from neglect and abuse as they age and become vulnerable. Perhaps it is the fact that parents lose some of their evolutionary value as they become dependent on others that makes a divine command necessary (evolution makes sure that parents invest in their children without requiring cultural mechanisms).

It is also interesting that the commandment is couched in language that connects parents to God, and the reward for obeying this command is that often promised for obeying God, that is, long life in your own land; also, the command to "honor" rather than merely obey your parents is reminiscent of the proper attitude toward God.[30] Jonathan Magonet suggests this command, which follows the command to honor God by observing the Sabbath, reminds us of the creative power of both God and parents. Yahweh, the lord of creation, is "a third partner alongside the parents in the creation of a new human being."[31] In suggesting a tie between the parents – the source of all kin relations – and God – the moral center of the community – this command may access the psychology of kin selection to reinforce the moral value of the group.

We may also see the psychology of reciprocation at work. Honoring your parents is a way of reciprocating for the resources they have invested in you. Is an individual who is unwilling to reciprocate the debt to parents likely to reciprocate to a neighbor if they can avoid it? Caring for aging parents who can no longer contribute to your inclusive fitness may be an act of altruism that signals one's commitment to moral obligations and enhances one's reputation in the community.

All of this is admittedly more speculative than I am comfortable with, and I want to avoid straining too hard to fit this within an evolutionary schema. My thesis does not claim that all religious laws embody evolutionary concerns, only that an evolutionary analysis can shed light on religious moral traditions. We may treat this command as a transition between moral concerns within the Decalogue and continue on to the rest. In this light we can note the command also marks a transition of the moral psychology underlying the Decalogue. The first four commandments serve the evolutionary goals of uniting the group into a moral community under the watch of a powerful and concerned deity, and of establishing signals of commitment to the moral bonds of society via commitment to that deity. Commandments six through ten shift our focus to the basic moral obligations to members of the community. They set out the conditions of reciprocation in terms of respecting the rights and obligations of fellow group members, as well as establishing penalties as means of discouraging and/or redressing acts of defecting from this social contract.

As we turn to a consideration of the remaining commandments we will find they largely serve as social constructions that express the evolved psychology of reciprocal altruism, both direct and indirect. Since not as much work is required to lay bare the moral strategy of these commands, our discussions will not always be as detailed as those of the earlier commands. However, we will detect other evolutionary concerns embedded in some of these commands that will require extra attention.

VI) You shall not kill. (Exod. 20:13)

From a critical stance this is one of the more controversial commands. On a plain reading it seems to stand in stark contrast to the penalty of death prescribed for a wide variety of offenses, and the numerous accounts of deadly violence, apparently divinely sanctioned, perpetrated by the Israelites against foreign people. A more nuanced reading of the command, one that more appropriately translates the Hebrew *rsh* as "murder" rather than "kill," will move us toward a deeper understanding of this prohibition. However, I am going to postpone such a discussion to Chapter 5, when we examine the question of religious violence. An evolutionary treatment of the sixth commandment will open a window into this crucial issue, and so warrants a separate treatment.

For our present discussion we will take "You shall not kill" to prohibit taking the life of a member of your community. The instinct to self-preservation is as basic and powerful as any of the other elements of our evolved psychology (though not necessarily the predominant instinct, as humans are often quite willing to give up their lives for any number of reasons). The need to protect the lives of our family, as well as our own, is a fundamental task in our reproductive strategies and we come ready with powerful emotional reactions to anything that threatens those lives.

Keep in mind that a family is a group of individuals sharing and investing in a common pool of genes. Theses individuals form a kin group. Because individuals in a kin group have invested resources in the members of this group, via kin selection, an assault on a member risks wasting those resources; those who waste their resources suffer in terms of reproductive success. Therefore evolution has equipped us to be very sensitive, on a personal level, to threats to our kin. How might we guard against such threats?

Our discussion of evolutionary morality highlighted the importance of reputation in protecting an individual from defectors and cheats. If I have the reputation of responding with irrational passion to an offense, I make it less worthwhile for others to risk offending me. If I have the reputation of being ineffectual or weak in responding to offenses, I make myself a target. One way to protect my family from harm is to gain the reputation of being a relentless avenger of offenses.

The murder of one member of a family is a terrible loss, but allowing my family to be seen as easy targets threatens our genetic future, and so the murder of a family member must be avenged. It is often said in critique of revenge killings that another death will not bring back a lost loved one. This is true, but the strategy is not to bring back a lost loved one but to discourage future attacks on the lives of other loved ones. A violent and deadly response to the murder of a family member does more than re-establish balance ("an eye for an eye"); it signals that such offenses will not be tolerated, that attacks on my family will result in grievous loss for you and your family and so serves as a motivation for you not to attack us again.

Note that it is not necessary that the actual murderer is the one who is killed in retaliation. The initial murder was not simply a crime against an individual; it was a crime against a group of kin, threatening the survival of the genetic line of that group. As long as revenge is taken on the family of the murderer the crime has been reciprocated and the message sent.[32]

Of course, now there is another family that has been assaulted and its genetic future threatened. This family can no more accept the threat to their security than the first family could; they too must seek revenge or risk gaining the reputation of being weak and vulnerable to attack – and so the cycle of violence continues. As we step back we can see how pointless it is, and how endless the violence must be as long as we continue to give in to the psychology that sustains it. The difficulty comes in acting on this insight, and this difficulty is twofold: (1) It is not reflective reason that is driving us in these cases, but deeply embedded emotional reactions, and (2) these emotional reactions are elements of an evolved strategy necessary for inclusive fitness. Individuals who do not successfully discourage attacks on their family do not pass on as many of their genes as those who do.

As difficult as it is to find a way out of this deadly logic, no society can thrive as a coherent unit that does not find a way out. Moral systems that function as formalized systems of indirect reciprocity provide a path out of the violence. The crucial step is for society to assume the role of avenger for individual wrongs. For a group of unrelated individuals to function as a coherent society there must be a basic principle of reciprocity to respect each other's right to life. When this reciprocal arrangement is violated the group as a whole must take revenge. In this way the balance demanded by reciprocity is re-established, and the group signals that if you violate the lives of people in my family you will be punished, not by me but by society. "You shall not kill," along with severe punishment for murder, is a universal aspect of social morality, and for just these reasons it is the way out of the socially destructive cycle of revenge killings.

The Decalogue imbues this prohibition with divine authority, and this is just what we should expect. Backing the law against killing with the prestige and power of the deity grants it greater credibility and makes it more effective. It is Yahweh who has set the ban against both murder and revenge killing and so it is not merely a human convention, backed only by the word of human authorities. When society seeks to regulate such passionate and primal urges the involvement of a god is often called for.[33]

VII) You shall not commit adultery. (Exod. 20:14)

To the modern ear this command sounds like a straightforward warning against violating the sanctity of marriage. It is often presented as a bedrock of "family values" and used to bolster traditional marital arrangements. However, the scholarly understanding of this commandment should give pause to those who would have the Ten Commandments serve as a moral guide in contemporary society. Adultery here is a very specific sexual relation: that between a married woman and a man other than her husband. Extra-marital sex between a married man and an unmarried woman was not considered adultery.[34] To understand the logic of this particular definition of adultery we must keep in mind the context of the Law: It is a contractual relationship between God and the free, adult males of the community. Laws six through ten set out the proper behavior of these males and establish the conditions for reciprocity necessary for them to live together. They set out what is mine and what is yours – for the males – and the penalties for violating these conditions. The seventh commandment addresses one particular example of what belongs to a male, that is, his wife, and so it does protect the sanctity of marriage – not as an emotional bond between two people (although it might be that) but as a property relation. The wife is the proper possession of the man and so having sex with another man's wife is a property offense against that man – and not just any offense but one so grievous as to warrant death for both parties involved: "If a man commits adultery with the wife of his neighbor, both the adulterer and the adulteress shall be put to death" (Lev. 20:10).[35]

It follows that extra-marital sex between a married man and an unmarried woman is not a similar violation and does not require the same penalty, although it can be penalized: "If a man seduces a virgin who is not betrothed, and lies with her, he shall give the marriage present for her, and make her his wife. If her father utterly refuses to give her to him, he shall pay money equivalent to the marriage present for virgins" (Exod. 22:16–17). A married man who has extra-marital sex with an unmarried woman does not commit adultery against his wife because the man is not his wife's property – marriage is not an equal relationship. His actions may constitute an offense, but if so it is not against his wife or the woman he sleeps with but against the father of the woman. Even then two conditions must be met: The woman must not be betrothed to another (for if she is then she has already become the property of another man and the crime is adultery, and punished as such) and she must be a virgin. Why is it an offense only if the woman is a virgin? Because by taking her virginity outside of marriage the offending male has now made her spoiled goods. If the woman had already *known* a man, she was already spoiled goods and no further damage was done, but in regard to a virgin his action has rendered the woman virtually unmarriageable, and has imposed an economic hardship on her father. That we are correct to see this as a property crime against the father is supported by noting the particulars of the penalty. The man has two ways to make amends: He can marry the woman – which erases the offense by relieving the father of the futile task of finding a suitor for his defiled daughter – or, if the father chooses, the offender may pay the father the going price for a virginal daughter. Could the Bible speak more clearly about the moral status of women?

Carolyn Pressler argues that this view of women as property extends to the treatment of sexual violence. There are, she tells us, two "rape laws" in Deuteronomy. Deuteronomy 22:23–25 provides the background for understanding these laws. There we are told that in the case of consensual sex between a betrothed virgin and a man who is not her betrothed, both are to be put to death – the woman because she consented, the man because "he violated his neighbor's wife." The first "rape law" (Deut. 22:25–27) specifies that if the betrothed virgin is in a situation where she cannot cry for help she is not to be punished because she could do nothing to stop the act, but the man is to be put to death. No specific justification is noted here and so it appears that his offense is the same as in the preceding verses: violating his neighbor's property, not forcing a woman to have sex against her will. The rape is not the crime; the crime is the property violation. This is made even clearer in the second "rape law" (Deut. 22:28–29): "If a man meets a virgin who is not betrothed, and seizes her and lies with her, and they are found, then the man who lay with her shall give to the father of the young woman fifty shekels of silver, and she shall be his wife, because he has violated her."

Whether you have consensual sex with an un-betrothed virgin or you rape her, the offense is against her father, and the penalty is the same: financial restitution. There is no penalty for the sexual assault – and the woman's compensation is to be married off to her rapist. This leads Pressler to a damning, and justified, accusation: "An examination of the Deuteronomic laws treating forcible violation of women leads to a sobering conclusion: these texts do what rape does. They eliminate women's will from consideration and erase women's right to sexual integrity."[36]

Curiously, as Pressler points out, there is one example of a penalty for sexual assault in the Law. In Deuteronomy 25:11–12 we have a scenario in which two men are fighting and the wife of one man comes to the aid of her husband and grabs the genitals of the other man. In this case, the woman, who is not seeking sexual gratification by this move but is, in fact, endangering herself on her husband's behalf, is to have her hand cut off and shown no pity.[37] Again, let us keep in mind just what the Bible says the next time we hear an argument for making it the moral foundation of society.

This reading of the seventh commandment seems at odds with a moral rule designed by an omni-benevolent deity to guide us to moral perfection. Its treatment of women and its disregard for the violation of a woman's personhood through rape are morally offensive and are repudiated within civilized society. How then can we reconcile them as divine commands of a morally perfect being?

We cannot.

This law, however, can be made consistent with an evolutionary function. From an evolutionary perspective, this interpretation fits with studies of sexuality and parental investment. A married woman who has intercourse with someone other than her husband creates doubts about the paternity of the child. It raises the threat that a man may be investing in some other man's child, and this is an evolutionary disaster for the man. On the other hand, a man who has sex outside of marriage does not raise the same danger, as long as his partner is not another man's wife.[38]

The different response to sex with a non-virginal unmarried woman follows a similar logic. An unmarried woman who has lost her virginity raises the specter of uncontrollable sexuality and, as this raises the threat of uncertain paternity within marriage – that woman's value as a mate drops precipitously. For a married man to have sex with an unmarried non-virgin is no offense at all since no man's interest has been harmed. Hence controlling the sexual behavior of women is of utmost importance

– to men – and since the Law is an arrangement between men, we get the laws that we do.

The evolutionary risks of uncertain paternity explain the strong and often violent emotional reactions to cases of infidelity. Adultery, as defined in the Bible, is a grave threat to the stability of society, and there must be not only powerful disincentives to such behavior but effective penalties to negate the need for personal vengeance in the case of such behavior – hence the penalty of death. In setting out a public penalty for a private offense the laws set the conditions of reciprocity through the severe punishment of violations. This encourages adherence to the rule of law by raising the cost of defection.

This evolutionary perspective also allows us to make sense of the outrageous disregard for the woman. The pain and humiliation that the violated woman feels does not threaten to disrupt the social cohesion of the group – as long as she is not married and her father can be compensated. Women, due to their inferior status in this patriarchal society, are not centrally addressed by the Law because the purpose of the Law is to maintain a functional and cohesive group and is concerned only with those with the power to disrupt that cohesion.

Now, to give an evolutionary justification of this sexist code is not to give a moral justification of it. We must keep in mind that an evolutionary account of morality lays out the origin and social function of our moral predispositions, *which is not the same thing as morally approving those predispositions*. And so, an evolutionist can argue that the seventh commandment's dismissive attitude toward women makes sense given the evolutionary origins of our moral sense without thereby endorsing that moral worldview. This is not, however, something a traditional religious interpretation can do.

VIII) You shall not steal. (Exod. 20:15)

On the most basic level this law functions to protect the belongings of the members of the community. Thomas Hobbes argued that in a state of nature there is no "mine" and "yours" until each member of the group has agreed to relinquish claims to those things claimed by another and this concession is reciprocated by each in turn. Even then, a third party is needed to wield the power to enforce these mutual agreements. This move is a prerequisite for the development of civilization, for without it no one can feel secure in their property and so an individual's time and resources are going to be directed toward protecting what necessities he or she has, rather than developing the industry and commerce that will benefit both the individual and the group. The command to not steal, issued by the governing deity and backed up by that being's power to detect and punish cheaters, is a fundamental step in establishing the conditions of reciprocal respect for the right to property held by members of an extended community. Of course, the notion of private property is a relatively late cultural construct and not a product of our evolved psychology. What is produced by our evolved psychology is a deep concern with reciprocal relationships, and once the practice of private property is established we will intuitively apply the standards of reciprocation to it.

Seeing this as a prohibition against property theft is the most direct reading of the command, but it is not the only reading, and perhaps not the original. It has been suggested that the original target was theft of a person (i.e., kidnapping) and that over time this was extended to cover all theft.[39] There are, as we might expect, different penalties prescribed for theft of property and theft of a person. Property theft was punished by fines; theft of a person, however, was a capital crime: "Whoever steals a man, whether he sells him or is found in possession of him, shall be put to death" (Exod. 21:16). In Deuteronomy 24:7 we get a more detailed elaboration: "If a man is found stealing one of his brethren, the people of Israel, and if he treats him as a slave or sells him, then that thief shall die; so you shall purge the evil from the midst of you."

Being kidnapped and sold into slavery was a real danger in an Ancient Near Eastern world with a widespread practice of slavery. To steal a person who was a member of the group was to deny all moral worth to that person and break the bonds of community. An offense that so severely threatened the fabric of community justified the imposition of the most severe penalty.

However, despite the social danger of stealing a person, owning and selling a person – even members of the community – was not prohibited. Sam Harris argues that the Biblical acceptance of slavery – a practice regulated in the Torah and accepted in the New Testament – is the most damning argument against the morality set out in scripture. The immorality of slavery, he points out, is perhaps the least controversial moral position in the modern world. It is universally condemned, and even those who practice it today dare not call it by its name. And yet on this clear moral truth, the Bible, Jewish and Christian, gets it exactly wrong.[40] Again, we must ask, how may one reconcile this abhorrent moral position and its supposed authorship by a morally perfect deity? And again we must answer: You cannot.

However, things look different from an evolutionary perspective in which moral laws are codes for regulating the behavior of group members toward one another with the aim of creating a cohesive social unit. A slave is not part of the moral community and is not evaluated for potential to cooperate and to reciprocate cooperation. A slave is a possession that is dealt with, however benignly, through coercion. The harm done to a slave threatens social cohesion by the harm done to its owner, and that is what needs to be addressed (e.g., "If the ox gores a slave, male or female, the owner shall give to their master thirty shekels of silver, and the ox shall be stoned," Exod. 21: 28–32). To be fair, we must note that the Law does set bounds for the proper treatment of slaves and accords them some minimal moral consideration (e.g., "When a man strikes the eye of his slave, male or female, and destroys it he shall let the slave go free for the eye's sake," Exod. 21:26). We can and should applaud this as a moral innovation in a world where the life of a slave was cheap. But even this innovation is in line with the logic of evolutionary morality as Hebrew slaves are accorded more extensive and specific rights than non-Hebrew slaves (see Exod. 21:1–11).

It is interesting that even a fellow Hebrew could end up a slave to his neighbor, but such a change of status had to be carried out as a legal trans-action, for example, through a purchase – that is, "when you buy a Hebrew slave" (Exod. 21:2) – or through transfer of property – "when a man sells his daughter as a slave" (Exod. 21:7). The condition of slavery is not itself a moral offense against your neighbor; the offense is the failure to follow the proper procedures in the act of dehumanizing your neighbor. It is those procedures that set the conditions of reciprocation that must be respected for society to function.

IX) You shall not bear false witness against your neighbor. (Exod. 20:16)

By this point in our discussion it should be obvious how this command fits into an evolutionary analysis. As the law specifies the subject of the prohibi-tion to be "your neighbor" it too functions to set the boundary of behavior expected of one member of the moral community toward another. It does not present a categorical prohibition – "You shall not bear false witness PERIOD" – and this implies that bearing false witness against a stranger, that is, an out-group member, is not a moral concern, at least not a central one. The central concern is the treatment of members of the group. As Childs informs us, "the term 'neighbor' (rea') refers to the full citizen within the covenant community."[41]

Bearing false witness causes a problem for communal living in at least two ways. To understand this we need to see that the phrasing of the command indicates it refers to behavior within some sort of legal procedure in which a person is called to bring testimony.[42] An individual is brought before the tribunal to bring a charge or answer an accusation involving another member of the community. To present false testimony prevents justice from being done, that is, it impedes proper reciprocation. But in addition to weakening the legal enforcement of communal reciprocity, bearing false witness does damage in another, perhaps more insidious, manner. It unjustly damages the reputation of the person under consideration.

We know that reputation is an important resource in social interactions. Testifying that your neighbor is a cheat may cause lasting damage to that person's reputation and impact negatively on the ability to provide for him- or herself and family – that is, it hurts the pursuit of inclusive fitness. And this is true even when the testimony is false. It is the public perception of being a cheat that does the damage, not the actual act of cheating.

So this command is not a general prohibition against lying. Lying may be a moral imperfection but it does not necessarily damage the moral bonds of society (a lie may not actually harm another – although, of course, it often does), and the commandments are concerned not with moral perfection but with the consequences of actions on the community.

> X) You shall not covet your neighbor's house; you shall not covet your neigh-bor's wife; or his manservant, or his maid-servant, or his ox, or his ass, or anything that is your neighbor's. (Exod. 20:17)

This is a most interesting commandment. Here we have a command that focuses not simply on an action but on an internal state, as the verb *hmd* "appears to denote a subjective emotion whereas all the preceding prohibitions were directed against an objective action."[43] Commentators have argued that the verb also covers the action stemming from coveting and not just the emotion.[44] This makes sense because the act of taking causes damage, even apart from the emotional motivation behind the act, and naturally this would be covered by the prohibition. Still, it is clear that the desire, or intention, of coveting is the target of this command. This comes across more directly in the Deuteronomic version (Deut. 5:21). There we read: "Neither shall you covet your neighbor's wife; and you shall not *desire* your neigh-bor's house, his field ..." (emphasis added). So, what is the significance of this commandment, and what make it so interesting?

We immediately recognize this as another in the series of commands setting the boundaries of individual property rights, and so our discussion of those rules can be extended here. What is interesting is the move to include an internal state in the command. It is not just the act of taking but the desire to have something that belongs to your neighbor – not in the sense of being envious of your neighbor's new oxen (or big-screen HDTV, as the case may be) and wanting to go out and get one for yourself, but in the sense of wanting *your neighbor's* oxen. Desiring to deprive your neigh-bor in order to enrich yourself is the crime. This, however, is not the sort of crime that can be legislated by a civil code, simply because it cannot be policed. How could we tell that a person is guilty of coveting if this does not express itself in action? Even if we were suspicious, how could we prove an accusation of coveting, distinguishing it from simple envy? However, this is just the sort of information that a full-access strategic agent, such as a god, can readily ascertain. Yahweh knows the evil in your heart; he need not wait until you act on your covetousness. You need a god to police this sort of law.

But why do we need such a law? Why not be satisfied that people refrain from acting on their socially disruptive desires? If we recall our discussion of emotions we should be able to answer this. Emotions motivate us to action. By coveting your neighbor's goods you prepare the grounds to act in a covetous manner, and that would be socially disruptive. Jealousy, envy, and resentment are powerful emotions that often lead to violent confrontations.

Also, emotions are signals of commitment. To be perceived by your neighbor as covetous may signal that you are not a trustworthy member of the community, that you cannot be relied on to respect the bounds of reciprocal rights that constitute the community – it may weaken the social compact between you and your neighbors. Of course, this only happens if you allow your desires to show in your mannerisms and expressions. If you can disguise these your covetous desires pose no problem. However, there has been a sort of cognitive arms race throughout human evolution endowing us with both the ability to disguise our true emotions and with tools for detecting faked and insincere emotional signals. In the end, the most effective way of not being seen as covetous is not to be covetous.

In this sense, this commandment displays a sophisticated understanding of human social interactions. By extending the command to the internal state, and not merely to the overt action, it promotes more than legal respect for our fellows; it promotes the conditions for true social harmony. As such, this command, though still rooted in our evolved psychology, opens up room for moral innovation.

Conclusion: The Evolved Law

At the outset I identified the goal of this chapter to be the presentation of the Judaic ethical traditions embodied in the Decalogue as expressions of deeply embedded psychological pre-dispositions produced by evolution. We have pulled from the Decalogue rules and precepts that display the logic of kin selection and reciprocal altruism. We have also identified elements of commitment theory, including the role of moral emotions and reputation in securing moral obligations, as well as examples of costly signaling, within the Mosaic Code. These findings not only support the thesis of this book but also shed light on some of the more puzzling aspects entailed by a literal reading of the moral code of the Ancient Israelites, and their conception of Yahweh. This strengthens the case for an evolutionary understanding of religion and religious morality.

The specific significance of this chapter is to provide an alternative mode of interpretation – a new hermeneutic tool, as it were – of one of the most important moral codes in Western history, that is, the Ten Commandments. We can trace their development from primitive strategies for promoting group cohesion, ultimately in support of individual reproductive fitness, to an articulated moral system designed to meet the particular needs of a people struggling to succeed in the competitions of life at a particular period of history – but still constrained and guided by the ultimate goal of group cohesion serving reproductive success.

We must wait until the final chapter to consider what this implies about the continuing relevance of the Ten Commandments. So far we have only looked at the pro-social function of evolved morality – the in-group code of conduct. We need to also carefully consider the implications of this in-group strategy for those outside the covenantal community. This will lead us into the topic of religious violence, and no evaluation of religious morality is adequate without addressing that topic. But before entering that treacherous terrain we must continue the project of defending the thesis of the book, and this requires we go beyond Judaism. My thesis is not that Judaism alone is an expression of evolutionary strategies or that there is something unique about Judaism as a religious tradition. My contention is that the approach we have just taken to Judaism may just as successfully be taken toward religious morality, in general, or at least to monotheistic traditions. To substantiate this we need to move on to another example: Christianity.

But before we move one, one more point. In discussing the tenth commandment I mentioned it as an example of moral innovation, and this requires an explanation. The command not to covet does not merely set a code of behavior but is an invitation to reflect on our desires and how those desires contribute to or damage our relationships. Once we begin to reflect we start on the path to taking some control over our emotions and moral intuitions. We may then make conscious choices about the type of persons we wish to be and the type of society we wish to create. This is an example of culture pulling at the leash of biology. The question, as always, is, How far may that leash be stretched? In this chapter we have seen that even some of humanity's most vaunted transcendent beliefs are ultimately grounded in an evolved psychology. Still, due to the great variety of social environments in which humans struggle for existence there is the possibility of great variation in how our moral psychology is expressed. This, in conjunction with our precious, even if limited, ability to reflect on our beliefs and emotions, creates the possibility for moral innovation. Just how much innovation is possible and how resilient innovation can be, given the pull of our moral intuitions, are vital questions yet to be addressed. Considering how this evolved psychology shaped Christian ethics will be a step toward answering these questions.

4 | EVOLUTIONARY RELIGIOUS ETHICS: CHRISTIANITY

Extra gentem nulla salus. (Outside the tribe there is no salvation.)

Setting the Task

In discussing Judaic moral traditions I pointed out how difficult it is to decide where to begin, given the complexity of Jewish history. I dealt with that problem by effectively ignoring it, whenever possible, and focusing on the text as we have it before us today. One might imagine that with Christianity and Christian ethical traditions no such problem exists. Here the tradition itself supplies the starting point: the life of Jesus of Nazareth. Of course there are debates over precisely when Jesus lived, but it is his life rather than the exact date that provides the origin point of Christianity. So, in this chapter at least, it appears we can put aside anxiety over historical origins and focus confidently on what the Christian scriptures tell us about Christian ethics.

Unfortunately, this is not the case, as most readers with any acquaintance with a scholarly approach to the subject recognize. A traditional telling of Christianity's origins as triumphal progress – from the foot of the cross on Golgotha to the emperor Theodosius kneeling at the foot of Bishop Ambrose, acknowledging the supremacy of the Church's authority in the world – is now widely seen, in scholarly circles as well as by the educated laity, to be at least a gross oversimplification and, more likely, a post-hoc reconstruction of Christian history functioning as propaganda.

With the 1945 discovery of ancient copies of alternative gospels, known as the Nag Hammadi library, scholars such as Elaine Pagels and Bart Erhman have opened the worlds of early Christian communities to a larger, non-professional audience.[1] The recent discovery of an alternative gospel attributed to Judas Iscariot caused a stir far beyond the academy, prompting coverage in popular presses and a television special.[2]

Anyone who has looked into the origins of Christianity, from any perspective other than a conservative confessional one, will have a sense that what emerges as the Catholic Church late in the fourth century was the result of historical processes that were marked by diversity and competition among conflicting understandings of what it meant to be a Christian. However, even this picture, that of different Christian traditions – Ebionites and Marcionites, Gnostics and Pauline, and so on – struggling toward orthodoxy and against pagans and Jews, is challenged as still being too simple a depiction of the first three centuries of the Common Era. Scholars are coming to recognize that the use of the word *Christian* as a term of identification has a complex and uncertain history.

By the time Jesus, and then Paul, turns up on the scene, Judaism was a heterogeneous complex of beliefs, traditions, and expectations.[3] To speak of *Judaism* as if this signified a unified religious practice and community is an abstraction that glosses over the historical picture as badly as speaking of a *Christian* tradition at this time does. As Judith Lieu writes, the early centuries of the Common Era were "a world of fuzzy boundaries where exclusive commitment was an anomaly,"[4] a period when "both Christianity and Judaism ... were diverse phenomena."[5] Daniel Boyarin argues that even as late as the second century the boundary between Christianity and Judaism was "so fuzzy that one could hardly say precisely at what point one stopped and the other began."[6] Boyarin says that during these early centuries, the various forms of Judaism and Christianity were "part of one complex religious family, twins in a womb, contending with each other for identity and precedence, but sharing to a large extent the same spiritual food, as well."[7]

It is only in the fourth century, after Christianity is embraced by Constantine, that we can speak with some confidence of Christianity and the Christian Church. However, this is far too late in the story for our purposes. We must begin our consideration of Christian ethics at an earlier point, when the boundaries were still fuzzy and group identity uncertain. Indeed, it is only by understanding this historical context that we can come to appreciate the development of a distinctive Christian moral tradition.

The material for our study will be the New Testament, specifically the Gospels and the letters of Paul.[8] I exclude non-canonical gospels, partly to prevent the discussion from becoming unmanageable, but more importantly because it is the canonical gospels, by their very status as canonical, that proved to be the most fit in the struggle for acceptance and that have most significantly shaped Christian moral sensibilities and identity.[9] The New Testament is a record of a nascent religious movement seeking to distinguish itself in a complex world.[10] This topic is ripe for analysis from a variety of approaches, and there is a rich literature on the topic, much of which informs the present study. As we explore the origins of Christian moral traditions we are looking for traces of evolutionary influence that may have shaped the particular forms Christianity has assumed. Reading these

Christian documents through the lens of evolutionary psychology may open a new path through familiar terrain.

In terms of the thesis of this book we should expect to find embedded in Christian ethics a system based on the psychology of reciprocation, which also triggers evolved preferences for kin, and which establishes a group identity by drawing a moral boundary between itself and others, marked by signals of commitment; and this system will be supported and enforced by a god who fits the template of a minimally counter-intuitive (MCI) being. This is a daunting task because it is on these very points that traditional Christian apologists insist that Christianity is unique. Christ taught us to "Love your enemies, do good to those who hate you" (Luke 6:27), which is a repudiation of the logic of reciprocal altruism; Paul tells us that in Christ there is "neither Jew nor Greek, there is neither slave nor free, there is neither male nor female; for you are all one in Christ Jesus" (Gal. 3:28), and what is this if not a rejection of all boundaries, a declaration of moral equality that rejects the moral distinctions of in-group and out-group? It is argued that Christ transcended the pull of our evolved psychology and freed us from such constraints.[11] Even if we are to grant the effectiveness of an evolutionary analysis of Judaic ethical traditions, it is argued that this religious tradition is just what Christ overturned.[12]

I want to be clear that I recognize that these criticisms appear to provide evidence against an evolutionary account, and to be equally clear that I reject that position and hold that Christianity, no less than Judaism, is open to an evolutionary analysis. This is not to deny that there is something distinct about Christian morality (although not anything radically novel, as much of what is distinct has its roots in developments in Judaism, particularly in the Prophets). Christianity does represent a new development in humanity's religious consciousness; it does present a different understanding of humanity's relation to the divine; it does provide the material for a new understanding of our moral relationship to others. But this does not preclude an evolutionary basis for this religious ethical tradition or argue for Christian exceptionalism (i.e., the idea that Christianity is uniquely distinct from other religions or moral traditions).[13] Recognizing a distinct, and in many ways novel, moral tradition is not at odds with an evolutionary explanation because, as we have discussed, evolution does not entail biological determinism nor preclude moral innovation. Still, the question posed at the end of the last chapter is relevant here: How far can innovation move away from its evolved roots? Does Christianity break the leash of biology? To address these questions we need to determine if we can make a case for an evolutionary understanding of Christian morality. However, first we need to consider a vital aspect of religious morality – that it is grounded in the will of a deity who can be relied on to function as an enforcer of the group's moral code; that is, we must consider how *Jesus*

Christ functions as a minimally counter-intuitive concept, interested in the moral behavior of the group.

Constructing the Christ

We have seen that the character of Yahweh in Jewish scriptures followed the pattern set down in the course of our evolution and uncovered by cognitive psychology. Yahweh fits into the ontological category of *person* but violates several of those categorical expectations. Our analysis of Yahweh was more focused on how that conception of a god fit into the ontological category of *person*, since Yahweh is presented as a cosmic figure that clearly transcends that category. Things are quite different with Christianity. With Christianity we begin with Jesus, who clearly fits into the category of *person* and who is recognized by all to have been a person[14] – a human being who was born and raised and died, who ate and drank, had friends and family, got angry, cried, and doubted. The job of the early Christian writers was to present this person as more than human, as divine. They had to construct a picture of Jesus that showed he also violated some of those categorical expectations, and to do so in a way that was memorable and morally significant. As we read through the gospels that is just what we find. The presentation of Jesus as *the Christ* fits that pattern set out by cognitive psychology for a minimally counter-intuitive concept. The categorical violations attributed to Jesus enable *the Christ* to assume the moral role necessary to support and enforce the religious ethics of emerging Christian communities. At the same time, the evangelists never stray too far from the category of *person*, for to do so would weaken the intuitive sense of realness that gives the concept its compelling nature.

As we explore the construction of *the Christ* in the canonical gospels we are not concerned with the historical Jesus. Trying to uncover the historical figure behind the gospel character is a fascinating and important project, but it is the Jesus of the gospels, irrespective of his connection or lack thereof to the historical Jesus, which has shaped Western civilization.

Let's start at the beginning with the birth of Christ. Interestingly, only two of the four gospels tell us anything about his birth. The gospels of Mark and the John[15] say nothing of Christ until he is a mature man, ready to begin his mission. Entailed in this, of course, is the recognition that he had indeed been born, but there was nothing about that birth that seemed noteworthy enough to include in their accounts. This is surprising given just how dramatic the birth accounts are in Matthew (1–2) and Luke (1–2:21), but this is not our concern here; our concern is with what those narratives reveal.

The general details of Christ's nativity are well known in the West from their role in Christmas traditions, regardless of religious affiliation. Those traditional Christmas stories and songs about the nativity, however, often distract us from a close reading of the texts, a reading that reveals two very different tellings of Christ's birth. These differences and how they get glossed over by contemporary Christmas traditions are interesting topics, but it is what they share that is key to our discussion, for both initiate the transformation of the *person* Jesus into the MCI concept of Christ – they literally prepare the way of the Lord.

These narratives work with the default understanding of Jesus as a *person*. He is born of a mother, Mary, into a human family with Joseph as father. Luke tells us that he was wrapped in swaddling clothes – because babies get cold and need to be kept warm – and eight days after his birth he was circumcised – because that is what happens to Jewish male infants. There is nothing worthy of note here and it is no wonder that Mark and John did not bother to mention such details. This is just what happens when *persons* are born, but of course there is more. The birth narratives do not simply to announce the birth of a *person* but signal this person is something more.

Both stories have the birth preceded by divine messengers telling of the coming wonder (an angel speaking to Joseph, in Matthew; to Mary, in Luke); both have the birth accompanied by celestial wonders (a star, in Matthew; an angel and a multitude of heavenly hosts, in Luke) and both tell of the visit of worshippers (three wise men, in Matthew; shepherds, in Luke). All of this indicates that this baby born in Bethlehem is no ordinary *person*; ordinary existence is interrupted by divine signs, the cosmos themselves speak to his significance. These memorable stories signal that this *person* requires our attention.

Matthew fills out his story with even more dramatic elements. He tells of the evil king Herod, who hearing of the birth of a potential rival sets out to destroy the infant. However, the child's parents are warned and save the baby. The child escapes the persecution and grows up in anonymity in a foreign land until he is ready to assume his true destiny. New Testament scholars point out that with this story Matthew is directly connecting the birth of Jesus to the birth of Moses. The formula found in Exodus of the birth of Moses, the destined savior of the Hebrew people who would estab-lish God's covenant with his people, is here adapted to tell the story of Jesus, destined to be the savior who establishes God's new covenant with the world. Moses' birth sparked a vicious response from Pharaoh, who ordered the massacre of all male infants in order to protect his hold on power, as Jesus' birth also provoked Herod into ordering a massacre of the innocents; Moses is saved by being placed in a basket and sent down the river where he is raised as an Egyptian in Pharaoh's court, not among his own people; Jesus is spared death when his parents flee with him to Egypt (quite a trip for an indigent couple with a newborn) where he is raised away from his people; Moses and Jesus both grow up and return to the holy land, fulfilling their destinies as saviors of the people. This effectively serves Matthew's goal of establishing Jesus as both the fulfillment of the Jewish scriptures and the beginning of a new phase in God's self-revelation.

But Matthew, whether consciously or not, is doing something more. He is appropriating a mythic schema, thousands of years old and used repeatedly to herald the coming of a powerful leader. This schema, with variations, was also used to tell the story of the Mesopotamian ruler Sargon (perhaps the earliest rendition of this myth, dating from the third millennium B.C.E), the Greek demi-god Herakles, and the legendary figures of Oedipus and Romulus and Remus, to name a few. The birth of each of these figures was accompanied by a danger that was avoided by having the child raised away from his true home until he could return to fulfill his great destiny. Another common element that shows up repeatedly, although not consistently, is that the child is born to a human mother but is fathered by a god. This element is shared by Matthew and Luke (but never mentioned by Mark or John): Christ was born of a virgin. He was not conceived, as *persons* are, through sexual union of a man and a woman. He was conceived through the Holy Spirit, because Mary had "found favor with God."

While this version of the story spares us salacious details of Yahweh coming down from heaven in Zeus-like fashion to ravish this unsuspecting mortal woman, the story of a woman finding favor in the eyes of a god and then finding herself pregnant with the son of that god is both so ancient and so familiar in mythic literature that it points to a basis not in fact but in psychology.

If we view gods as MCI concepts then it follows in an intuitively acceptable way that gods have sexual desires. Indeed in many cultures it is the sexual desires and mating of the gods that explain much of the universe, from the creation of the cosmos to the growing of crops. So it is quite a natural idea that gods would seek sexual satisfaction, and since gods are imagined in human form they will naturally be attracted to humans with beautiful forms. Also, male gods generate expectations in line with those generated by powerful mortal males and so stories of gods taking whichever woman found favor in their eyes sounds familiar. Stories of gods – male and female – mating with humans proliferated throughout ancient literature, and the Bible is no exception. Genesis gives us a snippet of just such a tale: "the sons of God saw that the daughters of men were fair; and they took to wife such of them as they chose. ... the sons of God came into the daughters of men, and they bore children to them. These were the mighty men of old, the men of renown" (Gen. 6:1–4).

Such stories may raise problems today, and raised problems for some ancient thinkers (Plato and Epicurus were just two who found such stories about the gods offensive) but they show up repeatedly and in vastly different cultural settings because they flow naturally from expectations generated by the ontological category of *person*, and so they have an intuitive plausibility about them; and they are memorable, attention-grabbing stories (humans continue to have a fascination with the sexual exploits of the mighty – indeed the gossip industry thrives on it). These stories are also well suited to serve as explanations for exceptional human beings. They signal that a particular human being, who may appear to be a member of the category *person*, transcends that category and has a divine nature as well (which in turn explains why they were so special). Matthew and Luke make use of a formula that heralds the entrance of a super-human figure into human history, and signals the communities that read these texts that Jesus was more than man.

In order for a god-concept to assume a central role in a community's moral life, that god needs to be more than a super-powerful being; the god must have the characteristics that suit it to play such a role. That god must be a full-access strategic agent; he must be an interested party in the affairs of the group; he must have the power to support the community and to enforce its moral code; and he must have the reputation that makes that enforcement credible. The god can further serve as a moral legislator and role model for the community. The character of Christ in the gospels meets all of these criteria.

Several of stories show us that Christ has access to knowledge that *persons* are not privileged to know. For example, we learn that at the age of twelve Christ was able to amaze the teachers in the temple "with his understanding and his answers" (Luke 2:46–47). More impressive, he was able to predict the destruction of the temple (e.g., Matt. 24:1–2); his own death (e.g., John 12:27–36); and his resurrection (e.g., Matt. 16:21). He is also able to share with his followers the signs that presage the end of time (e.g., Matt. 24:3–8) and the timing: "Truly, I say to you, this generation will not pass away till all has taken place" (Luke 21:32). This is just not the sort of information to which a *person* has access.

More significant for morality, Christ has access into the hearts and minds of others. He knows that despite his bluster, Peter will not stand up for him after his arrest but will deny him (Matt. 26:34). He knows that Judas is planning to betray him (John 13:21–27). He recognizes that despite their show of piety and virtue, the Scribes and Pharisees "outwardly appear righteous, but within [they] are full of hypocrisy and iniquity" (Matt. 23:27–28). Jesus Christ has access to all the relevant information needed to judge moral interactions, far more than is available to mere mortals.

Christ, as full-access strategic agent, is in that prime position to serve as moral judge for the community, and he is intensely concerned with the moral behavior of the people. He proclaims, "Think not that I have come to abolish the law and the prophets; I have come not to abolish them but to fulfill them" (Matt. 5:17). Christ characterizes his mission as one of moral salvation: "For God sent the Son into the world, not to condemn the world, but that the world might be saved through him" (John 3:17). And that salvation is achieved by adhering to moral standards: "If you keep my commandments, you will abide in my love, just as I have kept my Father's commandments and abide in his love" (John 15:9–10).

This passage tells us that not only is Christ an interested party in moral interactions but he also serves as a moral role model. Christ supports the moral code of the community by embodying it, telling us to love one another "as I have loved you" (John 15:12). Indeed, throughout the gospels Christ's life is set before the community as the ideal for all members of the group. Not just his words but his actions become moral guidelines for the community.

Jesus Christ has access to our inner most thoughts; he cares deeply about morality and displays the moral character expected of those in the group. These traits qualify him to assume the role of enforcer of the group's moral code. To play this role well, however, Christ, or any god-concept, must be understood to have both the inclination and the power to reward and punish, and this is well attested to by the gospel authors.

After proclaiming that he has come to fulfill the Law, he warns that "Whoever then relaxes one of the least of these commandments and teaches men so, shall be called least in the kingdom of heaven; but he who does them and teaches them shall be called great in the kingdom of heaven" (Matt. 5:19). This sets a punishment for violating the moral code but also signals the social nature of that code. Breaking the Law is not simply an act with personal consequences. Bad behavior may influence others and set them down the wrong path, and this will be held against you. Mark gives a more emphatic teaching on the sin of leading others astray: "Whoever causes one of these little ones who believe in me to sin, it would be better for him if a great millstone were hung around his neck and he were thrown into the sea" (Mark 9:42). Dire consequences indeed! Aside from the severe punishment, what is also interesting about this passage is how Christ qualifies this admonition – the punishment is for those who morally endanger not just any child but those "little ones who believe in me." This qualification helps to establish the boundaries of the moral group, which we will turn to later, but significant here is that Christ identifies himself as the symbol of morality. To believe in him is to put yourself on the side of morality; to reject him is to side with evil, and those who reject him can expect to suffer the consequences.

When Christ sends out his disciples to spread the word to surrounding towns he informs them that those towns that reject them (and so reject Christ's teaching) face terrible judgment when the kingdom of God comes, in fact, "it shall be more tolerable on that day for Sodom than for that town" (Luke 10:12). Sodom and Gomorrah were well known to be filled with people who committed vile acts offensive to God, and would naturally face damnation on the day of judgment – but it will be even worse for these other towns! And why? Because they are filled with evildoers who violate the laws of God? No, at least we are not told that. We are simply told that they have failed to accept the word of Christ. That is enough to merit condemnation. This signals in a powerful way that Christ embodies morality, and rejecting morality, by rejecting Christ, will be severely punished. If Christ is committed to punishing towns for refusing his disciples, what can individual sinners expect? We are not left to guess: "so it will be at the close of the age. The Son of man will send his angels, and they will gather out of his kingdom all causes of sin and all evildoers, and throw them into the furnace of fire; there men will weep and gnash their teeth." But the righteous need not fear, for they will "shine like the sun in the kingdom of their Father" (Matt. 13:40–43). These examples make clear that Christ is committed to enforcing the moral code and that he does so by discouraging defectors with punishment and rewarding the good.

There is a passage, however, that seems to speak against this picture of Christ as moral enforcer. In John we hear Christ proclaim, "If any one hears my sayings and does not keep them, I do not judge him; for I did not come to judge the world but to save the world" (John 12:47). This seems to be at odds with the picture we just developed. If Christ is not going to judge those who hear his word and reject it (and note how inconsistent this is with the Christ of Matthew and Luke), then he is not going to be very useful in strengthening the moral bonds of the group. But even in John, the gospel that seeks to portray Christ as love, we are quickly assured that defectors from the moral code will certainly face judgment: "He who rejects me and does not receive my sayings has a judge; the word I have spoken will be his judge on the last day" (John 12:48). And on that last day the fate of the defector is no less terrifying in this gospel of love than it is in the synoptic gospels: "If a man does not abide in me, he is cast forth as a branch and withers; and the branches are gathered, thrown into the fire and burned" (John 15:6). If an MCI concept is going to play a morally significant role for a group of believers it must be portrayed as committed to punishing defectors and rewarding cooperators. Despite efforts to portray Christ as a God of love and forgiveness, he must also be portrayed as a God of vengeance, and this is just what we find in the gospels.

Of course, being committed to enforcing the moral code of the group is not very effective unless you have the power to back up your threat. In our discussion of Judaism we saw that the Israelites were often reminded of the power of Yahweh, who created the cosmos with the power of his words and who rained destruction on the enemies of Israel. This is a god with the power to make good on his word. What about Jesus?

One salient fact about Christ is that he is the son of God, sent by the Father to do his bidding: "the Father who sent me has himself given me commandment what to say" (John 12:49). His relationship with the Father allows others to enter into communion with the Father: "He who has my commandments and keeps them, he it is who loves me, and he who loves me will be loved by my Father" (John 14:21). Indeed, Christ proclaims that he is the only path to the Father – "no one comes to the Father, but by me" (John 14:6) – and it is through Christ that one earns the approval of the Father: "if anyone honors me, the Father will honor him" (John 12:26). To drive this home even more directly, "I and the Father are one" (John 10:30). This explicitly connects Christ and his work to the power of the Father, and this Father is the same god that so clearly signaled his power to the Israelites in the Hebrew Scriptures. Anyone this close to such a deity is someone with power worth respecting.

But of course we are not led to believe that Christ himself is without power, even if that power comes from God. Some of the most memorable gospel stories about Jesus signal the unique powers of Christ. It would be too cumbersome and unnecessary to list the various miracles attributed to him. What is significant in these stories are the types of powers attributed to Christ: Christ has the power to provide the resources the community needs (the multiplication of the loaves and fishes, e.g., Matt. 14:13–21); he has the power to heal the sick (e.g., Mark 6:53–56); and he can cast out demons, freeing individuals from terrible mental and emotional afflictions (e.g., Luke 9:37–43). These are powers are very close to the everyday concerns of people trying to deal with the precariousness of life. These stories signal that not only does Christ have powers that other *persons* do not, but that he has powers that are important to people's lives. Beyond this we are shown that Christ has power over the forces of nature. He can walk on water (Matt. 14:22–27), dissipate storms (Mark 4:35–41), and perhaps most important of all, has power over death itself (e.g., John 11:38–44).[16] A being with this degree of power and these kinds of power is a being powerful enough to mete out rewards and punishments.

These miracle stories make Christ a memorable and significant figure in the life of the community, and in relaying these stories the evangelists never allow our attention to stray too far from the moral import of Christ. In the story of the paralytic man Jesus first cleanses the sufferer of his sins, then heals the body (Matt. 9:1–8). The authority to forgive sins is of particular importance, for forgiveness is a way of reconciling one with the community that has been offended; it offers a renewal of commitment to that group and continued membership in society. By claiming the power to forgive sins Christ becomes the gatekeeper to the community. Those who are forgiven may be admitted back into the fold, while the unforgiven are cast out. Not only does Christ have this power but he can bestow it on mere mortals. When he says to his apostles, "Truly, I say to you, whatever you bind on earth shall be bound in heaven, and whatever you loose on earth shall be loosed in heaven" (Matt. 18:18), he imbues the leaders of the community with that crucial authority to police the morality of the group.

We may always be thwarted in our efforts to connect the Jesus of the New Testament to the Jesus of history (and I say this without denying the fascinating strides that have been taken toward this goal) and much that is said of Jesus is clearly of a legendary nature. The importance of the gospels is in their success in constructing out of the historical materials available to them a character of *Jesus the Christ* that was well designed to play a moral role in the then emerging Christian communities. Given the dominance of the religious traditions that centered on this character throughout the next two millennia, and its continued worldwide influence, the New Testament presents one of the most effective religious concepts in history.

To truly appreciate its effectiveness we must turn to the moral code it supports and the community it helps to sustain. For an MCI concept, such as *Christ*, to be effective on a wide scale, it must connect to a morality that taps into evolved psychological predispositions. Does Christ's moral message do so or does it transcend our evolved moral natures? Does the moral tradition set out in the New Testament seek to establish a universal moral code or does it fulfill its evolutionary function of regulating in-group behavior, establishing the boundaries of the group, and providing signals of commitment to that group? To these difficult questions we now turn.

Setting the Boundaries: Christian and/or Jew?

The supposition that Christ came to abolish any boundaries dividing human from human is a significant challenge to an evolutionary analysis of Christianity. This position is famously expressed by Paul's statement, quoted earlier, that in Christ, "There is neither Jew nor Greek, there is neither slave nor free, there is neither male nor female; for you are all one in Christ Jesus" (Gal. 3:28). This is a common theme in the Pauline letters. In Romans, Paul assures us that "God shows no partiality" (Rom. 2:11). In 1 Corinthians he rails against divisions in the church, reminding his readers that "we were all baptized into one body – Jews or Greeks, slaves or free – and all were made to drink of one Spirit" (1 Cor. 12:13). And it is not just Paul who advocates this view; it is set out in the gospels, as well. In John, Jesus declares that he has come "to save the world" (John 12:47) not to save the members of a particular group. Jesus is the "true light that enlightens every man" (John 1:9). Indeed, we are told that the very last command Christ gave to his disciples was: "Go therefore and make disciples of all nations" (Matt. 28:19).

This, it is argued, makes Christianity distinct and marks a new epoch in morality. Every other moral tradition, religious or secular, may advocate an in-group bias, but the teachings of Jesus explicitly reject that bias. Christ introduced a universal morality into human history, one inconsistent with an evolved moral psychology that creates distinct moral boundaries. Christian ethics, then, transcend evolutionary ethics; and this transcendence of our evolved moral psychology may even speak to "a divine source"[17] – which, of course, is exactly what Christianity claims.

This reading of Christianity must be addressed if we are going to make a plausible case for an evolutionary reading. I have argued that morality developed to define and sustain a community, setting it apart from rival groups, and that the key to understanding the moral tradition of a group is to see how it contributes to group identity formation, marking out those individuals committed to the group from those who stand apart. A moral code that does not serve these functions *is* inconsistent with an evolutionary analysis. Therefore, to support my thesis we need to demonstrate that Christianity does not transcend this evolutionary moral logic, that while Christianity does extend the boundaries of the moral community, it nevertheless establishes a boundary and imbues that boundary with ultimate moral significance. Not only is boundary-setting a concern of Christian ethics, it is a central concern, and much of that moral tradition works to signal commitment to the in-group enclosed within that boundary. A closer reading of the texts, as well as a consideration of the historical setting of Christianity's origins, will suggest a different understanding of Christian *universalism*.[18]

What later comes to recognize itself as Christianity has its origins in first-century Palestine, during a period that has been described as the "heyday of Jewish sectarianism."[19] Scholars recognize that during this period Judaism was struggling to respond to the challenges presented by Hellenization, a process that was cultural and intellectual, as well as political. This early form of globalization spread Greco-Roman ideas and practices throughout the Ancient Near East, undermining traditional systems, while also offering new ways of being in the world, and the Jews of this period were no different in being both offended and attracted by these new ways.

By challenging traditional practices and beliefs, Hellenism challenged group identity and led to the "fuzzy boundaries" that characterized the period. Loosening traditional boundaries opened up new possibilities, and one novel possibility was the choice of which group to identify with.[20] While this may have initiated a period of "creativity and adaptation"[21] in religious expressions, it also posed disturbing challenges. If boundaries are fuzzy then individuals may cross them from both sides, and this undermines the conditions of a functioning moral code. In-group members may cross out of the group without reciprocating for the benefits of membership they have already enjoyed; outsiders may cross in to exploit the cooperation and sociality that has developed within the group, with no intention of contributing to the group. In this situation, how do I know who I can trust to reciprocate cooperation and who should I avoid as a possible cheater? If I cannot answer these questions with some degree of certainty then my cooperation becomes foolish, a waste of resources on those who will not contribute to my own inclusive fitness. As we have seen, evolution makes us very wary of this danger. The breakdown of established group boundaries may provide a heady sense of freedom, but it can be no more than a transitional phase if society itself is not to collapse. This challenge resonates in a deeply emotional and psychological manner, and it demands a response.

One response is to crack down on boundary crossing, to re-affirm the traditional boundary and police it vigilantly. We saw that costly signals of commitment, such as circumcision and Sabbath observations, take on added significance in times of uncertainty. It is not surprising to learn that during this period of Jewish history they came to have particular importance. Of circumcision, Shaye Cohen writes that it is "only in Maccabean times" that this practice is seen as "the essential mark for Jewish identity or as the sine qua non for membership in the Jewish polity"[22]; and Tessa Rajak writes that the "Sabbath was central to the identity of Jews living among Gentiles."[23] Both of these practices were recognized by the Romans as distinctively Jewish.

These practices may signal one's membership in Judaism, but in a period of transition the very understanding of what it meant to be a Jew was itself contested. Such a situation is a fertile breeding ground for the rise of competing sects.[24] The appearance of numerous sects during this period is well attested to, with Sadducees, Pharisees, and Essenes being some of the more notable. And of course it is just in this period that a group of Jews from Jerusalem and the Galilee began to develop a sect centered on the teachings of Jesus of Nazareth.

The origins of Christianity are part of the development of first-century Jewish sectarianism. The early Christians were one of several groups of Jews struggling to redefine their understanding of Judaism and forge an identity for themselves as the true children of the covenant. For a sect to be successful it must both connect itself and distinguish itself from a more established tradition. To claim validity for its perspective it must criticize the original tradition as corrupted, while affirming some selected aspects of that tradition that it claims to preserve. In the terms of our evolutionary analysis, the sect becomes the in-group, drawing a boundary around itself that distinguishes it from the older tradition, now denigrated to the status of out-group. The sectarians, in turn, are seen from the perspective of the traditional group as defectors who threaten the stability of the in-group.

As we turn to the New Testament we will find that a central concern is to distinguish Christianity from Judaism, while claiming the mantle of heirs to the covenant, and we will recognize numerous Christian practices and moral innovations are means of signaling this distinction and one's membership in the new in-group. This function of the moral tradition found in the New Testament is more complicated than this, however. In signaling its distinctiveness from Judaism, Christianity needed to avoid the opposite danger of identifying itself with paganism. Thus Christianity represented, or sought to represent itself as, those of a third race, "neither Jew nor Greek."[25]

In the gospels the boundaries of the community are in flux. In Luke, Jesus is confronted with this very issue. He had just taught that we should love our neighbor when he is asked, "And who is my neighbor?" This is significant as it indicates confusion about the boundaries of the group. When those boundaries are clear then my neighbor is readily identifiable. In a more stable, traditional Jewish society this question need not arise, but that is not the world of first-century Judea, and so Jesus recognizes this question must be addressed, and he does so with the parable of the Good Samaritan (Luke 10:25–37). In this famous story the hero is a member of a reviled out-group who stops to aid a stranger in need, while two others that might have been expected to be moral role models (a priest and a Levite) ignore the suffering of a fellow Jew. This brief parable says much. "Neighbor" is now defined as the one who provides aid and comfort, regardless of ethnicity. The focus has shifted from group identity to moral behavior. This parable also teaches that ethnicity is not a reliable signal of commitment to cooperate. The priest and the Levite fail to provide aid to a fellow Jew, that is, to a fellow member of the in-group. This behavior signals that one cannot be relied on to cooperate, which undermines the whole project of group living.

This parable is proposed to be a perfect example of Christ going beyond evolutionary morality.[26] Jesus here rejects any boundary between one people and another, and makes moral values the means by which we are to judge others. There is something to this claim. Jesus does indeed reject ethnicity as a condition of in-group membership, and he does turn the focus to moral values, but this does not entail a rejection of the binary thinking of in-group/

out-group. It indicates instead that the boundary between the two is being redefined. Part of that redefinition is setting out what one is not, how the new in-group differs from the old in-group being left behind. The Good Samaritan story is part of this process; it claims that being heir to the covenant is no longer dependent on one's Jewish ethnicity.

This is seen repeatedly throughout Luke, the gospel that is believed to have been directed to a largely gentile audience. A particular concern to Luke is to make the case that Jesus, while Jewish and the Messiah expected by the Jews, did not come just for the Jews. This position is flagged early on in Luke's version of the genealogy of Jesus, which he traces back past Abraham, father of the Jews, to Adam, father of all humankind (Luke 3:23–38). The message is also driven home, without much subtlety, in the story of Jesus healing a centurion's servant. A centurion sends a messenger to Jesus to ask him to heal his slave. Jesus goes to the man's house to do so, when he is met by an anxious centurion who tells Jesus that he is unworthy to have him enter his home, and asks that Jesus merely say the word and he knows his servant will be healed. Jesus is very impressed by this and before healing the man's slave declares to the crowd that had gathered, "I tell you, not even in Israel have I found such faith" (Luke 7:1–10).

In Israel he has not found the faith demonstrated by this centurion – that is, by a man who not only is not Jewish but is a Roman soldier, a member of the hated, oppressor class. Even one such as this had more faith than any supposed fellow in-group member.

Of course, this is not unique to Luke, but is characteristic of the New Testament in general. In Mark, it is a centurion at the crucifixion who recognizes Jesus's true identity: "Truly this man was the Son of God!" (Mark 15:39) while bystanders, presumably Jews, mock him in his suffering. Matthew, who also tells the story of the centurion's slave, not only notes the centurion's superior faith but goes further and has Jesus add: "I tell you, many will come from east and west and sit at table with Abraham, Isaac, and Jacob in the kingdom of heaven, while the sons of the kingdom will be thrown into the outer darkness; there men will weep and gnash their teeth" (Matt. 8:11). In a concise way, this statement both denigrates the Jews ("sons of the kingdom"), who will be cast out, and offers to those outside the in-group the benefits of membership.

If Luke is the more gentile-oriented gospel, Matthew seems to have been written for a community of Jewish Christians. Matthew, of all the gospels, is most concerned with connecting Jesus with Jewish prophecy. We have already seen how Matthew's telling of Jesus' birth appropriates the narrative of Moses' birth, equating Jesus' significance to that of the founding figure of Judaism, but this focus is also found in Matthew's version of Jesus' genealogy. Where Luke traces Jesus' lineage to Adam, Matthew starts with

Abraham, the father of the Jewish people, and traces the line down to Jesus. Although Matthew places greater emphasis on Jesus' Jewish credentials, all four gospels make a point of that connection. It is part of the dynamics of sectarianism that the sect must affirm its identity as the true expression of the original tradition, while rejecting that older tradition as corrupt. This was even more imperative for Christianity.

In the Roman world religion was always ancient. The gods existed from time immemorial and so traditions centering on the gods should also be ancient. There may be innovations, or newly introduced traditions, but these needed to be grounded in antiquity. To have a "new religion" just did not make sense and tainted such movements as superstitions deserving of suspicion. Now, whatever their ambivalence toward Judaism, it was an ancient religion and so worthy of some respect. In fighting for a place in a Roman world Christianity needed to make the case that it was not a new religion but was in fact the true fulfillment of ancient Judaism.[27]

The gospels also set out this complex relationship between Christianity and Judaism in their treatment of the moral code itself. Jesus is frequently concerned to demonstrate just how the new moral message he brings surpasses the ancient Judaic code, while at the same time recognizing the worth of that code. We have already heard Jesus proclaim that he has come to fulfill the law (Matt. 5:17), but after making himself clear on that point he proceeds to set out a new understanding of the law. This teaching is known as the Antitheses, because Jesus sets out his position on the law as an antithesis to the traditional teaching. These take the form of "You have heard it said ... but I say to you."

He sets out six of these (Matt. 5:21–48), all commentary on moral injunctions taken from the Mosaic Law. We can just pick out two to see their significance:

> You have heard that it was said to the men of old, "You shall not kill; and whoever kills shall be liable to judgment." But I say to you that everyone who is angry with his brother shall be liable to judgment. (Matt. 5:21–22)

> You have heard that it was said, "You shall not commit adultery." But I say to you that everyone who looks at a woman lustfully has already committed adultery with her in his heart. (Matt. 5:27–28)

Jesus here cites two of the Ten Commandments, validates them, but then goes beyond them. He teaches not that the old law was wrong or has been left behind but instead that it does not go far enough. These laws had not been properly understood by the older tradition, and this is why that tradition needs the reform he brings. I would not suggest that Jesus' teaching here is simply a device for establishing the boundaries of the new sect, but it is one of the functions of his teaching.

We can see this again in those passages where Jesus refers to the Decalogue. All three synoptic gospels tell the story of Jesus being asked what must be done to gain eternal life. Jesus begins his answer by listing the commandments. While there is some variation in the wording and order in the accounts, all three have Jesus identify five commands: Do not kill, do not commit adultery, do not steal, do not bear false witness, honor your father and mother (Mark 10:17–20; Matt. 19:16–19; Luke 18:18–20). More telling are the ones he does not cite. He makes no mention of the first four commands – nothing about graven images, about keeping the Sabbath, no reminders of being liberated from Egypt; in other words, nothing in the Decalogue that was specifically related to Jewish history or Jewish identity. In this story Jesus both affirms the importance of the Law while moving it away from its Jewish moorings.

Perhaps the most significant aspect of Christian morality, in terms of redefining the boundaries of the group, is the position it takes on Sabbath practices, dietary laws, and circumcision, practices that serve as costly signals of commitment to Judaism. To reject these particular practices was to signal that one had opted out of the moral contract, or at least that one could not be trusted not to opt out. We also noted that these practices became more significant in times of great social stress, such as in first-century Judea. Jesus could hardly find a more effective way to signal that there was a new community on the rise than to reject these practices.

In terms of dietary laws, Jesus proclaims: "Hear and understand: it is not what goes into the mouth that defiles a man, but what comes out of the mouth, this defiles a man" (Matt. 15:10–11). The Jewish leaders heard and clearly understood, as Jesus' disciples inform him that the Pharisees were offended at this teaching, and well they should have been. Jesus is effectively erasing the distinction between kosher and non-kosher foods. This not only rejects a signal of commitment to the Jewish community, thus signaling his break from that community, but argues, in effect, that this identifying Jewish practice is morally confused: "Do you not see that whatever goes into the mouth passes into the stomach, and so passes on? But what comes out of the mouth proceeds from the heart, and this defiles a man" (Matt. 15:17–18). He goes on to say "to eat with unwashed hands does not defile a man" (Matt. 15:20), thereby rejecting the Jewish practice of ritual purification before meals, another identifying signal. In Jesus' view these practices are empty rituals, devoid of moral significance. From the perspective of cognitive psychology we recognize that these practices had great moral significance, not as intrinsically good or bad acts, but as signals of commitment to the moral expectations of the group. In rejecting these,

Jesus signals his break from that group, and also begins to establish the groundwork of his new community.[28]

One of the most provocative of Jesus' teachings concerns the Sabbath. All four gospels contain an account of Jesus healing on the Sabbath and inciting deadly rage on the part of the Jewish authorities. John adds a second Sabbath miracle story, while the synoptic gospels drive the point home by coupling two Sabbath violations. Clearly, this aspect of Jesus' teaching struck a chord among his followers.

One Sabbath day, we are told, Jesus and his disciples were walking through a corn field, when his disciples, feeling hungry, began to pick grains to eat. A seemingly innocuous act, it provokes a rebuke from the Pharisees: "Look, your disciples are doing what is not lawful to do on the sabbath" (Matt. 12:2). Jesus responds by reminding the Pharisees of when David and his men were hungry and entered the temple to eat the bread that had been brought for sacrifice, bread meant only for priests; he also tells the story of the priests violating Sabbath restrictions while attending to the temple. He then declares: "I tell you, something greater than the temple is here. ... For the Son of man is lord of the sabbath" (Matt. 12:3–8).

This is another brief story rich in meaning. Jesus signals a break from the traditional group, but not an absolute break. By reinterpreting Sabbath observations in a way that draws upon aspects of Jewish history, he does not so much reject that tradition as argue that the Jews have not properly understood it. He is not a sinner, but instead has a deeper understanding of this Jewish practice than do the Pharisees. But then he does something much more than correct a misunderstanding of doctrine: He declares himself the lord of the Sabbath.

From the perspective of traditional Judaism, this is outrageous. The Sabbath is the Lord's day, a day to remember what Yahweh has done for his people, a day to symbolically join with Yahweh in his rest. Now Jesus is placing himself above the Sabbath. He is equating himself with God – a charge made explicitly in John's stories of Jesus' Sabbath miracles (John 5:1–18). We can understand that on religious grounds alone this is behavior that cannot be tolerated, but when we call to mind the significance of Sabbath observations, and that violations were to be punished by death, the reaction is not surprising: "The Pharisees went out and took counsel against him, how to destroy him" (Matt. 12:14).[29] Jesus' teachings concerning the Sabbath signaled in an unmistakable way a rejection of solidarity with the established in-group and his intention to remake the community around a new moral covenant.

This refinement of the new Christian community, and its distinction from Judaism, is a central concern for Paul, as well. Much has been written about how divisions and competition within the new Christian communities shaped the doctrines of orthodoxy embedded in the canonized text. While this is relevant to our discussion, it is so complex that we could easily get lost in it. For the sake of focus, let's look at one important part of this story, Paul's teachings on circumcision. Paul is so concerned with this that he mentions it in five of the seven undisputed letters; we consider two – Romans and Galatians – to see how this teaching develops.

Paul recognizes that circumcision is not only a sign of identification with the in-group but also a sign of salvation through the Law, which is consistent with it being a costly signal of commitment to the moral contract of the in-group. By taking on the tradition of circumcision he is treading on sensitive ground. Paul, however, is preaching a new moral contract; he is seeking to establish a new moral community grounded in the death and resurrection of Jesus Christ. In this mission the Jewish custom of circumcision is proving an obstacle. The requirement that all males of the covenant be circumcised asks one thing when the male is an eight-day-old child, quite another when that male is fully grown. It takes little imagination to understand why the requirement that prospective converts to Christianity first undergo circumcision presented a hurdle to Paul's mission. But the question of circumcision had deeper significance. It was a sign of commitment to the established in-group that Paul, a herald of the new sect, was seeking to replace. And he makes this move not by completely repudiating the old ways but by reinterpreting this ancient practice in light of a new moral emphasis. Paul sets out his argument in Romans:

> Circumcision indeed is of value if you obey the law; but if you break the law, your circumcision becomes uncircumcision. So, if a man who is uncircumcised keeps the precepts of the law, will not his uncircumcision be regarded as circumcision? Then those who are physically uncircumcised but keep the law will condemn you who have the written code and circumcision but break the law. (Rom. 2:25–27)

Circumcision should not be understood as a physical sign of righteousness because circumcised men can and do break the law. So what does their circumcision represent?

Since they have acted immorally it becomes in effect uncircumcision. But if circumcision is symbolic of inner righteousness then one who obeys the law, even though he is physically uncircumcised, is the one who is truly the circumcised. Paul is moving away from circumcision as a sign of the covenant. This becomes explicit as the passage continues: "For he is not a real Jew who is one outwardly, nor is true circumcision something external and physical. He is a Jew who is one inwardly, and real circumcision is a matter of the heart, spiritual and not literal" (Rom. 2:28–29).

In keeping with the strategy of the sect, Paul claims the mantle of historic Judaism by claiming to see more deeply into the true meaning of that tradition, thereby appropriating that tradition for the new group, while at the same time moving the group in a new direction. He provides further support for his redefinition of what it means to be a Jew by pointing out that Abraham, the father of the Jews, was chosen by God because of his righteousness, and then was circumcised, proving that the inward state is the true sign of the covenant, while the physical manifestation is only a symbol (Rom. 4:1–12).

In Galatians we find the issue has become terribly contentious, as Paul takes a much more strident tone. In Romans, physical circumcision was unnecessary, at best an outward symbol of inner righteousness; in Galatians it becomes an actual impediment to enjoying the benefits the new Christian community: "Now I, Paul, say to you that if you receive circumcision, Christ will be of no advantage to you … you are severed from Christ" (5:2–4). He is so incensed by disagreement over this issue that he wishes those who cause controversy on this "would mutilate themselves!" (Gal. 5:12). Why the vehemence? Because this is not simply a doctrinal dispute; it is a dispute over signals of commitment to the moral bounds of the group. Circumcision is a signal of commitment to the moral codes of the old in-group that determined righteousness by obedience to the Law. Paul is not simply rejecting that particular signal; he is rejecting the moral system itself. In the new Christian community the in-group will be bound not by the Law but by faith in Jesus Christ. This is why Paul goes to such lengths to argue against the Law – it is the code that bound an old community that was now to be superseded by the community of Christ, a community with its own moral covenant and its own signals of commitment. By rejecting the Law we reject allegiance to the community it binds.[30]

Before continuing we need to consider a criticism. My claim is that Christianity represents a new in-group with its own boundaries separating it from an out-group, thus undermining the claim of exceptionalism based on Christianity's supposed universalism. But all we have seen so far is that Christianity distinguishes itself from Judaism, which is not the same thing as establishing Christianity as a new in-group. Judaism, from a Christian perspective, was flawed by its narrow focus. Christianity expended so much energy in distancing itself from Judaism just because Judaism represented the in-group/out-group divide that Christ came to erase. For Christians to make the case that they are not Jews is not the same thing as establishing a new in-group.

This is a fair charge, and if we had no more evidence of in-group/out-group thinking in the New Testament we would have to concede the point. But this is not the case. Christians do not merely distinguish themselves from Jews; they set up a newly defined in-group, bounded by a moral code, with distinct signals of commitment, and in doing so clearly define an out-group, comprised of more than just non-Christian Jews.

The Third Race: Christians as In-Group

While setting the boundaries of the new in-group is a concern for Paul, the gospel writers make it clear that this new group is grounded in the teachings of Christ. There is a telling episode in which Jesus is teaching and his disciples interrupt him to say that his mother and brothers are looking for him. Jesus replies, " 'Who is my mother, and who are my brothers?' And stretching out his hand toward his disciples, he said, 'Here are my mother and brothers! For whoever does the will of my Father in heaven is my brother, and sister, and mother' " (Matt. 12:48–50). As in the parable of the Good Samaritan, Jesus here redefines the boundaries of the group, in this case by rejecting family ties as definitive. My group is determined not by blood or ethnicity but, as with his redefinition of "neighbor," by moral values.

In an article very much in the spirit of this work, David Lahti discusses Jesus' teaching from an evolutionary perspective. He analyzes the Sermon on the Mount and finds in it 105 statements making moral claims.[31] Not one, according to Lahti, makes familial relatedness or ethnicity a basis for moral distinction.[32] Lahti argues that as individuals from groups of different ethnic or tribal identities begin to interact regularly, "a shared values aspect to social norms should increase in emphasis, relative to the shared kinship aspect."[33] Lahti grounds this claim in evolutionary thinking: In increasingly complex environments, social cohesion based on kinship gives way to one based more significantly on indirect reciprocity.[34]

In his redefinition of family, Jesus does more than reject ethnicity as a sign of community; he upsets the very social order. Roman society, not merely Jewish society, saw itself grounded in the stability of the family. The *paterfamilias* and the *pater patriae* were not merely honorifics but models of authority. To disrupt the one was to threaten the other – and this is just what Jesus does. In Luke, Christ sets out the cost of discipleship: "If anyone comes to me and does not hate his own father and mother and wife and children and brothers and sisters, yes, even his own life, he cannot be my disciple" (Luke 14:26). This is revolutionary talk. If you don't give obedience to your father, how likely are you to pay allegiance to the emperor? And Jesus is not simply saying, "Don't listen to your father," but hate your father, and mother, and all in order to follow him.

Scholar of early Christianity Wayne Meeks reminds us that a major problem Romans had with the early Christians was the social disruption this new cult threatened to bring with it.[35] It was not so much that they followed a new god, but that they seemed not to respect the family values of Roman society. As another scholar points out, the Romans' concern matches contemporary fears that modern-day cults are "seducing children away from parental control."[36] And according to some texts, this was a well-founded fear. The non-canonical *Acts of Paul and Thecla* tells a story that would make modern-day parents cringe. Thecla is a young woman bethrothed to be married until she hears Paul preaching on the virtues of virginity. She is so taken by this that she spends all her time sitting at her window listening to Paul speak in the street outside. Her mother is beside herself, but nothing she says has any influence. She calls in Thecla's beloved to intervene, but he too is unsuccessful. Thecla announces that she will not marry him, but instead will commit herself to the virtuous virginity preached by this strange man outside her window. Her family, we are told, went into deep mourning, and can we be surprised? Their daughter has rejected her vows, repudiated their authority, ignored their pleas, and put herself on a collision course with the laws of society (by converting to an illegal cult), and all because of the teachings of some charismatic street-corner preacher. Is this not the story of any number of families who saw their children succumb to the attraction of modern cult figures such as Jim Jones or David Koresh?

Jesus' position on family is designed to disrupt allegiance to traditional authority structures and transfer it to himself. He fully recognizes the upheaval this will cause and embraces it: "Do not think that I have come to bring peace on earth; I have not come to bring peace, but a sword. For I have come to set man against his father, and daughter against her mother ... and a man's foes will be those of his own household. He who loves father or mother more than me is not worthy of me" (Matt. 10:34–37). This is quite a price to ask, but Christ makes it clear that it will be worth it. "And every one who has left houses or brothers or sisters or father or mother or children or land for my name's sake, will receive a hundredfold and inherit eternal life" (Matt. 19:29).

Of course, the point of such social disruption is not simply to rebel against authority. It is the first stage in establishing a new social order, one in which allegiance is withdrawn from traditional sources of authority, such as family or tribe, and transferred to the new group. Jesus begins this process by denying all established social relationships and centering the new group on allegiance to himself. In doing so he solidifies the moral bonds of that group, because Christ is a full-access strategic agent, interested in the moral doings of the group and with the power to reward and punish.

To follow Christ one must give up all one has, surrender ties to all other groups, relinquish all old identities. But this does not mean one stands alone; it is a prelude to joining a new community. Those who follow the will of God are a true family with Jesus and so with each other – this is a new in-group. Christians are not simply non-Jews; they are not pagans either. They represent a distinct group. This point is given great emphasis in the gospel of John, which stresses the distinction between Jesus' followers and the "world." In John's opening chapter we are told that Christ "was in the world, and the world was made through him, yet the world knew him not" (John 1:10). Not only does "the world" not know Jesus, it hates Jesus, and why? "[B]ecause I testify of it that its works are evil" (John 7:7).

The "world" hates Jesus because he brings moral judgment against it. Clearly, his moral code is not of the world and so those who follow it "are not of the world, even as I am not of the world" (John 17:14). Moral systems are means for establishing a basis for social cohesion and coopera-tive interactions. A new moral system indicates a new social entity, and this constitutes the new in-group. An in-group implies an out-group, here identi-fied as the "world" – those who not only stand outside the group but who threaten the group. Jesus warns his followers of the persecution they face because they follow him, that is, because they commit to this new group (Matt. 10:16–22).

This is our evolved moral psychology at work. Those who stand outside the group are a danger because they have not committed to the group and so are not bound by the moral code that makes social interaction safe. They, in turn, see us as threats to their group and so we can expect hostility from them. This is a fundamental cognitive predisposition that constitutes a basic moral orientation. Christianity may claim to be universal in scope, but as a moral code it bears the marks of an in-group/out-group mentality. Jesus himself expresses the epitome of such binary thinking: "He who is not with me is against me. And he who does not gather with me scatters" (Luke 11:23). And there are moral consequences for being on the right side, for Christ warns, "[E]very one who acknowledges me before men, I will acknowledge before my Father in heaven; but whoever denies me before men, I also will deny before my Father in heaven" (Matt. 10:32–33). There is a sharp divide between those who are in communion with Jesus and those who are not, and rewards and punishments follow accordingly.

Christian apologists of course recognize this. There are those who accept Jesus and those who do not; there will be the saved and the damned. So, how can some argue that Jesus abolished the divisions of in-group thinking? What is the basis for the claim of universalism? The typical response to such questions is that in Christ, all are welcomed – Jew and Greek, male and female, slave and free. No one is excluded based on ethnicity or nation-ality or any other sign of group identity. Since all of this is left behind as one follows Christ, the boundary of the group is opened for all to cross. Holmes Rolston III sees this as a decisive point against an evolutionary account of Christianity. He writes,

Any account of in-group altruism to achieve out-group competitive success is powerless to explain the universalism in the major world faiths. If the function of a religion is to provide fervent loyalty for a tribal group, urging one's religion on aliens is exactly the wrong behavior. ... Missionary activity is helping to ensure the replication of genes unlike one's own. ... That would be altruism of the most self-defeating kind! This preaching to the unconverted is not predicted by theory, nor explained retrodictively.[37]

This is a useful passage to dissect. It is cogently argued, by a respected thinker, striking directly at the thesis of this book, and it gets the evolutionary account all wrong.

The first sentence sets the challenge: In-group altruism cannot explain the major world faiths, such as Christianity, because of their universal aspirations. The key argument for this is that "urging one's religion on aliens is exactly the wrong behavior" because such behavior is "helping to ensure the replication of genes unlike one's own." This sounds like solid evolutionary thinking, for acting in a way to promote genes not one's own is a sure path to evolutionary disaster. This would be a clincher of an argument – *if* kin altruism were the only type of altruism. If that is, we could not provide an evolutionary mechanism to account for altruistic behavior directed toward non-kin.

But this is not the case. Reciprocal altruism and indirect reciprocity are just two of the mechanisms for extending altruism beyond the clan level. Rolston, of course, is aware of these mechanisms; he is just not impressed with them. He says the "pseudo-altruist will have to say that such missionaries were just setting up a world moral climate in which they themselves were most likely to prosper genetically," and then claims "it is difficult to see how they prosper to the detriment of others who are the beneficiaries of this allegedly pretended altruism."[38]

First, let's do away with the talk of "pseudo" and "pretended" altruism. There is nothing fake about evolved altruism. As we discussed, the ultimate cause of altruism is to promote conditions conducive to an individual's inclusive fitness, but it does so by creating cognitive/emotional predispositions to act altruistically. These predispositions are the proximate causes of altruistic behavior and are sincere motivations (or may be sincere motivations) to help others.

The question is, are missionaries – those agents of a religion's universalism – creating a moral climate in which their in-group may prosper genetically? Yes, that is exactly what they are doing. An evolutionary function of morality is to create a climate in which pro-social behavior may flourish. This means creating a climate in which individuals can secure adequate resources for themselves and their kin and, just as importantly, in which they are protected from threats to their resources and their kin. How does missionary work promote this? Missionaries spread a religion and that religion's moral code. This means it spreads its group's moral commitments to new in-group members, as well as spreading belief in the group's MCI being, that is, the god who oversees the group's moral code and metes out rewards and punishment. By spreading one's religion one is extending the boundaries of the in-group to include more individuals who might otherwise have been out-group members. Out-group members pose a threat to my group and indirectly (though perhaps directly) to me and my kin. Reducing their numbers, and therefore hopefully the strength of the out-group, reduces their threat. Is it hard to see how this is beneficial to the members of the in-group?

Rolston does not see it, and this is because he conceives of the costs and benefits of reciprocity in direct terms; he wants to know how the missionary prospers to the detriment of the beneficiary of this altruistic sharing of religion. But the point of altruism is not to benefit at the detriment of the recipient, but to benefit in return when the recipient reciprocates, directly or indirectly through the strengthening of the in-group. How do you strengthen the group? Make it stronger, more effective than competing groups. As Lahti points out, for a group whose boundaries are marked by values, such as Christianity, the "spread of one's values enlarges the group."[39] Also, keep in mind that the historical situation of early Christianity was a period of fuzzy borders and religious diversity, with various religious sects competing for a place in society and for adherents. In this situation, John North argues, Christianity's "active mission to convert gained the initiative for them."[40] *Universalism* provided the new sect with a competitive advantage against other groups – it was culturally adaptive.

If we insist that arguments based on reciprocity demonstrate how a particular act of altruism translates into a quantifiable increase in genes for the altruist, then we are rarely, if ever, going to find such arguments satisfying – but this is a badly distorted view of how our evolved moral systems work. So the final line of Rolston's quotation – "preaching to the unconverted is not predicted by theory, nor explained retrodictively" – is mistaken. An in-group bounded by shared values rather than shared kinship, struggling in a social environment with larger established out-groups, gains a competitive advantage by enlarging the group through spreading its value system. This is in line with the logic of indirect reciprocity, and explains the universalizing aspect of Christianity.[41]

Meeks points out that a universalizing strategy is consistent with sectarian logic. If a sect is breaking away from the established in-group, and setting itself in distinction to that group, it is because that group has become corrupted. In turn the sect promotes its moral view as the pure one, with the true moral vision; "it judges, it believes, with the judgment of (the one) God."[42] This universalist stance can take different forms. The group may withdraw from the corrupt world into its own purified world, as some groups of Essenes did, or it may seek to convert that world, as some early Christians did. Withdrawal may provide a certain moral satisfaction, but it does not make for success in the competition for resources, thus making the group vulnerable to larger out-groups (e.g., the Roman legions). Proselytizing holds out a greater chance for success and survival, and so the development of universalist aspirations can be explained by the principles of cultural group selection.

We may grant that there are good evolutionary reasons for adopting universalism as a strategy, but does that mean Christianity transcends in-group/out group thinking? Not at all. While all may join the in-group, there is still a membership that comes with a price, along with rituals of initiation, and those unwilling to pay the price to join the club are set apart, in both this world and the next. Christ did say to make disciples of all nations, but this is a universalism advocated by numerous totalizing ideologies, for example, Soviet Marxists, who sought to bring all the nations into their communist in-group. A totalizing strategy in which your group becomes the only group may be a sort of universalism, but certainly not the sort that Christians should want to boast of.

At this point a Christian might admit that there is a boundary dividing the in-group from the out group but claim that Christianity's special worth stems from the fact that this boundary is one of moral values. If moral values become the key criterion for in-group membership, then bringing everyone into the group is to bind humanity into a universal moral community – and this would be a universalism to boast of. David Lahti argues that this is just what Jesus has done: "The in-group, delineated primitively on the basis of kinship, is recast in the Sermon on the Mount on the basis of shared values."[43]

This shift from tribalism to values as a basis for constituting the in-group does represent a moral innovation, introduced in the West on a major scale by Christianity (although not necessarily invented by Christ, as it has precursors in the Jewish prophets and is predated by Stoic philosophy and some Eastern systems of thought). It is an innovation that may well represent a high-water mark for human morality (I return to this in the final chapter). However, as admirable as this signal of commitment is, it is not the only way to identify members of the Christian in-group. It shares the field, and eventually yields the foreground, to another signal commitment to the group: having faith in Jesus Christ – and this is a fateful shift that again casts Christian universalism in a different light. And so we need to turn the discussion to signals of commitment.

Putting on Christ: Christianity's Signals of Commitment

In distancing itself from Judaism, Christianity rejected many of the practices that signaled commitment to Judaism. But for any group to function as a group there must be ways of identifying who is in and who is not, who can be trusted as a partner in social cooperation and who is a risk. There must be signals of commitment, the costlier the better, and Christianity developed its own repertoire. In discussing these signals we need to keep in mind that the construction of Christian identity was much more "fragile" than is sometimes supposed.[44] In a period of fluid religious and cultural identifications a focus on the finished canon can give the appearance of a homogeneity that did not exist. The texts are the end product of this process of clarifying fuzzy borders and negotiating identity, the statement of the group that gained predominance by the mid-fourth century. However, since this is the group that assumed the mantle of orthodoxy and shaped future understandings of Christianity, their texts are a valuable resource for a study of group identity formation.

Two central signals of Christian identity were baptism and the Lord's Supper, or Eucharist. Baptism is a ritual rich in meaning, not only as a sign of entry into the new group but as a rejection and condemnation of the old group. In contemporary Christianity baptism is a celebration introducing a new member, often an infant, to the group. This has great significance for the community, but little for the initiate. The infant, born to in-group members, does not commit to the group through baptism but instead is committed by its parents. Whatever spiritual importance this may have, it is not experienced as such by the infant. This was not the case during the early period of Christianity. Baptism was not merely an initiation ritual that washed away sin but also was a conversion experience. A prospective member, often an adult, was making a choice to enter into this new group, leaving behind old affiliations – and this was not a morally neutral move. Meeks writes, "By making the act of washing the central act of initiation itself, Christianity had from the beginning implied a boundary between an impure society and a pure community."[45]

The conversion process in some early Christian communities emphasized in dramatic fashion the moral nature of the commitment one was making. Meeks discusses a third-century document, known as the *Apostolic Tradition*, which describes the process in some detail, and notes its focus on boundary issues and moral evaluation: "candidates are screened before they are even permitted to take instruction, and people with morally suspect occupations ... are excluded or required to change their jobs." There is continued screening and instruction that could last up to three years. This period of instruction could be accompanied by "repeated exorcisms" that "dramatize a picture of the world outside the church as a realm under the devil's power." Meeks contrasts this with purification rituals of initiation into pagan mystery cults. In those cases what was to be kept pure was the sacred space of the rituals, but in Christian rites "what is kept pure is the community." The initiation is "the anchor and the beginning point for a process of moral re-education that is conducted by and within the community of converts."[46] So, while today baptism may not seem like a very costly signal of commitment, in its original context this rite could be a time-consuming, emotionally demanding, and social process in which one was scrutinized by the community for signs of sincerity in committing to the group and in which one denounced the world being left behind. As such it functioned as a costly signal of commitment to the group. The intense scrutiny of moral character is just what we should expect of a group that members choose to join rather than are born into, and it is consistent with our understanding of Christianity's shift to a values- rather than kin-based system of membership.

The sharing of a sacred meal, the Eucharist, is another signal of commitment that held more weight in the ancient world than it may today. As Williams Irons pointed out, religious rituals provide opportunities for members of the group to observe one another for signs of sincerity or possible signs of defection. The more social the ritual and the more often it is celebrated, the more effectively it can perform this function. The tradition of a sacred, shared meal served this purpose well. Meeks also recognizes the value of the Eucharist in securing the group: "because it was celebrated more frequently than baptism, it provided more occasions on which the implications of that special identity for appropriate modes of behavior could be impressed on participants."[47] The New Testament provides evidence that this practice did indeed offer an opportunity for moral scrutiny and instruction.

In 1 Corinthians, Paul addresses a series of complaints concerning the community he helped to establish at Corinth. It appears that the communion meal had become a bit undisciplined. Some members were coming early and eating their fill, leaving nothing for latecomers, who then went hungry; others seemed to be getting drunk. Paul is outraged: "What! Do you not have houses to eat and drink in? Or do you despise the church of God and humiliate those who have nothing? What shall I say to you? Shall I commend you in this? No, I will not" (1 Cor. 11:17–22). This hints at a deeper problem than mere boorish behavior. The sharing of a meal was a basic social practice in the Roman world, one with clear social implications. Your dinner guests could raise your social standing. The arrangement of the settings and even the quality of the food served often reflected social status. In other words, the hierarchical nature of Roman society was reflected in and reinforced through dinner parties. So the shared meal of the Christians was a feature common to the larger social environment. What offends Paul is that at Corinth the Christians seem to be conducting this meal as the pagans do, with the wealthy and powerful taking more than their share, while the poorer members were left with scraps. The point of this practice, however, is to remember Christ, to remember that worldly ways have been left behind.[48] When Christians share a meal they must leave social status behind, they must "wait for one another," that is, they must act like Christians. To eat and drink "in an unworthy manner" is to profane "the body and blood of the Lord" and court judgment (1 Cor. 11:27–34).

Paul not only instructs Christians how to behave appropriately but reminds them that this is the "Lord's Supper," a symbolic re-enactment of Christ's last supper when he instructed his disciples to "Do this in remembrance of me" (Luke 22:19). Invoking Christ is a reminder that the community is bounded by this powerful deity who has set the pattern of behavior and the criteria for membership – it is not a merely cultural practice – and there are moral consequences for failing to adhere to those commitments.

We see in these two rituals not only signals of commitment to the group but a clear message that the key criterion for membership is moral behavior. This point is made repeatedly by Jesus throughout the gospels. We have already seen Jesus define his family as those who do the will of God (Matt. 12:50), and this is a common theme: "Not every one who says to me, 'Lord, Lord,' shall enter the kingdom of heaven, but he who does the will of my Father who is in heaven" (Matt. 7:21; see also John 14:23; Matt. 7:15–19).

Doing the will of God – the Supreme Being who establishes the moral code for the group and reinforces that code with rewards and punishment – is central to Christianity, as it is to many religious ethical traditions. Given Christianity's rejection of ethnicity as a criterion of membership, these moral values become more significant. But if moral behavior is what distinguishes in-group from out-group, then that behavior had better be distinctive – if not, then how can it signal one is a Christian? This was clearly a concern to Paul. It raises the question of whether Christian moral standards were distinctly different from those of "the world." We will look more closely at the moral code set out in the New Testament in the next section, but for now we can say that in terms of its moral code, Christianity did not stand out as unique, or even all that different from other codes in their social environment.

Wayne Meeks again provides one of the best discussions of this issue. He points out that the vices and virtues enumerated in the New Testament do not contrast with lists that could be drawn by Greco-Roman moralists of the time.[49] The moral standards Christians set for themselves to emulate were certainly higher than the ones followed by many in ancient Roman society, but this is not the appropriate contrast (i.e., between moral teachers and the morality of the masses). The comparison must be with other, non-Christian moralists of the time; those who critiqued common behavior and argued for a higher ethical standard. Here one can find much of Christian morality echoed or presaged by numerous moralists, such as Epictetus,

Plutarch, the Stoics, Musonius Rufus, as well as Jewish moralists – all of them sharing the same cultural environment as the early Christians. This leads Meeks to conclude that "Jesus did not arrive in Galilee proclaiming a complete, systematic, and novel Christian ethic. ... There has not ever been a purely Christian morality, unalloyed with the experiences and traditions of others."[50] If Meeks is correct, and I believe he is, then how could moral values serve to distinguish Christians from other groups in their environment? There must have been something distinctive about them. Meeks agrees and says that we need to consider these moral standards in the context in which they functioned and found their meaning.[51]

What distinguished Christian moral standards, at least in the mind of Christians, is that they are not simply the conclusions of human reason, as were the codes of the Greco-Roman moralists. They represented the word of God, revealed through his Son, Jesus Christ. This then presents another way of signaling commitment to the moral code of the group, and in a way that is distinct to the Christian in-group: signaling commitment to Christ, which is perfectly in line with the logic of evolved religious morality sketched out earlier. Christ is the divine being who legislates and enforces the group's moral code. Signaling commitment to this being signals commitment to the group's morality that he oversees. Christianity takes advantage of this option, and commitment to Christ, that is, faith, stands alongside following Christ's teaching as criteria for membership. In fact, by the time Paul has set the grounds for what is to become orthodox Christianity, faith in Christ surpasses all else as the defining element for membership in the Christian community. But before we turn to Paul we can see this move set out by Christ himself.

We have seen, in stories such as that of the centurion's servant, that faith in Christ is greatly rewarded. The power of faith is further attested to when Jesus teaches that to have "faith as a grain of mustard seed, you will say to this mountain, 'Move from here to there,' and it will move; and nothing will be impossible for you" (Matt. 17:20). Jesus also makes it quite clear that he himself is the object of this powerful faith. He proclaims, "And I tell you, every one who acknowledges me before men, the Son of man will acknowledge before the angels of God; but he who denies me before men will be denied before the angels of God" (Luke 12:8–9). Speaking in the third person, Christ teaches, "He who believes in him is not condemned; he who does not believe is condemned already" – and why? "Because he has not believed in the name of the only Son of God" (John 3:18). It is those who "acknowledge" and "believe" in Jesus who stand on the right side of God. In fact it is only those who believe who can be made right with God: "I am the way, and the truth, and the life; no one comes to the Father, but by me" (John 14:6). This is an incredibly important claim: Christ provides the one path to God, therefore anyone who fails to believe in Christ is cut off from God. This is the in-group/out-group mentality. To fail to "abide" in Christ is to be "thrown into the fire and burned" (John 15:6), while those who believe "though he die, yet shall he live, and whoever lives and believes in me shall never die" (John 11:25–26). These are powerful motivations to believe in Jesus and powerful incentives to follow the moral code that binds the Christian in-group.

Clearly for Paul this is the primary lesson Christ brought, that salvation comes through faith. Throughout his letters Paul drives home the point that it is not through the Law but through accepting the sacrifice and resurrection of Christ that one is justified in the sight of God. This is the central message of his letter to the Galatians. The law was given through Moses to guide the people until they were ready for the fulfillment of God's promise of salvation. That has now been fulfilled by Christ Jesus and so the law is surpassed: "Now before faith came, we were confined under the law, kept under restraint until faith should be revealed. ... But now that faith has come, we are no longer under a custodian; for in Christ Jesus you are all sons of God, through faith" (Gal. 3:23–26).

This not only serves to distinguish Christians from Jews but reorients the moral world of monotheism. The Law was the means to righteousness before God; by fulfilling the law one lived in accord with God's will. Paul shifts the emphasis from law to faith, from what you do to what you believe, and this is the fateful shift. With faith as the ultimate criterion for in-group membership policing other members for sincerity of belief and for proper doctrinal beliefs becomes, for the first time in the history of religion, the central concerns of a religious moral tradition. This re-prioritizes the moral standards set out in the gospels. There Jesus identified his group, his family, as those who do the will of God, that is, those who do what is morally correct. Now, behavior becomes secondary to belief. This moral view is also set out in the gospels, but with Paul's influence it becomes the predominant one. And this, more than anything else, contributes to the conflicts, both doctrinal and physical, that mark Christian history from the moment orthodoxy is established in the church. We will explore this in greater depth in the next chapter. For now suffice it to say that faith in Christ has become the ultimate signal of commitment to the Christian in-group and marks the boundaries of that group in a very sharp manner. The prospect of a universalism in which group membership is marked by moral behavior is superseded by the more common method in which membership is established by signaling loyalty – faith – to the group.

But before turning to our next issue, religious violence, we need to spend some time with the moral logic of Christianity. For on this topic too have apologists argued Christianity is an exceptional moral creed, not subject to evolutionary analysis.

Loving Your Neighbor and Turning the Other Cheek

Christ's teachings on familial relationships turned traditional family values on its head. Still, he did not abandon the language of familial obligation. We are to reject our natural families so that we may commit ourselves to our new family in Christ – in whom we are all brothers and sisters because we all share the one true Father. This rhetoric taps into the underlying psychology of kin selection in a very familiar way. However, identifying who is kin and who is non-kin is not a straightforward task – as I commented, people do not come with a scarlet K to facilitate kin identification. Therefore, various environmental cues must serve as kin-estimators. Since evolution works with a satisficing strategy, that is, adopting strategies that tend to produce the best results overall and with all things considered, the mechanisms for kin altruism need not be precise. This gives us the flexibility to respond to a variety of cues and these may be cultural ones. That this evolved moral preference for kin can be shaped by cultural cues means religion can direct, or re-direct, and enlarge the scope of these evolved mechanisms.[52]

This rhetoric of kinship (e.g., "brothers in arms," "a band of brothers," "the human family," "the fatherland" or "motherland," "children of god") is prevalent in so many contexts because it triggers, with varying degrees of intensity, the powerful psychology of kin selection, which generates kin altruism – and this can endow the social and moral bonds between unrelated individuals with the emotional coloring typically granted to blood relatives. This is a lesson that has been intuited by political leaders, moral reformers, and religious figures throughout history – and Jesus was no exception.

Defenders of Christian exceptionalism are unlikely to dispute this or even to be bothered by it. Changing people's moral habits is very difficult, even when you have the right message. So why would Christ fail to employ such an effective strategy for the greater good of moral improvement? This response is perfectly reasonable. If our goal is moral improvement, it is better to work pragmatically with the realities of human nature than to insist on some morally pure motivation that leaves actual humans unmoved – as long as the moral message is not compromised.

It is the moral message that is of primary concern, and it is here that Christianity finally transcends any evolved moral psychology, say the apologists. This is what makes the morality of Christianity stand apart from other admittedly noble pagan moral codes. The morality preached by Jesus transcends the pull of evolutionary morality by rejecting reciprocation as a basis of moral behavior. Let's take a look at this.

In Matthew, Jesus is confronted by the Pharisees, who challenge him to identify the greatest of the Laws:

> And he said to him, "You shall love the Lord your God with all your heart, and with all your soul, and with all your mind. This is the great and first commandment. And a second is like it, You shall love your neighbor as yourself. On these two commandments depend all the law and the prophets." (Matt. 22:35–40)

Jesus is not issuing new commandments here; both clauses of this teaching are in the Torah.[53] But even if these formulations are not original, what is distinctive is that Jesus makes these the very foundation of the moral law. How do these stand up to an evolutionary analysis?

The first clause – "You shall love the Lord your God with all your heart, and with all your soul, and with all your mind" – commands us to commit ourselves to God absolutely and on the deepest level possible, that is, to the MCI being who serves as the moral guide and enforcer for the community. Complete commitment to such a being entails commitment to the moral code he prescribes, a code that promotes social cohesion and a stable environment in which members may pursue their inclusive fitness. Such a commitment signals one is a trustworthy partner in social interactions because one recognizes the god who oversees those interactions. That Jesus makes this the foremost commandment makes sound sense from the perspective of evolved religious morality.

What about the second clause, "You shall love your neighbor as yourself"? A case can be made that this too is consistent with our evolved morality. Jesus introduces it by saying, "And a second is like it" ("it" being the previous clause commanding complete commitment to God). How is loving your neighbor as yourself like loving God completely? There are of course theological answers, which I will not entertain. More to the point is that there is an answer based in religious moral psychology. Loving God completely signals a deep commitment to the moral code of society that allows society to function; to love your neighbor as yourself is to put your neighbor at the center of your moral concern, closer even than kin. Such a moral goal, even if only approximated, promises to reduce, if not eliminate, the intra-group conflict that can destabilize a society and threaten the good of all its members. To commit yourself to loving your neighbor as yourself is to signal in a powerful way one's commitment to the group.

We can see that social harmony is the goal of this command by the considering its original formulation in Leviticus. There it reads: "You shall not hate your brother in your heart, but you shall reason with your neighbor, lest you bear sin because of him. You shall not take vengeance or bear any grudge against the sons of your own people, but you shall love your neighbor as yourself" (Lev. 19:17–18). This is a telling passage, with its repeated transition from speaking of kin to speaking of neighbor, essentially conflating the two in terms of moral consideration. It clearly indicates a concern with social harmony within the group ("the sons of your own people") and toward that end admonishes us to love our neighbor as ourselves.

Now, social harmony within the community is a laudable moral goal, and Jesus may be hitting on an effective formulation to foster such harmony; that this is consistent with an evolutionary analysis does not mean that Jesus is simply giving expression to an evolved psychology. He may, in fact, as Christians would claim, be going beyond the worldly calculation of cost and benefits. In order to exempt Christ's instruction from an evolutionary explanation – to make the case that this indicates a higher moral source – we need to divorce this command from the psychology of reciprocation. An evolutionary analysis of "love your neighbor" would hold that this rule promotes pro-social behavior (which contributes to the pursuit of inclusive fitness for social beings like us) either by encouraging cooperation by ensuring reciprocation, whether direct or indirect, or by the threat of punishment for those who fail to reciprocate. Does Christianity rise above the moral psychology of reciprocation?

Many believe that Christianity does. Patricia Williams makes this claim explicitly in an article entitled, interestingly enough, "The Fifth R: Jesus as Evolutionary Psychologist." She claims that Jesus was an "astonishingly perceptive evolutionary psychologist"[54] and that he "seems well aware of the human desire for reciprocity and its offshoot, justice, and he constantly *discourages* seeking them" (emphasis added).[55] Jesus' talent as an evolutionary psychologist, according to Williams, is evinced by his insight into the workings of reciprocation and by the fact that he offers a way to transcend it. These insights, she hypothesizes, "probably came from the divine source."[56] Michael Chapman, citing with approval Williams's assessment of Jesus' contributions, writes that Jesus showed us the way to "escape from our own all-too-human evolutionary traps."[57]

It is not merely Christ's command to love your neighbor that is cited as evidence of leaving reciprocity behind; the command that "whatever you wish that men would do to you, do so to them" (Matt. 7:12) is often cited. Rolston, for example, says that the rule "Do to others as you would have them do to you" is not simply a tribal rule but "could be a universal truth."[58] Philip Rolnick proposes "love your enemies" as a candidate for exemption from evolutionary analysis. It "creates," he says, "real dissonance with sociobiology's imperialistic accounts of selfishness."[59]

What these sources share is a belief that the moral code preached by Jesus, in at least some of its prescriptions, cannot be explained as expressions of an evolved moral psychology because it moves beyond the logic of reciprocation. These are important counter-arguments to the thesis of this book. In fact, in my experience this is the key stumbling block in trying to extend this analysis to include Christianity. Even if this analysis sheds light on Judaism, it has been argued, it cannot apply as effectively to Christianity because Christianity is universal and because Jesus repudiates the logic of reciprocation. As I have already discussed, and I hope answered, concerns about an evolutionary account of universalism, this question of reciprocity within Christian morality is the major hurdle to be cleared.

My claim that Christ's moral teachings do not transcend our evolved moral psychology rests on the fact that the motivation for following the moral code is that this will result in a reciprocation of good to the agent, and this is exactly the condition that underlies evolutionary accounts of altruism, particularly that of indirect reciprocity. Evolution has made the hope/expectation of reciprocation a basic psychological orientation that deeply infuses our moral sense, and this moral sense is given expression in a variety of ways by the diverse moral systems, secular and religious, that humans have developed. And we will see that this, in fact, is just what Jesus does in the gospels. He sets out a system of indirect reciprocity in which altruistic acts are reciprocated, not by the recipient of the benefit (as in direct reciprocal altruism) nor by the community (as in non-religious examples of indirect reciprocity, although this too is an important reward for Christian altruists) but by God.

Let's begin with one of the central moral lessons of Jesus, the Sermon on the Mount. In this teaching Jesus tells the multitude that had come to hear him:

> But I say to you that hear, Love your enemies, do good to those who hate you, bless those who curse you, and pray for those who abuse you. To him that strikes you on the cheek, offer the other also; and from him who takes away your coat do not withhold even your shirt. Give to everyone who begs from you; and of him who takes away your goods do not ask them again. And as you wish that men would do to you, do so to them. (Luke 6:27–31)

This is inspiring morality that radically departs from our moral intuitions. Jesus here seems to be demanding a complete re-orientation in our moral outlook, and this new outlook appears to reject the logic of reciprocation completely. He advocates giving without restriction, and with no expectation of reciprocation – *such altruism could not have evolved*. An individual who practiced this form of altruism would have been crushed in the struggle for reproductive fitness, having little for him- or herself, much less enough to raise offspring to carry on the individual's genetic line. If such an altruist were by chance to arise in a group, they would quickly be marked a sucker to be taken advantage of by less naïve individuals pursuing their own inclusive fitness. Furthermore, even if we can give an evolutionary analysis of "love your neighbor," as I have suggested, such an analysis of "love your enemy" seems beyond the pale. "Love your neighbor" promotes social cohesion, from which I may benefit, but "love your enemy," that is, "love the members of the out-group," weakens my position to the advantage of my enemy. This flies in the face of evolutionary logic – or so it seems. Let's continue with the text:

> If you love those who love you, what credit is that to you? For even sinners love those who love them. And if you do good to those who do good to you, what credit is that to you? For even sinners do the same. And if you lend to those from whom you hope to receive, what credit is that to you? Even sinners lend to sinners, to receive as much again (Luke 6:32–34).

This is an intriguing critique of reciprocal altruism: To give in order to receive earns no credit, for *even sinners do that*. To give in order to receive is the basic logic of reciprocal altruism: I sacrifice for someone in my in-group because I expect, consciously or not, to be paid back, directly or indirectly – but Jesus points out that even sinners do that. Sinners are those in the out-group, or in-group members who defect from the moral code; in either case, they are the corrupt *other* who stands outside the community of the blessed – and even these out-group members practice reciprocal altruism within their own groups. In part, Jesus is setting a standard to distinguish those in the group from those not in the group, consistent with the evolved function of morality. Be that as it may, it still may be argued that Jesus repudiates reciprocity as a moral motivation – you get no credit for doing what even sinners do. But does this not suggest that you do earn credit for acting better than sinners do?

The text continues: "But love your enemies, and do good, and lend, expecting nothing in return; and your reward will be great, and you will be the sons of the Most High; for he is kind to the ungrateful and the selfish. Be merciful, even as your Father is merciful" (Luke 6:35–36). Two things are happening here: (1) Jesus presents God the Father as the model for moral behavior, and God is kind to those who do not deserve it, and (2) Jesus introduces a motivation for striving to be like God: Your reward will be great – and this re-introduces the notion of reciprocation. You are not simply to imitate God as your moral role model, although you are to do that ("be perfect, as your heavenly Father is perfect," Matt. 5:48), but you are to do so because this will reap you great rewards – your moral goodness will be reciprocated. The logic of reciprocal altruism becomes explicit as Jesus continues (Luke 6:37–38):

"Judge not": why? "and you will not be judged"
"condemn not": why? "and you will not be condemned"
"forgive": why? "and you will be forgiven"
"give": why? "and it will be given to you; good measure, pressed down,
    shaken together, running over, will be put into your lap"
"For the measure you give will be the measure you get back."

There could not be a clearer explanation of the logic of reciprocation: Do good so that you may benefit.[60]

And it is not just the Sermon on the Mount that presents this moral logic. In Matthew Jesus tells the parable of the unforgiving servant who, having been forgiven a substantial debt by his master, refuses to forgive a much smaller debt owed to him by a fellow servant. When the master learns of this he is outraged and sends the man to jail until his debt is paid. Jesus concludes, "So also my heavenly Father will do to every one of you, if you do not forgive your brother from your heart" (Matt. 18:23–35). This echoes the message contained in the prayer known as the *Our Father* where Jesus teaches us to pray: "And forgive us our debts, as we have also forgiven our debtors" (Matt. 6:12). Nor is this logic lost on Paul, who writes to the Galatians that "whatever a man sows, that he will also reap ... and let us not grow weary in well-doing, for in due season we shall reap." Interestingly, Paul concludes this expression of reciprocal altruism with a nod to kin selection in the service of the in-group: "So then, as we have opportunity, let us do good to all men, and especially to those who are of the household of faith" (Gal. 6:7–10).

What is distinctive about the reciprocal altruism advocated in the New Testament is that divine indirect reciprocity supplements ordinary human reciprocity and serves to encourage altruism even when reciprocation does not appear likely. Time and again we are told the cost incurred by acting morally will be repaid by God in the next life. In the famous parable of the sheep and goats, those who have provided for the most vulnerable members of the community – the hungry, naked, and sick – are the blessed who will inherit the kingdom (Matt. 25:31–40). When Jesus tries to override the innate predisposition toward genetic kin he promises eternal rewards: "And every one who has left houses or brothers or sisters or father or mother or children or lands for my name's sake, will receive a hundred-fold, and inherit eternal life" (Matt. 19:29–30). And when he tries to bolster the courage of his followers in the face of persecution, he holds out the prize of salvation to those who remain true: "for they will deliver you up to councils; and you will be beaten in synagogues. ... and you will be hated by all for my name's sake. But he who endures to the end will be saved" (Mark 13:9–13). Great rewards are needed for the tremendous sacrifices Christ demands.

In each of these examples altruistic sacrifice is called for in situations in which the reciprocation that would make such sacrifices cost-effective does not seem possible, either because the recipient is in no position to reciprocate (e.g., is poor or sick) or because the cost of moral behavior is so exceptionally high (e.g., giving up your family and/or your life) that extraordinary reciprocation would be required to balance the scales. In fact Jesus goes even further and encourages his followers to beware of giving to those who can reciprocate. In Luke, Jesus uses a parable about giving a banquet to make this point:

> When you give a dinner or a banquet, do not invite your friends or your brothers or your kinsmen or rich neighbors, *lest they also invite you in return, and you be repaid.* But when you give a feast, invite the poor, the maimed, the lame, the blind and you will be blessed, *because they cannot repay you.* You will be repaid at the resurrection of the just. (Luke 14:12–14; emphasis added)

Christ is asking more of his followers than seems intuitively reasonable and so he must raise the stakes in terms of benefits to counter-act the pull of those moral intuitions.

If we return to a consideration of the historical and social context of early Christianity we can see the importance of this rhetorical move. We know that the challenges brought by Hellenism led to dynamic social environments that instigated changes in moral and religious traditions. Traditional Jewish expectations had looked for the rewards of moral behavior to be provided in this life, in terms of land, children, and long life. During the period of the persecution under Antiochus Epiphanes (second century B.C.E.) – a major force for introducing Hellenism into Jewish culture – this expectation was severely challenged. Many who remained faithful to the ancestral ways died in the persecutions, while those who defected from the group and embraced Hellenism were rewarded. Scholars trace the origins of Jewish apocalyptic literature to around this time, with the book of Daniel being the most famous of such works. If God does not reward the faithful in this life, then either God is an ineffective moral enforcer, and so useless to the community, or there is another mode for God's reciprocation for our sacrifices – if not in this life, then there must be another life in which the rewards come. This option was not appealing to all Jews of the period; however, it did present an alternative to the dire prospects of abandoning the God of their ancestors. It provided a way to adapt to the changing social realities while maintaining loyalty to their established in-group, or in some cases to reform the in-group around a purer understanding of the tradition, as occurred with the rise of sectarianism. Christianity is a result of this process.

Christianity comes out of a larger intellectual milieu of apocalypticism. This worldview of an impending end-of-times brings the promise of future reward for the in-group, along with future punishment for defectors and out-group members, into the rhetorical repertoire available to early Christian moralists. The early Christian, or proto-Christian groups, were defectors from established Judaism and had also opted out of the pagan in-group. They were socially vulnerable and limited in their ability to provide the material rewards or social stability that allows indirect reciprocity to function. This is not to deny that these communities were proficient at providing real-life services to their members, or to underplay the role that this played in the appeal and ultimate success of Christianity. But in the early years of the Common Era, as is true of so many periods in history, material existence was precarious for much of society, much of the time. More politically connected or economically secure groups would have had a real advantage in such environments. However, a group that could draw on the hope of future bliss had an important resource that could help even the playing field.

In providing an evolutionary analysis of Christian morality I am not assessing the moral worthiness of these teachings – that is the task of the final chapter. But I am arguing that an evolutionary analysis sheds a different light on this moral tradition. Rather than standing above the pull of our evolutionary heritage, the Christian tradition, as set forth in the New Testament, was shaped by and drew from this evolved psychology. The cultural tradition of Christianity has not broken the leash of biology. Beneath the rhetoric of a transcendent morality lies a moral logic that has its ultimate source in our pursuit of inclusive fitness. The naked self-interest (although a properly qualified self-interest, broadened to include kin and fellow in-group members) beneath the noble moral rhetoric comes out clearly in a passage from Paul's letter to the Romans. Paul writes, "Repay no one evil for evil, but take thought for what is noble in the sight of all. If possible, so far as it depends on you, live peaceably with all. Beloved, never avenge yourselves" (12:17–19). This is the moral high ground, a truly admirable ideal. It is directly followed by: "but leave it to the wrath of God; for it is written, 'Vengeance is mine, I will repay, says the Lord.' No, 'if your enemy is hungry, feed him; if he is thirsty, give him drink; for by so doing *you will heap burning coals upon his head*'" (12:19–20; emphasis added). This certainly does not seem a very *Christian* thing to do – and certainly puts a different spin on "love your enemies" – and yet Paul is the major architect of Christianity; and this was not an isolated moral slip in Christian thought, to be passed over in embarrassed silence. This same sentiment is explicitly endorsed by St. Thomas Aquinas,[61] who argues that part of the reward for the blessed – those who have lived a life of Christian charity and love – is to witness the horrific suffering of the damned, even, we may assume, when those damned were loved ones in life. There is something very powerful at work here, something very different from the gospel of love, of which Christians are so rightly proud. There is also a gospel of hate and enmity embedded in the moral tradition of Christianity; and with an evolutionary perspective we can see that both of these gospels have their roots in the same ground – the in-group/out-group mentality that infuses our moral instincts. In the next chapter we turn to an examination of this shadow side of religious morality.

5 | RELIGION, VIOLENCE, AND THE EVOLVED MIND

Still, I knew there was only a thin line between the good shepherd and the butcher. (Stanley Moss[1])

Setting the Task

On September 20, 2001, President Bush in his "Address to a Joint Session of Congress and the American People" drew a distinction he believed was important for the nation to grasp. Speaking to Muslims, he said,

> We respect your faith. ... Its teachings are good and peaceful, and those who commit evil in the name of Allah blaspheme the name of Allah. The terrorists are traitors to their own faith, trying, in effect, to hijack Islam itself.

In another address, he continued this line of thought:

> The enemy tries to hide behind a peaceful faith. But those who celebrate the murder of innocent men, women, and children have no religion. (November 8, 2001)

The President presents us with a distinction between Islam as a religion of peace and the violence done in the name of Islam, which perverts its true nature. Politically, this was an important message to send, but is this a valid distinction or an accurate portrayal of religion? I say "religion," and not merely Islam, for this same distinction is drawn time and again by apologists of numerous faiths in order to distance their religion from an atrocity done in its name.

President Bush and other defenders of the faith are addressing a central paradox for many believers in the modern world: How can a religion, which they see as a force for good, so often and so easily generate hatred and violence? And we can see that from the West Bank to Northern Ireland to Gujarat, India, to Badr City, Iraq, to abortion clinics in America, violence is readily couched in religious terms. The traditional response in defense of religion is to take the approach President Bush took: Draw a distinction between the religion and what is done in the name of that religion or by its faithful. Indeed, the late Pope John Paul II made this distinction central in his review of the violent aspects of Christianity's history.

John Paul II made headlines with his willingness to recognize and apologize for Christianity's ugly record of persecution and discrimination against Jews, Muslims, and Christians who deviated from the path. In these important efforts at reconciliation the Pope consistently drew a distinction between the Church, which cannot sin, and the "sons and daughters" of the church, who committed atrocities in misguided zeal. In his famous Jubilee Homily he asked forgiveness, not for the Church which is "a marvelous harvest of holiness" with "total dedication to Christ and to our neighbors," but rather for "the infidelity to the Gospel that certain of our brothers and sisters have fallen into" (March 12, 2000). In an earlier reference to anti-Semitism, the Pope accepted Christian culpability but with a proviso: "I do not say on the part of the Church as such"; the problem stems from "erroneous and unjust interpretations of the New Testament regarding the Jewish people" (October 31, 1997). This is also a position advocated by some scholars, such as Charles Kimball, who in his work, *When Religion Becomes Evil*, distinguishes "corrupt forms of religious expression," that is, those that are violent, from "authentic, life affirming forms."[2] Even Jessica Stern, a leading expert on terrorism, in her study of religious terrorists wonders "how a person so obsessed with good and evil, with such strong faith, could be led so far astray"[3]; implying, of course, that strong faith and violence are somehow incompatible.

This approach to religious violence may be understandable, but it is ultimately untenable and prevents us from gaining any useful insight into either religion or religious violence. Bruce Lincoln has argued that the impulse to separate religion from the violence done in its name "rests on an understanding of what constitutes religion that is simultaneously idealized and impoverished."[4] It is clearly an idealized understanding that can see religion only in terms of its virtues, but more significant is that it is an impoverished understanding of religion, and it is impoverished because it is idealized, and so refuses to consider the complexity of the interplay between religious beliefs and practices, and other motors of human behavior.

Failure to recognize this clouds many public discussions of religion and violence. Since 9/11 it is common to hear it asked, "Is Islam a religion of violence?" Or in a more ecumenical vein, it may be asked whether Islam or Christianity or Judaism or Hinduism or Sikhism or ... are religions of violence, and then the debate ensues. However, in these terms the debate is a superficial one, often subject to the personal biases of those involved. Approaching the subject of religious violence in these terms is misguided because it works with an essentialized understanding of religion that does not correspond to realities of religion as it is lived and experienced, and that no scholar of religion would accept. To ask if Islam, or any other religion, is a religion of violence or a religion of peace is to inquire into its true nature, its essence, and then to judge whether that essence is violent or not. But what is the essence of Islam? Is it Islam as practiced by Sunnis? By Shiites? What about Sufis or Alevis? Who decides? Even within those traditions it is not possible to derive a definitive answer, and not because we do not know enough about those traditions, and not because Islam is a de-centralized religion, but because religious beliefs and practices are constantly interacting with, shaping, and being shaped by the myriad aspects of an individual's and a culture's experiences and history, resulting in diverse expressions of Islamic religiosity.

Even in a more centralized, hierarchical religion such as Catholicism, how can we uncover its essence? What is true Catholicism? One might be tempted to say Catholicism is what the Vatican says it is, but that definition would not work for many who strongly identify as Catholics, while taking stances inconsistent with Vatican rulings (e.g., on birth control). Further complications abound: Do we look at Catholicism pre- or post-Vatican II or, for that matter, pre- or post-Reformation? From a disinterested position it is just not possible to determine "true" Catholicism.[5]

This more nuanced understanding of religion is vital to a consideration of religious violence, but carries its own pitfalls. Given that we cannot identify the essence of a religion and judge it peaceful or violent, then perhaps, it may be suggested, we need not talk about violence being religious at all, and instead focus on the individual and organizational conditions that lead to violence. This also is a mistake. While we cannot make wholesale judgments such as "Islam is peaceful" or "Christianity is violent" we cannot deny the causal role played by religious beliefs and practices in so much of the violence that mars our history and our world. To look at that history, and to recognize the continued involvement of religious rhetoric and religious movements in justifications of violence, and then to dismiss those religious elements as irrelevant or incidental not only demonstrates an impoverished conception of religion but ignores the psychology of both violence and religion. Mark Juergensmeyer has referred to "a strain of violence that may be found at the deepest levels of religious imagination."[6] We need to understand that strain, without falling into the trap of essentializing.

But if we cannot point to an essence of a religion, then how can we assess that religion? If there is no "Islam" or "Christianity" but merely a menagerie of Islams, Christianities, and so on, then what can we say about Islamic or Christian violence?

While it may not be possible to identify an essence of Islam or a true Catholicism, it certainly is possible to speak sensibly about "Islam" and "Christianity." We may not be able to identify a set of beliefs and practices definitive of a religion but we can readily distinguish an adherent of Islam from an adherent of Christianity. There are shared traits, or family resemblances, to borrow Wittgenstein's metaphor, that allow us to make useful, if general, characterizations of particular religions. Sufis and Sunnis may have very different ideas about what it means to be a good Muslim, but they both connect those conceptions to the Qu'ran and the teachings of Mohammed, and not to the teachings of the Vatican. Similarly, Mel Gibson and Benedict XVI certainly disagree on what constitutes the Catholic faith, but neither would include the teachings of Mohammed in their faith. In speaking of religion and violence, actually in speaking about religion at all, we must be careful not to read general statements as if they were categorical, but we must also avoid the opposite error of what I call radical nominalism, in which any general statements about religion, or a religion, are deemed illegitimate because they do not extend to all manifestations of that religious tradition.

In seeking to understand religious violence I believe Juergensmeyer is correct to find the violent strain in the religious imagination. The position I will defend is that violence done in the name of religion is not a perversion of religious belief, as many apologists would like us to believe, but flows naturally from the moral logic inherent in many religious systems, particularly monotheistic religions, and that this moral logic is grounded in our evolved psychology. This does not mean that religions are violent belief systems, for as we have seen these religions are also inherently powerful sources of morality. Religious morality and religious violence both spring from the same source, and this source is the evolutionary psychology underlying religious ethics. To support this thesis we will return to religious moral traditions, as set out in seminal texts, and look for the psychological seeds of violence in Judaism and Christianity in order to discern the structure of religious violence, and then we will use that structure to analyze contemporary religious violence.

Devoted to Destruction: Sanctified Violence and Judaism

Thus far we have looked at morality as a means for establishing a sense of community and a code of in-group behavior. In serving this function morality also identifies an out-group and implies an out-group ethic. The key consideration within a group is to promote pro-social behavior by ensuring reciprocation among group members. The flip side of this membership is exclusion. If you are not family or neighbor, then you are an outsider. Outsiders are not invested in the group and so have less motivation to cooperate or to reciprocate cooperation and, therefore, may pose a danger to the community. For all the constructive morality found in religion, we find an equally prominent place for warnings against outsiders.

To consider this flip side of morality let's return to the sixth commandment. On Mt. Sinai God enshrines "You shall not kill/murder" as a divine command (Exod. 20:13) yet the first order Moses gives upon descending from the mountain is for the execution of those who had fallen into sin while he was gone:

> then Moses stood in the gate of the camp, and said, "Who is on the Lord's side? Come to me." And all the sons of Levi gathered themselves together to him. And he said to them, "Thus says the Lord God of Israel, 'Put every man his sword on his side, and go to and fro from gate to gate throughout the camp and slay every man his brother and every man his companion, and every man his neighbor.'" And the sons of Levi did according to the word of Moses; and there fell of the people that day about three thousand men. And Moses said, "Today you have ordained yourselves for the service of the Lord." (Exod. 32:26–29)

As we pointed out in our earlier discussion of this commandment, it is *murder* and not *killing* that is prohibited, and so since it is God who has ordered the death of these three thousand, and it is God who sets the law, this does not count as murder – it is not the illicit taking of life. Still, examining just what counts as killing and not murder will give us important insight into the extent of this command and into the nature of the moral system promulgated by Yahweh. As we shall see, it is one not shy about spilling blood.

Indeed, throughout the Mosaic Law we find numerous actions that are to be punished with death. Not only is a murderer to suffer the death penalty (Exod. 21:12), but also those who commit adultery (Lev. 20:10), bestiality (Exod. 22:19), and blasphemy (Lev. 24:16), as well as those who profane the Sabbath (Exod. 31:15) or curse their parents (Exod. 21:17) – to name just a few.

After having received the law Moses leads the Hebrews on what can be described as a blood-soaked trek to the Promised Land. We are told, for example, that when God delivered the land of Heshbon to the Hebrews they "utterly destroyed every city, men, women, and children; we left none remaining" (Deut. 2:34). They then moved onto the land of Bashan where they "smote him until no survivor was left to him." The passage continues,

And we took all his cities at that time – there was not a city which we did not take from them – sixty cities. ... And we utterly destroyed them, as we did to Sihon the king of Heshbon, destroying every city, men, women, and children. (Deut. 3:4–6)

In case we might be tempted to think the extent of this killing was an excess brought on by the heat of battle, rather than an intentional slaughter, we read in Numbers of a case in which Moses angrily chastises the army generals for not killing all the inhabitants of a city. In their defeat of the Midianites the Hebrews took as captives the woman and children, after slaying all the men. Moses, we are told, "was angry with the officers of the army," asking them, "Have you let all the women live?" (Num. 31:14–15) He corrects their error by instructing them thus:

Now therefore, kill every male among the little ones, and kill every woman who has known man by lying with him. But all the young girls who have not known man by lying with him, keep alive for yourselves. (Num. 31:17–18)

Nor can we attribute this horror to the weakness of humans perverting God's goodness and mercy, for these are all divinely ordered massacres. In Hebrew this practice is referred to as *herem* (*hrm*) or the *Ban* – "under which all human beings among the defeated are 'devoted to destruction.'"[7]

This is a very difficult concept for many modern believers to integrate into their conception of an all-good, merciful God. What sort of God would order the wholesale slaughter of entire peoples? The image of God as warrior is found throughout the Hebrew Scriptures (e.g., Exod. 15:3), and just as people can romanticize war and idealize warriors, God-as-warrior has been embraced by many believers in all three monotheistic religions. But can we romanticize a warrior who slaughters innocent children and little babies? Can we idealize when war is really genocide? And it is not simply that God sanctioned the human impulse to murder enemies as a concession to the primitive state of humanity's moral development – in Numbers he threatens his people that if they do not utterly destroy their enemies, "I will do to you as I thought to do to them" (Num. 33:56). In fact, Yahweh repeatedly insists on total destruction. We just read of Moses' anger at his general's failure to complete the massacre, but he is clearly acting as God's agent here, responsible to God for the people's failure to complete the slaughter. This reading is supported by the account of Saul, the first king of Israel, God's anointed one, and his fall from grace.

God had devoted the Amalekites to destruction but the people, under Saul's leadership, spared king Agag, after butchering all his subjects. Saul did not do this from compassion but saved Agag and the best of the livestock for a later sacrifice. Yahweh is incensed. He sends his prophet Samuel to finish the job – "And Samuel hewed Agag in pieces before the Lord" – and to inform Saul that he has lost the both the Lord's favor and his throne (1 Sam. 15:9–33).

An even more terrible response is related in the story of Achan, who during the destruction of Jericho – where they "utterly destroyed all in the city" (Josh. 6:21) – took some spoils from Jericho for himself rather than devoting them to destruction. Yahweh learns of this and warns Joshua, Moses' successor, that he will turn away from his people unless the offender is punished. When Achan hears of this, he confesses his sin. Joshua then gathers together all of the stolen items, and all of Achan's possessions, and *all of his children*. Then "all Israel stoned him with stones; they burned them with fire and stoned them with stones" (Josh. 7:10–26).

Yahweh is apparently satisfied with this response and reassures Joshua of his continuing love by giving to the Israelites "the king of Ai, and his people, his city, and his land," instructing them to "do to Ai ... as you did to Jericho." But as an added bonus Yahweh forgoes the complete ban and grants to his people "its spoils and cattle ... as booty for yourselves" (Josh. 8:1–2). The Israelites accept this offering with a passion and the slaughter of Ai continues until "all of them to the very last had fallen by the edge of the sword ... all who fell that day, both men and women, were twelve thousand, all the people of Ai" (Josh. 8:24–25). This is how God-the-warrior leads his armies.

Today, such a warrior would be put on trial for crimes against humanity.

So, it is no wonder that many believers pass over these stories or try to interpret them away. Yet if we are to take the Bible as an accurate portrayal of Yahweh, then we must hold Yahweh morally accountable for this murderous violence. Nor can we excuse Yahweh for being a product of his times, a consideration we might want to extend to frail humans. The actions of a timeless being cannot be explained away with cultural relativism, and more telling is that there is never a scriptural repudiation of the Ban.[8]

What, then, can we make of this? What to make of a God who on the one hand commands "Thou shall not murder" and on the other commands the complete annihilation of entire communities? One other strategy available for absolving God of the sin of genocide is to point out that from a historical perspective there is little reason to believe any of these genocidal events ever happened. Reconstructing the historical realities behind the text based on archeology and comparative studies of other ancient communities suggests a much different and much less violent story of the emergence of the Hebrews as an identifiable people in the land of Canaan.[9] This might allow some rehabilitation of the moral character of God but does not change the case against the Biblical depiction of God. For whether or not any of this divinely sanctioned slaughter occurred, the Bible is clear that the slaughter was divinely sanctioned.[10] To read the Bible for an indication of the nature of Yahweh is to come away with a morally disturbing and contradictory picture. But of course the approach adopted here is to read the Bible not as divine self-revelation but through the lens of evolutionary psychology, and from that perspective these seemingly conflicting aspects of Yahweh come into a more coherent focus.

Morality develops as a system to promote within-group cohesiveness. This cohesiveness is an advantage to the group in competition with other groups. Morality is a code of how to treat those in my group; it is not designed to extend, at least not in the same way, to those outside the group. Since these others are not bound by the same moral code they must be treated as potential cheaters; since their reproductive success is not tied to the success of our group they are not invested in our group and so cannot be expected to engage in altruism or reciprocation. Those outside the group are in fact a potential threat to my group's survival. The peoples the Hebrews encountered on their journey were obstacles that needed to be overcome in the interest of group survival. As such the moral injunction "you shall not murder" did not apply to them.[11]

The sixth commandment is not a pure moral rule that protects the sanctity of human life per se. It is a legislation of appropriate in-group behavior and so applies only to fellow group members. In a seminal paper on this topic, John Hartung points out that the equation of *human* with *Israelite* (i.e., in-group member) not only is found in the Bible but is confirmed in the Talmud and is reinforced by the great twelfth-century Jewish philosopher, Maimonides. Hartung argues that this equation underlies Judaic teaching on the crime of murder.[12] To kill a fellow group member is murder, and thus forbidden; to kill an outsider is not. This is not what one might expect of a divine law, but it is just what to expect of a law shaped by our evolved moral psychology. If we look more closely at some examples we will detect that evolved psychology at work.

We can see this, for example, in how the slaughter was regulated. A very specific distinction is set forth in Deuteronomy:

> When the Lord your God gives it [a foreign town] into your hand you shall put all its males to the sword, but the women and little ones, the cattle, and everything else in the city, all its spoil, you shall take as booty for yourselves; and you shall enjoy the spoil of your enemies, which the Lord your God has given you. Thus you shall do to all the cities which are very far from you. ... But in the cities of these people that the Lord your God gives you for an inheritance, you shall save alive nothing that breathes, but you shall utterly destroy them. (Deut. 20:13–17)

This geographic distinction raises the concern of boundaries. The enemy at a distance must be eliminated as a military threat and so all the males must be killed, but the women and children may be "enjoyed." But with towns closer to the land of the Israelites all living things must be destroyed: not just the men who pose a military threat to the group, but the women, and children, and cattle! Something else is at play here. Susan Niditch, in her valuable discussion, points out that the imposition of the Ban touches on concerns of purity and pollution – and this may allow us to make sense of this distinction.

Anyone deemed banned, or anything associated with people who worshipped a different god, has by that fact been rendered unclean, an "abomination" (e.g., Deut. 7:26). As Niditch puts it, "the language of revulsion is visceral: You must detest it and abhor it for it is *herem*."[13]

In our discussion of our evolved moral sense we did not touch on issues of purity and contagion, but it certainly can be argued that this is a significant part of our evolved religious moral sense. Evolutionary psychologists see contagion-avoidance as a basic part of our mental tool kit. Developing a powerful emotional and physical repulsion in the face of possible contaminants, that is, disgust,[14] was a vital adaptation. Humans who were viscerally repelled by possible sources of contaminants, such as foul smells, rotting food, excrement, and dead bodies, had an advantage over those who had to learn through trial and error which things were safe and which harbored possibly lethal infectants. It is easy to see why evolution selected for contagion-avoidance to be a quick and intuitive cognitive response.[15] Haidt has argued persuasively that concerns with purity are as much part of our moral sense as concerns with kin and reciprocity.[16]

This mental tool plays a key role in understanding the Ban. By characterizing these foreign people as "abominations" and as "unclean" the text triggers our evolved contagion-avoidance systems. Contaminated things need to be disposed of, and even slight contact with a contaminant is enough to ruin the whole thing. Think of the "fly-in-the-soup" scenario: Certain insects, such as flies and roaches, set off a contagion-avoidance response in many people. To find such an insect in one's soup in a restaurant will probably lead one to demand the food be taken away. Imagine if the waiter responded, "Why should we replace the whole bowl of soup, the fly was only in one part of it?" It may in fact be true that the insect touched only one part of the food, but that is typically sufficient to want to dump the whole dish. Once one part is contaminated we see the whole thing as ruined. The same logic is at work here: The town is polluted and so everything in it must go. "And you shall not bring an abominable thing into your house, and become accursed like it; you shall utterly detest and abhor it; for it is an accursed thing" (Deut. 7:26).

And what is it that has polluted these people? They have worshipped another god. But so have the people of cities far away. Why may the spoils of those towns be enjoyed? Yahweh justifies this harsh treatment of neighboring towns as necessary so that "they may not teach you to do according to all their abominable practices which they have done in the service of their gods" (Deut. 20:18). But – we must push the issue – why then not kill everyone in the distant towns? Are their women and children not as much a source of foreign practices and abominations? Why are the Israelites allowed to enjoy them? Does this not raise the risk of contamination? And if not, then why are the women and children of the nearer towns a risk?

This distinction becomes clearer if we see these stories not as historical accounts of military conflict but as explanations, as perhaps many Biblical tales were, of conditions contemporary to the time of the texts' composition, perhaps hundreds of years after the supposed occurrence of the event – in this case enmity and competition between Israel and its neighbors. On this topic, James Kugel discusses the strange persistence of a Canaanite presence in Israel, attested to by the Bible. In Deuteronomy 20 we are told that at the time of the entrance of the Hebrew people into the Promised Land, God identified Canaan as one of the cities devoted to absolute destruction. Yet in Judges we hear that Canaanites continued to live among the Israelites and "equally surprising … Israelites lived 'in the midst of the Canaanites' (Judg. 1:27–35; 3:5–6)."[17] Why should that be the case? We saw how Yahweh reacted when poor Achan took a few shekels' worth of banned goods. How could the Israelites have failed so miserably in imposing the Ban that there were still Canaanites in their midst and not have paid a terrible price?

The theory – still controversial – that there was no massive invasion of the Hebrews into Canaan but that instead the Hebrew people, however and wherever they originated, shared the land of Palestine with other peoples, allows us some insight into the psychology of the Ban. The people living near the Israelites posed the greatest danger, not necessarily in military terms but in cultural terms. For a group to survive, in a literal sense or in a cultural sense, it must establish and maintain a sense of identity. It does so, partially, by setting boundaries around itself, literal but also moral and psychological boundaries. God, we have seen, represents and enforces the moral code that binds a group together. In psychological terms, other gods and foreign worship are threats to the coherence of the group. The closer the groups, physically and culturally, the easier the exchange of customs and ideas, and the greater the threat to the coherence of the group's identity. Research is beginning to suggest that the differences between the early Hebrews and their Canaanites neighbors were not significant. As Kugel puts it, summarizing this research, "at least a good part of what was to become the future nation of Israel had probably always been there – or, to put it somewhat sharply, 'We have met the Canaanites and they are us.' "[18]

Our consideration of the evolved moral psychology of Judaism explained the value of a "jealous god" as an enforcer of community norms. Such a god is also extremely useful in policing the boundaries of the community. We can see the regulations concerning the Ban against outsiders as an extension of Yahweh's jealousy, serving the purpose of strengthening, and limiting, group identity. Those out-groups near to us, and so most likely to interact with us, must be seen as completely off-limits, lest they infect us with their ways.[19]

Those who live at a greater distance do not pose the same level of risk. Bringing in members of those out-groups to be slaves does not threaten the cohesion of the group, since as slaves they are marked as inferior and so are unlikely to be a source of cultural contamination; they are not poised to trigger prestige-biased cultural selection mechanisms. We might say the same thing about Canaanite slaves, but the text is not concerned in this case with survivors and slaves; it is concerned with marking everything Canaanite as impure, to be avoided at all costs, and at all measures.

Furthermore, by allowing his people to enjoy the spoils of war, at least some of the time, Yahweh is being a good leader rather than a controlling tyrant. He is depicted as a generous commander who certainly expects his due but is sure to share the spoils of war with his followers. We know that it was important for an ancient leader to keep the troops happy by allowing them to rape, pillage, and plunder a defeated enemy people, while naturally taking his share. Yahweh, as the Lord of Hosts (a military title), is simply acting the part of a good general. Since we know that our evolved template for *gods* is based on our expectations from the ontological category of *persons*, this would have been an intuitively right description of a divine warrior-king – it was just the way military leaders acted in the ancient world.

But as Yahweh is divine he will demand a different kind of spoil. The most valuable spoils go to the commander, and the most valuable spoils are the defeated people. A human commander would take these spoils in the form of slaves, but gods take them in the form of sacrifice. Human sacrifice to the gods is found in many ancient religious traditions. While this practice is apparently repudiated by Yahweh when he has Abraham exchange a ram for Isaac, the Ban indicates that Yahweh had not totally given up the taste for human blood. Niditch argues that at least in some circumstances the Ban was viewed as a sacrifice to Yahweh, as giving to God his due. She points out that the "ban as sacrifice requires a wider view of a God who appreciates human sacrifice."[20]

This, again, is an uncomfortable portrayal of a God who is understood to be morally perfect, but, again, such an understanding is a theological construction. Belief in gods intuitively follow templates based on our expectations of *persons*, with minimal violations of those expectations. From that perspective, this portrayal of God makes perfect sense.

Niditch also suggests another function of the Ban is that it serves a psychological role. Niditch notes that all cultures find ways to deal with "the horror of having taken human life."[21] Given humanity's bloody history, and the bloody world we now inhabit, it seems strange to speak of the horror of taking life. We readily acknowledge that war is hell, but this often refers to the death and destruction caused by war. Niditch points out, however, that as terrible as these evils are, the great psychological damage that comes from taking life in war is well documented.[22] A recent work by David L. Smith puts this in an evolutionary perspective.[23]

The predisposition to use violence, even lethal violence, in the pursuit of survival and reproductive success is part of the human condition, part of our evolved psychology, and is something we share with many non-human animals. This is particularly true of our closest relative, the chimpanzee.[24] Evolutionary psychologist David Buss argues that there must have been important adaptive advantages to killing because it comes with such dire risks. Violent encounters raise the possibility of one's own death, and as Buss reminds us, "it's astonishingly bad to be dead."[25] Being dead cuts off any further reproduction, prevents an individual from further investing in offspring, and, in fact, makes their future more vulnerable, as those offspring are not only denied the resources the dead person had provided but are denied that person's protection. However, on the other hand it is also "astonishingly advantageous to get a rival out of the way." This enhances one's own inclusive fitness by eliminating a competitor, eliminating or at least reducing the threat of competition from that rival's genetic lineage, and protects one's kin from the possible hostile intent of that rival.[26]

Killing other human beings, then, is not a pathology; it is not (necessarily) the work of twisted, evil people. It is a behavioral strategy in the competition for reproductive success. Buss and Smith do a good job of supporting the view that killing is a natural part of the human condition.[27] I recommend both works to the reader but I will not rehearse their arguments here; we do not need to devote much time to arguing that murder comes readily to our species. Instead, let's turn to the flip side, the moral revulsion we often feel at the thought of killing other humans – for this too is part of our nature. And it stems from our evolution as a social species.

The challenge of pursuing our inclusive fitness within a social environment, of creating a social environment in which there can be both social cohesion and individual reproductive success, was and is the key task for humans. In our discussion of the sixth commandment in Chapter 3 we saw how disruptive murder can be to the community. Since being dead is "astonishingly bad" for the kin group as well as the individual, unregulated killing would set off a cycle of retaliatory violence that could undermine the entire society. All societies find ways to regulate killing within the group. But laws, moral codes, and religions come relatively late in the history of the species, and to have reached that point humans must have solved, to some degree, the problem of intra-group violence. Just as we evolved cognitive tools that allow for altruism, we evolved tools to inhibit the killing of others like us.

Smith paints a moving picture of the psychological scars suffered by an alarmingly high number of soldiers, and argues that this is evidence of evolved emotional guards against killing other humans, and the costs that come with violating that prohibition.[28] But as Niditch commented, human societies have developed means for overcoming this psychological barrier to killing – very successful means, we must add. The basic strategy is simple: If the prohibition is against killing other humans, then portray the enemy as other than or less than human. Dehumanization of the enemy is, of course, a familiar phenomenon. Smith, however, points out that these dehumanizing strategies involve methods for triggering aspects of our evolved psychology.

He pays special attention to three such triggers: predators, prey, and parasites.[29] We have evolved responses to members of these three categories. Humans spent a good part of our history as a source of nutrition to numerous predators. Surviving meant finding ways to detect, avoid, and whenever possible eliminate predatory threats. The cognitive/emotional tools that make this possible were essential to our species' survival. By casting the enemy in terms of predators these deep psychological predispositions are triggered and we are primed to treat other humans as predatory animals or monsters – anything but fellow humans.[30] And "when the predator-detection module is triggered, the result is unambiguous: we either fight or flee." Smith continues: "In war, the soldier's predator-detection module can be switched on by other human beings. When this occurs, the enemy is no longer experienced as human. He is perceived as a dangerous beast that must be killed."[31]

Of course, while avoiding predators was a key task, so too was playing the role of predator to other animals. Early human hunting may often have been little more than scavenging the leftovers from other predators, but humans eventually developed into fearsome hunters, and this has left its mark on our psyches:

> Perceiving the enemy as a game animal is another way to sidestep the taboo against killing human beings. When this happens, the enemy is dehumanized without being demonized: they are not monsters, but neither are they people. They are innocuous game that can be gunned down for sport.[32]

More pertinent to our present discussion is the strategy of characterizing the enemy as parasites. Parasites are unclean and threaten our health – they provoke disgust and trigger our contagion-avoidance system. Parasites are not treated with halfway measures, they do not provoke moderate responses: "We try to wipe them out, to exterminate them completely. It follows that when the antiparasite module is activated and turned against fellow human beings, the stage is set for genocide."[33] By casting the enemies of the Israelites as "unclean" and "abominations" the Bible triggered this powerful response and set the ground for sanctified genocide.

Susan Niditch suggests the Ban provided another method for overcoming our inhibition against taking human life. Deeming the enemy as devoted to complete destruction freed the Israelites from any moral agonizing over whom to kill or when to show mercy – all belonged to God. Furthermore, since the enemy was God's portion they were thereby imbued with a certain value – they were after all worthy to be sacrificed to God.[34] This helped to avoid the dehumanization that often accompanied war. However, as John Collins points out, we may wonder if "the Canaanites appreciated the honor."[35] And given the language of abomination, we may wonder how much value was actually accorded to the enemy. However that may be, in connecting the slaughter to the will of the divine being – the source of the group's moral law – the Biblical text provided another means for facilitating the taking of human life.

The Ban also touches on the psychology of reciprocity. Collins points out that the sacrifice of the enemies and their goods is assumed to win "the support of the deity. ... there is assumed to be a connection between the fulfillment of the ban and success in battle."[36]

Another evolutionary strategy is evident in the story of Moses' reaction to his lax generals, when he instructs them to spare the virgins among the Midianite prisoners. This clearly was not done from compassion for he had no compunction about ordering the death of older women and male children. In the brute terms of reproductive fitness the young girls were resources for the propagation of the community, while the older women and boys would have been a drain on the resources of a nomadic people. Moses' actions seem coldly calculating to modern readers and not what one would expect of a religious hero, but to the degree that morality serves evolutionary ends Moses ably fulfilled his role as moral leader of his community. Again, we have an example of a Biblical story that causes great perplexity as a story about a morally superior deity, but makes perfect sense as a story of how evolved strategies to enhance reproductive fitness are expressed in the idiom of religion.

Rape is a horrible but undeniable part of war. As Smith puts it, "Rape occurs in virtually all armed conflicts. In war, the female body becomes a resource to be seized and exploited."[37] It was a staple of ancient warfare that women from defeated enemy groups became sexual resources for the males of the victorious group. Whether in the Roman telling of the Rape of the Sabines, or in Homer, or in Exodus, women were part of the spoils of war.[38]

Treating women as spoils of war is a deeply dehumanizing act, and one we would expect a morally enlightened deity to denounce (although we have already seen how women's humanity is treated in the Bible), but it pays off in crude reproductive terms. Yahweh does not denounce it, nor Moses prohibit it, because they are not expressing a higher moral code. They are advocating a moral code that promotes the inclusive fitness of their group. This is not a moral critique peculiar to the Hebrew Scripture, for this behavior is not unique to the Hebrews[39]; it is, though, a cautionary lesson in treating Biblical morality as if it were something other than it is.

So, it is hoped that this has allowed us to understand how the same moral code that instructs us not to kill can also, and coherently, promote mass slaughter. The sixth commandment applies in a different way to those inside the group than it does to those outside the group. However, we have seen that "you shall not kill" was often suspended within the group, as well. How is this to be explained?

Actually, the same moral logic that sanctions violence against out-groupers supports the imposition of the death penalty toward in-group members. Morality sets the bounds of appropriate in-group behavior and serves as a signal of commitment to the group. Breaking this code poses two problems that need to be addressed. For one, say in the case of theft, it creates an imbalance that needs to be rectified. More important, perhaps, is that a violation may signal a break from the group that may cast the perpetrator into the category of the out-group. As such, the former in-group member becomes a potential threat and is outside the bounds of moral treatment. Some such breaks can be rectified by a willingness to accept the punishment of the group, but some cannot.

We can see this logic at work by looking at two very different capital crimes: murder and profaning the Sabbath. In the case of murder, the death penalty seeks to restore the balance disrupted by the crime. "An eye for an eye" is the flip side of "do unto others" and so this punishment flows from the logic of reciprocal altruism. However, in profaning the Sabbath no member of the group is harmed. There is no imbalance to be corrected. To understand the severe punishment for this crime we need to remember that Sabbath observations serve as a signal of commitment to the group. By profaning the Sabbath one is signaling that he has opted out of this arrangement and is no longer a trustworthy member of the community. In the logic of evolutionary morality you are either in the group or out of the group, and if you are out, moral laws no longer need apply to you.

We have seen how important commitment to the group is in terms of the functioning of evolutionary morality. Given this, it follows that the God who oversees that code would be willing to use the most severe punishment to police the boundaries of the group. This is portrayed in a dramatic fashion in the story of Phinehas. In this tale Yahweh is once again angry at the unfaithfulness of his people, some of whom are having sexual relations "with the daughters of Moab" (Num. 25:1). We know that the Bible often discusses faithlessness to God in terms of sexual infidelity. Here the two are again connected, as Yahweh is upset lest playing the "harlot" with the Moabites leads to bowing down to their god Ba'al. Phinehas, zealous in his devotion, noticed an Israelite who has brought home a foreign woman; he follows the man to his home. There he takes a spear and "pierce[s] both of them, the man of Israel and the woman, through her body" (Num. 25:6–8). This pleases the Lord for, as he tells us, "Phinehas was jealous with my jealousy among them, so that I did not consume the people of Israel in my jealousy." (Nonetheless, we are told that 24,000 Israelites were wiped out by plague before Yahweh's jealousy was abated by Phinehas' act; and, of course, the people are then directed to smite the Midianites – just in case we thought Yahweh was going soft; Num. 25:9, 16–18.)[40]

This story is instructive. It forcefully tells the Israelites that they too can participate in God's justice. If they uphold the law by punishing transgressors then Yahweh need not punish them – and with Yahweh's reputation it is clearly in everyone's interest to make sure that he does not get involved. Punishment, and the threat of it, has been shown to be a crucial element in promoting pro-social behavior, as you will recall from Chapter 1. The prospect of punishment lowers the risks associated with social cooperation by raising the potential costs of cheating and defecting.[41] However, it comes with its own challenge, as punishing brings a cost. If this cost is shared by the group then it is less costly to any one individual, but there is the danger of free-riders here, just as there is the free-rider problem with altruism (second-order, as opposed to first-order free riding). The story of Phinehas addresses this problem in two ways: (1) Phinehas and his entire lineage are given special blessings by God: "Behold I give him my covenant of peace; and it shall be to him, and to his descendants after him" (Num. 25:12–13). Not only is the cost of punishing offset by divine reward but the psychology of kin selection is triggered by extending the reward to Phinehas' offspring. (2) The costs of not punishing are born by the whole community. If not for Phinehas, Yahweh's jealousy would have consumed them all – and the Bible has made it very clear that Yahweh is not given to idle threats. In a community without an effective system of punishing crime everyone suffers. An individual may rationalize that his single failure to contribute to social punishment cannot do that much harm, but in a society with a god such as Yahweh in charge the danger is too great – you do not want to leave punishment to him.[42]

As we peruse the Hebrew Scriptures we see that violence is not only tolerated but commended. But this is not random, mindless violence. It is violence with a purpose, and that purpose aligns with the ends of an evolved moral sense. Evolved moral psychology serves to promote pro-social in-group behavior, and the Law imposes violent sanctions on those violations that most threaten in-group cohesion (i.e., murder, adultery). To promote adherence to this in-group moral code the use of violence is justified against those who fail to signal commitment to the group (i.e., Sabbath violations) and against those who fail to respect the boundaries between in-group and out-group, which makes defection and/or invasion more possible (e.g., the story of Phinehas). As the group is the subject and place of moral commitments, it advocates the use of violence to protect the integrity of the group, both physically and culturally (e.g., the use of the Ban). Finally, and not incidentally, since the group's moral code is presented as divine law, promulgated and enforced by the deity, it embeds all of this violence in religious terms, imbuing this violence with a sense of moral rightness and moral necessity.

In her study of religious violence, *The Curse of Cain*, Regina Schwartz begins by looking at the story of Cain, the first murderer. He murders in a jealous fit because God has rejected his offering but blessed his brother's. She asks, "What kind of God is this who chooses one sacrifice over the other?" And she answers, "This God who excludes some and prefers others, who casts some out, is a monotheistic God – monotheistic not only because he demands allegiance to himself alone but because he confers his favor on one alone."[43] This is, I believe, a fair appraisal, but it is important to see that this aspect of the monotheistic God is not a contingent feature of his nature, a function of the way he happens to be depicted in the Hebrew Scriptures. Rather, given that *Yahweh* is a development of the ancient Israelites as they struggled for survival as a people and a culture, as they struggled to establish an effective moral code to promote their survival, he could not be anything but a God who favored one (the Israelites) over others (the non-Israelites). *Yahweh* as a minimally counter-intuitive concept is constructed using the template provided by our evolved moral and religious psychology, and as such serves the moral needs of group living.

We have discussed how the expression of our evolved morality changes as Christianity develops out of ancient Judaism; now we need to see how this development relates to the question of religious violence.

The Blood of the Lamb

At some time or other you have probably heard it said that one significant difference between the Old Testament and the New Testament is that the

God of the Old Testament is a God of justice, while the God of the New Testament is a God of love. This is often presented as if it were some wise insight into the Bible, which is then supported by the numerous stories of God's wrathful vengeance that marks so much of the Old Testament, in contrast with Christ's emphasis on God's fatherly, forgiving nature. If you have heard this it was probably from a Christian, as there is in it an implicit, faintly anti-Semitic, criticism of Judaism, with a suggestion that God in the Old Testament needed to be so strict because of the obstinate behavior of the Jews. That behavior was so bad, and so incorrigible, that God decided a new covenant was called for, hence Jesus. I do not mean to charge all those who make this distinction between the two portrayals of God with anti-Semitism, but I do want to point out that this distinction is heir to a very ancient bias against Jews. In the Gospels and in the letters of Paul, Christian identity formed, in part, by distancing Christians from Jews and arguing the Jews had misunderstood God's will. In the early centuries of the Common Era this distancing took on more virulent tones, with more serious consequences.

Rather, I want to charge proponents of this distinction with a superficial reading of the nature of God as revealed in the two Scriptures. Clearly, on the surface one can make the point that the New Testament lacks the holy warfare that plays such a dramatic role in Hebrew Scriptures. There is nothing in the gospels comparable to the Ban. But does this mean that God has lost his taste for blood? That he has foregone his call for human sacrifice? This would mark quite a significant change in the nature of God – and raise its own theological difficulties, for how can an infinite being change? Of course, we are interested not in theological justification but in psychological explanation. In attempting to account for the starkly different portrayals of God in the Bible we need to attend to the different social conditions that underlie the creation of those two portrayals, and the way God, as an MCI concept, is altered in response to those conditions.

We have already done this in our analysis of Christian morality. I have argued that the qualities of *univeralism* and *exceptionalism* attributed to Christ's moral vision can be grounded in our evolved psychology just as readily as Judaic traditions; Christianity set a distinction between an in-group and an out-group, just as Judaism had. Christianity did set the boundaries of that divide differently than did Judaism. It had different requirements of its members and set out different signals of commitment, yet Christianity is marked by all the elements of an evolved religious morality as much as is Judaism, so too in its conception of the MCI concept that oversees the moral bonds of the group. God for the Christians, just as God for the Jews, is conceived to be a full-access strategic agent; an interested party in moral matters; a moral role model, legislator and enforcer. At this deeper level of analysis the God of the New Testament functions just the way the God of the Old Testament functions.

So, why the starkly different pictures? This template for constructing a god is given different expression in different cultural situations.[44] The God of the New Testament is constructed in response to the particular social and political pressures experienced by proto-Christian groups in the first centuries C.E. In the last chapter we set out how these particular pressures shaped the presentations of God and Christ. Here we need to examine how these pressures shaped Christianity's relationship to violence.

In our consideration of Judaism we saw that the grounds for religiously justified violence stem from concerns with policing the boundaries of the group. This pertains to Christianity, as well. While Christianity drops ethnicity and nationality as criteria for group inclusion – "neither Jew nor Greek" – it does set a criterion, that is, faith in Christ – "you are either with me or you are against me." And if you are against me, if you are not part of the Christian in-group, you earn none of the benefits (i.e., salvation) but instead bear the heavy costs (i.e., damnation). This comes across in the famous parable of the sheep and goats. Speaking of the final judgment, Christ tells us,

> Before him will be gathered all the nations, and he will separate them one from another as a shepherd separates the sheep from the goats, and he will place the sheep at his right hand, but the goats at his left. Then the King will say to those at his right hand, "Come, O blessed of my Father, inherit the kingdom prepared for you from the foundation of the world." ... Then he will say to those at his left hand, "Depart from me, you cursed, into the eternal fire prepared for the devil and his angels." (Matt. 25:32–41)

What is particularly notable about this passage is the severity of the treatment toward those in the out-group. In the Jewish Scriptures, those outside the group merely suffered death, here they suffer eternal torment. Christianity not only established an in-group/out-group divide, it raised the stakes for being on the wrong side of that divide. Throughout the Gospels, the opponents of the Christians are categorized not merely as dangerous or evil but as in league with the devil. This comes out most dramatically in Christ's parable about good seeds and bad seeds. First he sets the stage:

> He who sows the good seed is the Son of man; the field is the world, and the good seed means the sons of the kingdom; the weeds are the sons of the evil one, and the enemy who sowed them is the devil; the harvest is the close of the age, and the reapers are angels. (Matt. 13:37–39)

The good seeds represent the in-group and they are the sons of the kingdom; while the out-group are like weeds, and are the sons of the devil – a clear distinction, with significantly different moral appraisals. The harvest, the time to reap what you have sown, is the coming end of the world; it is not in this world but the next when the benefits of being part of the in-group are paid, as well as the costs for being outside the group. In identifying the reapers as angels Christ signals the divine nature of the coming judgment. And just what will be the outcome of this judgment? Christ is quite explicit:

> Just as the weeds are gathered and burned with fire, so will it be at the close of the age. The Son of man will send his angels, and they will gather out of his kingdom all causes of sin and all evildoers, and throw them into the furnace of fire; there men will weep and gnash their teeth. The righteous will shine like the sun in the kingdom of their Father. He who has ears, let him hear. (Matt. 13:40–43)

Let him hear, indeed. Could the message be any clearer, or the stakes any higher? Those who reject the word of Christ are not merely confused or misguided; they are the children of the evil ones. Christ here employs the standard strategy for dehumanizing your opponents: Equate them with something non-human, such as devils and weeds, as this helps to overcome the evolved inhibitions against killing those of your kind. The image of the out-group as weeds can also trigger our evolved repulsion against parasites. Weeds are useless plants that threaten the health of the garden, and we all know what to do with weeds – you get rid of them.

Now it may be countered that Christ is not advocating the use of violence by members of the in-group against the out-group, although that point seems to have often been lost on Christians who have repeatedly throughout history taken Christ at his word and literally given out-group members and defectors over to the fire. Indeed, Christ is doing something more: He is elevating the in-group/out-group to cosmic levels, and this has dangerous consequences.

Elaine Pagels points out that in "the ancient world ... it is only Essenes and Christians who actually escalate conflict with their opponents to the level of cosmic war."[45] Understanding this escalation is a complicated task, but an explanation rooted in evolutionary logic may be suggested. As radical, minority sects within first-century Judaism, both the early Christians and Essenes had little temporal power to exercise in defense of their group and so were less able to punish those who defected. If the cost of defection is low, the likelihood of defection increases. This raises the cost of cooperation. A group cannot survive under such circumstances. Divine retribution then assumes a more essential role. An individual could, theoretically, enjoy the benefits of membership in a Christian community, then defect before reciprocating and avoid punishment by being absorbed back into the more powerful majority group. However, in doing so they were now aligning themselves with the enemy of God and could have no hope of escaping divine justice.

We may understand this shift away from a physical punishment of opponents in this life toward a spiritual punishment in the next as an example
of the same evolutionary moral logic found in our discussion of Judaism,
but applied to the specific environmental conditions of early Christianity,
rather than as a repudiation of that logic. Interestingly, Spinoza made a
similar point on this subject in his insightful 1670 work, *Theological-
Political Treatise*. In discussing the proposed distinction between the Jewish
ethic of hating your enemy and the Christian ethic of loving your enemy,
Spinoza sees the difference entirely due to differing socio-political circumstances. He points out that Christ's injunction to turn the other cheek has
its precursor in Lamentations, where Jeremiah writes "let him give his cheek
to the smiter, and be filled with insults" (Lam. 3:30). Spinoza argues that
these admonitions to submit to your enemies come at times of oppression.
In more socially stable periods such principles cannot hold because they go
counter to the requirements of a just community.[46]

This is a sound analysis in keeping with the functioning of evolved morality, and support for this comes from the fact that as soon as Christianity
acquired the role of the dominant group within Roman society, it quickly
resorted to the more familiar, mundane means of punishing defectors. When
in the fourth century the emperor Constantine removed legal prohibitions
against Christianity and began to bestow imperial favor, long-simmering
within-group distinctions came to the fore. Christianity was in its final stage
of emerging as a distinct religious culture and questions of orthodoxy had
become more pressing than the need to distinguish Christians from Jews
and pagans (not that these concerns went away). For a group that was
distinguished by faith, just what that faith consisted in became more significant, and so too did signals of commitment to the group, which in this
case often took the form of correct belief.

The heterogeneous Christian world was always marked by doctrinal
differences, as well as by efforts to do away with those differences. Pagels
relates the story of Tertullian, the early church father famous for his struggles with "heretics." A heretic, following the Greek root of the term, is one
who makes a choice. In this case, it is one who chooses what to believe.
For Tertullian heretics were the enemies of the true church; as Pagels
informs us, "Tertullian insists that making choices is evil, since choice
destroys group unity."[47] When speaking of a group defined in large part by
belief we can see that Tertullian is not exaggerating. To allow choice in
belief is to make it an individual matter, but if it is an individual matter
how can it function as a signal of group commitment, and without signals
of group commitment how can we promote social cohesion? Choice and
belief need not play this role, but with the move from salvation through
acts to salvation through faith, belief assumed this vital moral function.
Given this, it is no wonder that when questions of orthodoxy replaced

concerns with bare survival the battles over beliefs would be passionate. And they were not only passionate, they were violent.

To take just one example, let's look at how an early Church debate on a theological question played out: the Arian controversy. This centered on the question of the nature of the relationship between Jesus, recognized by both sides as the Son of God, and God the Father. One side of the debate, that championed by Bishop Athanasius, later to be St. Athanasius, held that God and Christ are co-equal in nature and in majesty; the other side, argued by an Alexandrian priest named Arius, held that while Christ is divine and is the Son of God, he is not co-equal to the Father but proceeded from the Father. In theological terms the Athanasian side held that the Father and the Son were *homoousios* (of the same substance) while the Arians held they were *homoiousios* (of similar substance).[48]

To contemporary ears this may seem like a parody of theological hair-splitting, of no practical significance. After all, both sides were devoted Christians; both worshipped Christ as the Son of God; both accepted his divinity and spiritual authority. Yet this theological battle raged for most of the fourth century, and this "battle" was not merely a metaphorical battle of words but often erupted into actual violence and bloodshed between the two sides. Richard Rubenstein's *When Jesus Became God* provides an informative treatment of this subject, describing an event that occurred some fifty years into the controversy:

> By the time the men at the front of the mob smashed through the prison gates, the crowd had grown until it had overflowed the square. ... Even for Alexandria, where riots were as common as Mediterranean gales, this demonstration was unusually large. ... A roar of approval greeted the splintering of the gates. Minutes later the invaders reemerged from the prison bearing their trussed-up quarry on their shoulders ... The mob's prime target ... was George of Capppadocia, the metropolitan bishop of Alexandria and titular head of Egypt's huge Christian community. ... Punishment was duly administered. George and his fellow prisoners died in the prison square, presumably as a result of lethal beatings. ... after the rioters killed their victims, they paraded their corpses through the city.[49]

They then added insult to injury and burned the bodies.

What was the bishop's crime that so enraged the mob of Christians to brutally, and illegally, murder their spiritual leader? He was an Arian, appointed to his post by the pro-Arian emperor Constantius II (for so central was this controversy that even the Roman emperors took sides and used their imperial power to intercede in the issue), and with confidence in his imperial backing George used his ecclesiastical authority to persecute those who opposed his theological position – pagans and non-Arian Christians (i.e., out-group members and defecting in-group members). Also feeding the fury of the crowd was Athanasius, exiled during Constantius' reign, who made secretive visits to Alexandria.[50] While we do not know what Athanasius said to the crowd we can find the seeds of violence in his writings.

Athanasius wrote a famed *Life of St. Anthony*, about a revered Egyptian ascetic and founder of Christian monasticism. In this work he makes use of Anthony's authority to oppose the Arians. He cites Anthony as denouncing the Arian heresy as "the last of all and a forerunner of Antichrist." Good Christians should "have no fellowship with the most impious Arians. For there is no communion between light and darkness." And this is not simply a human dispute; "Creation itself is angry with them."[51] This led Anthony to warn his Christian in-group: "Only defile not yourselves with the Arians, for their teaching is not that of the Apostles, but that of demons and their father the devil; yea, rather, it is barren and senseless, and without light understanding, like the senselessness of these mules."[52]

Here in the writings of the saint we see the lethal strategy of identifying your opponents as non-human – they are demons and mules, the children of the devil. We see the particular Christian strategy of elevating the stakes of the dispute: The out group is on the side of darkness and has offended "creation itself." We also find the language of defilement that triggers our contagion-avoidance systems. Again, we have a revered spiritual authority using language designed to incite and justify the use of violence against those in the out-group. What is perhaps most remarkable about this tale is the nature of the divide between the in-group and the out-group. That which separated Christian from Christian – which led to numerous instances of mob violence, approved if not instigated by church fathers, and to alternating periods of exile and excommunications of those on each side of the divide – was the issue of whether Christ was of the *same* substance or of *similar* substance to God the Father. Edward Gibbon has wryly commented that critics of Christianity "of every age have derided the furious contests which the difference of a single diphthong excited between the Homoousians and the Homoiousians."[53]

It may seem incredible that our cognitive predisposition to divide the world into in-groups and out-groups can be triggered by so trivial a difference as a "single diphthong," but Gibbon has a take on this that is very much in line with our evolutionary analysis. He notes that such a metaphysical topic as the difference between same and similar substances would likely provoke only calm and thoughtful discourse even among a society of philosophers – who might be expected to actually care about such questions. But with Christianity "the Logos," that is, the Word, "had been revealed as the sacred object of the faith, the hope, and the religious worship of the Christians." Since Christianity rejected the usual signs of group membership – for example, tribalism, ethnicity – doctrinal issues, that is, what constitutes right belief, assumed central importance. This changed things dramatically. Even metaphysics could provoke passionate concern:

> Those persons who, from their age, or sex, or occupations, were the least qualified to judge, who were the least exercised in the habits of abstract reasoning; aspired to contemplate the economy of the Divine Nature: and it is the boast of Tertullian, that a Christian mechanic could readily answer such questions as had perplexed the wisest of Grecian sages. ... These speculations, instead of being treated as the amusement of a vacant hour, became the most serious business of the present, and the most useful preparation for a future life.[54]

Now, of course, the fact that such an abstract distinction became "the familiar topic of private meditation and popular discourse"[55] does not mean that the common Christian understood what that distinction implied in philosophical terms. Indeed it is a topic of such philosophical complexity that even highly educated Christians, then and now, cannot fully articulate the distinction. So why would the average Christian care enough about the dispute to attack, kill, and then desecrate the body of their bishop? Because the distinction divided the Christian world into in-group and out-group, and given our evolved psychology that divide sets the boundaries of the moral community and identifies threats to that community. With the diminishing of the pagan threat to Christianity internal divisions came to the fore and with ferocity.

Doctrinal dispute turned violent is not unique to the Arian controversy but is a common feature of Christian history, and regularly endorsed by its moral leaders: Augustine justified the use of imperial force to compel schismatics to conform:

> Wherefore, if the power which the Church has received by divine appointment in its due season, through the religious character and the faith of kings, be the instrument by which those who are found in the highways and hedges – that is, in heresies and schisms – are compelled to come in, then let them not find fault with being compelled, but consider whether they be so compelled.[56]

Luther justified the slaughter of peasants who read too freely into the Gospels (i.e., deviant in-groupers):

> Therefore, whosoever can, should smite, strangle, and stab, secretly or publicly, and should remember that there is nothing more poisonous, pernicious, and devilish than a rebellious man. Just as one must slay a mad dog, so, if you do not fight the rebels, they will fight you, and the whole country with you.[57]

He also justified violence against that perennial out-group, the Jews:

> First to set fire to their synagogues or schools and to bury and cover with dirt whatever will not burn, so that no man will ever again see a stone or cinder of them. This is to be done in honor of our Lord and of Christendom, so that God might see that we are Christians, and do not condone or knowingly tolerate such public lying, cursing, and blaspheming of his Son and of his Christians. ... Second, I advise that their houses also be razed and destroyed.[58]

So much for turning the other cheek.

As Spinoza pointed out, turning the other cheek is good advice in times of oppression when any other action would be futile. Once the social environment of Christianity changed, Christianity took a very different, more typical attitude toward responding to threats. This does not mean that the ethic of turning the other cheek was repudiated; it remains a staple of Christian moral exhortation and no doubt is a guiding principle for many Christians. But to not reciprocate harm with harm strains against our evolved moral psychology, and while it is possible to pull against that biological leash it requires greater effort, and this is more difficult when the social conditions allow us to repay our enemies with punishment. Now, this is not a criticism of Christianity as a moral system. As a cultural expression of our evolved psychology Christianity ably expresses the elements required of an effective bond for the community, and those elements include mechanisms of reciprocation, punishment for defectors and cheats, and means of identifying the moral community. What is being critiqued here is the claim often made on Christianity's behalf that it represents a higher moral system, one based on transcendent principles, and *as such* commands our allegiance. This is not so. Whatever its merits – and there are significant merits – Christianity's status as a moral system must be evaluated in the same manner as any other moral system; it is not by its nature an exceptional system.

In assessing Christianity we must look not only at its merits but at its demerits, and they too are significant. The particular danger that Christianity presents stems, interestingly, from its most highly touted merit: its universalism. As we discussed in the previous chapter, Christ's moral message is often held as superior, for it is for all humans – not just for the Jews or the Romans, not just for the well born or successful, but for all of humankind. All may be saved; all are worthy of moral concern for all are God's children. This is a vitally important moral advance, not unique to Christianity but certainly promoted by Christianity more effectively than by any other system (in the Western world, at least). But there is a flip side to Christian universalism and this is exclusivism – anyone can be a Christian, but only Christians may be saved.[59]

Marc Shell sets out the dire consequences of this:

[T]he Christian union of all humankind into a single brotherhood encouraged a certain intolerance. The doctrine crucial to Christianity that "all men are brothers" … turned all to easily into the doctrine that "only my brothers are men, all 'others' are animals and may be treated as such."[60]

Shell made this statement in the context of a discussion of the Christian reconquest of Spain, which resulted in the expulsion or conversion of Jews and Muslims. This followed a period of relatively peaceful co-existence among Muslims, Jews, and Christians under Muslim rule – a situation that made Spain, according to Shell, "for hundreds of years … the most tolerant place in Europe."[61] This reconquest gives us another example of Christian rhetoric designed to trigger moral disregard for the out-group: Jews who converted to Christianity often lived under suspicion of having converted as an expedient rather than sincerely and were labeled *marranos*, or pigs – dirty animals that can serve to trigger contagion-avoidance mechanisms.

The problem is that Christian universalism does not do away with the in-group/out-group divide. It does not see all humanity as an actual group – although there is rhetoric to suggest this – instead, it sees all humanity as a possible group. All may join[62] but those who do not constitute an out-group. And the rhetoric used by Christians, from Christ and Paul to Augustine and Luther, clearly and consistently designate out-group members as less than human, often as demonic. There is no sense in this tradition that the out-group members can be humans who simply are not part of "us." Shell points out that both Jews and Muslims had a conception that there were out-groups that deserved a degree of moral consideration, but the universalism of Christianity does not allow for such a category.[63] The potential for an out-group member to convert may accord them some moral worth, but given the stakes involved that moral consideration was a fragile reed.

In fact, that potential to become in-group members was a double-edged sword. It made all non-Christians the source of moral concern – they could be brought into the fold – but the consequences for being outside the group (i.e., eternal damnation) was so severe that moral concern for the out-group members could, and often did, justify coercive measures.

If you are not part of the group you are damned; if I care for your immortal soul then I must do whatever I can to bring you into the group. This mindset is grounded in the teachings of Christ. In the parable of the wedding banquet (Matt. 22:1–14) Christ tells of a king who invited guests to his son's marriage feast but the invited would not come. The king is angered and has his troops kill all those who refused the invitation. He then sends his servants to go throughout the town and compel whoever they find to come to the feast. It was this parable that Augustine used to justify the use of imperial force against heretics. We see this same ethic in Paul, who instructs the church at Corinth how to handle a sinner in their midst: "deliver this man to Satan for the destruction of his flesh, that his spirit may be saved in the day of the Lord Jesus" (1 Cor. 5:5).

Moral concerns for the out-group members, throughout the history of Christianity, often took this strategy to heart: Burn the body to save the soul. As morally reprehensible as contemporary Christians may find this moral logic, it cannot be said to be a perversion of Christ's message; it is grounded in Christ's moral worldview.

This comes out dramatically in the period Marc Shell is discussing. The reconquest of Spain gave us one of the most virulent examples of religious violence in history, the Spanish Inquisition. The Inquisition, whether in its Spanish or Roman versions, was a church-sanctioned use of violence and torture against heretics, false converts, and those suspected of dealing with the devil. In other words, it was a mechanism for policing the boundaries of the group. Its victims were in-group members whose signals of commitment were deemed insufficient, because they either held the wrong version of religious doctrine or were suspected of fraternizing with the enemy (e.g., witches as servants of Satan). The flames of the Inquisition burned most fiercely during times of social instability (the conjunction of the plague, the new ideas of the Renaissance, and the challenge of the Protestant Reformation prepared the ground for the Roman Inquisition; the effort to return Spain to Catholic control spurred the Spanish Inquisition), and this fits with our understanding of evolved psychology. When the group is most vulnerable, firming up the bonds that hold the community together is most important and defectors most dangerous.

The Inquisition, of course, is a standard example used to question the moral behavior of Christianity. How could a church devoted to the Prince of Peace sanction such violence? The standard apologetic response is that the Church was not to blame, but rather the weakness of the humans who acted in the name of the Church must bear the responsibility. This is a feeble defense, and given our understanding of evolved religious morality it is just confused. Morality evolves as a means for establishing group cohesion to enable the group to respond to threats from other groups and to create conditions conducive to its members' pursuit of their inclusive fitness. When the group is threatened by external enemies or by internal divisions it is essential to firm up the group's boundaries and the commitment of its members to group solidarity. For a cultural system such as Christianity, in which belief often serves as signals of commitment to the group, deviation from orthodoxy will be processed as defection, and a threat to the group. Defectors, as well as out-group members, do not enjoy the benefits of in-group moral consideration. The Inquisition was not a perversion of Christian morality, it was an effective expression of that moral system –

when this is understood from an evolutionary perspective. This, of course, is not to excuse the horrors committed by Christianity; we are assessing the functioning of the moral system, not approving it.

Another defensive move in the face of institutional religious violence is to blame the corrupting influence of temporal power on the purity of the Christian moral vision. Certainly, the combination of political power and universalist/exclusivist worldview is a perilous mix. In an important discussion of the dangers of Christian universalism, religious scholars Daniel and Jonathan Boyarin warn that "universalism plus power produces imperialism and cultural annihilation as well as, all too often, actual genocide of those who refuse to conform." They continue: "Christian universalism, even at its most liberal and benevolent, has been a powerful force for coercive discourses of sameness, denying, as we have seen, the rights of Jews, women, and other to retain their differences."[64]

We must acknowledge that access to temporal power did indeed change Christianity, and we must also acknowledge the nature of that change. Access to the powers of state did not introduce a violent impulse into Christianity; it merely gave it the means to actualize that intrinsic aspect of the Christian system. If the violent strand of Christianity has not yet been adequately revealed, then we need only return to the Bible and peruse the closing book of the Word of God to complete the argument.

The book of Revelation presents itself as a vision granted by God to "his servant John." This vision is the unfolding of the apocalypse, the end of the world. This book is, in my estimate, the most horrific story ever put to paper. In it we are witness to the final wrath of a vengeful God, the image of God that supposedly is only to be found in the pages of the Old Testament. But this God of Revelation is so fervent in his destructiveness that the Ban seems a model of moderation and restraint. In Revelation is foretold the coming of the four horsemen who "take peace from the earth, so that men may slay one another" and are given a quarter of the earth "to kill with sword and with famine and with pestilence and by wild beasts of the earth" (Rev. 6:4, 8). But this is just the beginning.

Next we hear of cosmic disasters: "the sun became black as sackcloth, and the full moon became like blood, and the stars of the sky fell to the earth" (Rev. 6:12–13). This is followed by a series of earthly disasters in which trees and grass and one third of all sea life is destroyed before the water itself is poisoned. Then we get a scene that seems to come from a Stephen King novel, except that even King could not conjure up such cruelty. Smoke comes up from a bottomless pit and out of the smoke come locusts, but no ordinary locusts. These locusts are given a charge:

> [T]hey were given power like the power of scorpions of the earth; they were told not to harm the grass of the earth … but only those of mankind who

have not the seal of God upon their foreheads; they were allowed to torture them for five months, but not to kill them, and their torture was like the torture of a scorpion, when it stings a man. And in those days men will seek death and will not find it; they will long to die, and death will fly from them. (Rev. 9:3–6)

Lust for the suffering of the out-group has never surpassed the standard set out in this book. It is not sufficient that those without the "seal of God" (read: the signal of commitment to the in-group) are punished, they must suffer so grievously that they beg for death – and then are denied that. And sparing the lives of these out-group members is not done from compassion, it is so they may suffer even more unimaginable horrors. I will refrain from describing the rest of these punishments, but they go on for another fourteen chapters, interrupted only by a chorus of rejoicing from those in heaven who praise God for his just ways. Needless to say, at the end all the evil out-group members die – but actually that is not the end. After they have suffered and died for their sins they are then resurrected for the final judgment, at which time if "any one's name was not found written in the book of life, he was thrown into the lake of fire" (Rev. 20:15).

There is perversity in the level of hatred and blood-lust in this book, a book that supposedly reveals the consummation of divine justice. To think that today there are people who read this book and instead of being nauseated or being outraged that their loving God could be saddled with such a tale, actually find in it comfort and pray for its fruition, is almost beyond comprehension. I am reminded of Epicurus' claim that the truly impious are not those who deny the existence of God but those who attribute to God things unworthy of his blessedness.[65] From this perspective, these people are the most impious Christians on the planet. But I am getting off track.

What we want to do is place this in the context of our evolutionary analysis, and in doing so we are assisted by a recent teaching on Revelation from Pope Benedict XVI.

In an address to an audience of the faithful, Benedict instructed them that the scenes found in Revelation are not to be taken literally but "should be understood against the backdrop of the dramatic experiences of the seven Churches of Asia which had to face serious difficulties at the end of the first century – persecutions and also inner tensions – in their witness to Christ."[66] This we know is a situation in which the temptation to defect from the group will run high, and defection from these early Christian communities would have been simple and have brought great benefits. We know that during some periods of persecution a Christian could avoid civil punishment by simply throwing a few grains of wheat onto the altar of a pagan god and would then be free of further harassment. This simple act, of course, would have been a signal of defection from the Christian in-group, and yet the consequences for not doing this simple act were dire. What could the Christian community offer to balance the equation? In these early centuries the churches did not have the ability to provide physical protection of its members from the Romans, and so continued commitment to the group might mean death. In such circumstances the promise of future rewards for present commitment to the group becomes absolutely vital to maintaining group solidarity.

Revelation's horrors constitute future punishment to the out-group for the evil they commit now, a warning to those tempted to defect from the group, and a promise of reciprocation of good to in-group members for the great sacrifice they make by remaining loyal in times of adversity. It appeals intuitively to our evolved moral psychology in a way that gives strength to a group almost wholly lacking in temporal strength:

> Thus, the Seer wants to tell us: trust in Jesus, do not be afraid of the opposing powers of persecution! The wounded and dead Lamb is victorious! Follow the Lamb Jesus, entrust yourselves to Jesus, take his path! Even if in this world he is only a Lamb who appears weak, it is he who triumphs![67]

So, Revelation is yet another example of religious teachings that seem to conflict with a higher moral source but that make sense as an expression of our evolved moral psychology.

Still, whatever the psychological goal of Revelation may have been, that goal is accomplished by setting out, under divine sanction, the use of terrible violence against those outside the group.[68] The ethical lesson being taught is not "Do not return hatred with hatred; violence with violence." It is clearly: "Hatred will be repaid with hatred; violence with violence." This is still an ethic of "an eye for an eye," not one of "turn the other cheek." It is an embrace of the use of violence to further the good of the in-group, and this is a lesson that has been embraced by numberless Christians ever since.

As we have completed our assessment of the violent strand in Judaism and Christianity we can see that this violence is no aberration, nor is it a corruption of some pure ethic of love. It is an expression of the evolved moral psychology that structures these religious ethical traditions. The very same evolved moral psychology that generates love, and sacrifice, and care – which represent the best expressions of religion – also generates hatred, bias, and violence. The line that determines whether religion generates love or violence is the line that defines the in-group from the out-group.

In looking at religious violence we have been analyzing ancient texts, but of course our ultimate concern is with the terrible suffering caused by religious violence in the world today. Before concluding this chapter we need to see what light this evolutionary analysis can shed on this problem.

A Case Study in the Evolved Psychology of Religious Violence: 9/11

Trying to understand religious violence and its role in tragedies such as the events of September 11, 2001 – or any of the other numerous examples in which Christians, Jews, Muslims, Hindus, and others perpetrate violence against each other – is far too complex for any single methodology to suffice. Yet it is because this phenomenon is so complex that any light that can be shed by a particular methodology is desperately needed. Thus my goal here is to see what insight may be gained into religious violence by looking at the role our evolved moral psychology may play.

From our study of Judaism and Christianity I believe we can discern a certain structure to the psychology of religious violence.[69] The initial move is to discriminate between an in-group and an out-group, with a set of practices and/or beliefs that function as signals of commitment to the in-group. Next, there is a differential in moral evaluation of the two sides of the divide: The in-group is owed a higher level of moral consideration and accorded a greater level of moral protection than those outside the group or those who defect from the group. Thus far, this structure is not unique to religious violence, it simply flows from the basic evolutionary strategies for allowing systems of reciprocity to develop and group cohesion to form. Religion comes into play with the integration of one or more minimally counterintuitive concepts (e.g., gods) into the moral matrix. *God* comes to represent the moral bonds that hold a community together and functions as both legislator and enforcer of the group's moral code. This gives that moral code a heightened sense of significance and obligation. Commitment to that god can then function socially and psychologically as a signal of commitment to the group. Also, by clothing the social code of the group in divine authority it can relieve the individual of responsibility for the consequences of his or her decisions ("If god commands, I must obey").

Consequent to this is that the out-group, by virtue of being the out-group, is not aligned with that god, or is not in proper relationship to that god. This further distinguishes the moral status of the two groups and leads to an escalation of the stakes at play. This becomes even more dramatic in universalist systems. In this case the out-group is not simply "other" but, in being aligned against God, is in league with evil itself. Inter-group conflict is no longer simply a competition between two groups seeking to promote their own interests, it is now a cosmic struggle with no middle ground available, and nothing short of victory acceptable.[70]

While we have drawn this structure from a study of Judaism and Christianity I do not believe it is unique to these two religions.[71] The specifics of a religious tradition will lead to variations in just how violence is generated and how it will be justified, but as the evolved moral psychology at play will be the same, the general logic behind religious violence will be similar. I can do no more at this point than to simply assert this position and leave it to another time, or to other scholars, to test this claim. However, by looking at the other monotheistic moral tradition we can gain greater confidence that this structure is common at least to monotheism.

A more detailed analysis of Islam from the perspective of evolutionary psychology is an important project, but one that is not attempted here. However, even a cursory review can detect evidence of the same evolved moral logic at play in Islam that we identified in Judaism and Christianity.

We find in Islam a delineation of an in-group and an out-group. Marc Shell has argued that the relatively peaceful co-existence of the three monotheistic faiths in Islamic Spain was made possible, at least in part, by the readiness of Islam to recognize that the world was not simply divided into in-group Muslims and out-group non-Muslims. By recognizing Jews and Christians as "Peoples of the Book," Spain under Muslim rule avoided the intolerance that flowed from Christian universalim.[72] This is an important point, and an appreciation for the religious harmony established by Muslim rule in Spain, compared with the inquisitorial violence wrought by their Christian successors, is a valuable antidote for facile and superficial judgments about Islam and its relationship to violence. However, despite this accommodation for Jews and Christians within Islamic society, these non-Muslim peoples of the book did not enjoy the same social status as full-fledged members of the in-group (i.e., Muslims). Still, more pertinent to our discussions is the line that Islam establishes as the outer boundary of the in-group: that between believers and non-believers.

Jews and Christians earn some in-group status, although of a secondary nature, because they worship the same God as do Muslims, and Muslims recognize Moses and Jesus as legitimate sources of sacred legislation. Therefore, although Jews and Christians do not appreciate the final revelation of God's word, nor fully understand the revelations they were given, they cannot be cast as out-group members since they are committed to the same God who oversees the bonds of Muslim society – as long as they continue to be faithful to that God. However, those who do not worship the one God – i.e. Hindus, Buddhists, atheists – have no commitment to the MCI being who oversees the Muslim community and so are treated to the same moral disregard/suspicion as out-group members are within Judaism and Christianity. There are believers and there are non-believers, and which side of the line you are on makes all the difference in the world.

We can find passages in the Qu'ran that establish this clear divide between the faithful and the unbelievers, along with the consequent demonization of the out-group:

> Allah is the guardian of those who believe. He brings them out of darkness into the light; and those who disbelieve, their guardians are Shaitans [Satan] who take them out of the light into the darkness. (Surah 2:257)

We also find very different moral codes for those on either side of this divide. While a Muslim is prohibited from killing a Muslim, no such prohibition applies to disbelievers:

> And whoever kills a believer intentionally, his punishment is hell, and Allah will send His wrath on him and curse him and prepare for him a painful chastisement. (Surah 4:93)

> When your Lord revealed to the angels: I am with you, therefore make firm those who believe. I will cast terror into the hearts of those who disbelieve. Therefore strike off their heads and strike off every fingertip of them. (Surah 8:12)

As Islam shares with Christianity a universalizing tendency, we find, as we would expect, a raising of the stakes. The fortunes of those on either side of the divide continue to diverge into eternity:

> A parable of the garden which those guarding against evil are promised: Therein are rivers of water that does not alter, and rivers of milk the taste whereof does not change, and rivers of drink delicious to those who drink, and rivers of honey clarified; and for them therein are all fruits and protection from their Lord. Are these like those who abide in the fire [the disbelievers] and who are made to drink boiling water so it rends their bowels asunder. (Surah 47:15)

By heightening the different fates of in-group and out-group members Islam lowers the cost of investing in the good of the group. The grotesque nature of the price of defection is a particularly effective and common strategy for discouraging defection, as our consideration of Revelation demonstrated.

We see the basic structure that generates religious violence is embedded in Islam, as it is in Judaism and Christianity. The question is whether this structure can be implicated in the 9/11 attacks. How much a role religion played in the motives and goals of the September 11th terrorists is open to debate; that religion was involved in the actions of that day and its aftermath is not. Indeed, religious scholar Bruce Lincoln has argued that the motives of the terrorists were "intensely and profoundly religious."[73] But religion played a role not only in the motives of the terrorists but in the response of President Bush. Both processed the situation in terms shaped by the evolved religious mind. If we take a brief look at some of the comments made by those involved in the plot, as well as comments made by the President after the event, we can see evidence of the evolved psychology of religion at work on both sides.

For example, we see the belief in God functioning to provide unity and confidence in the group as it struggles with competing groups:

> Remember the words of Almighty God. ... Remember: "How many small groups beat big groups by the will of God." And His words: "If God gives you victory, no one can beat you." (Mohammed Atta)[74]

We also see it in President Bush's claim:

> In this struggle, God is not neutral. (Bush, 9/20/01)[75]

Also evident in the rhetoric is the in-group/out-group divide:

> These events have divided the entire world into two camps, the camp of the faithful and the camp of infidels. May God shield us and you from them. (Osama bin Laden, 10/7/01)[76]

> Every nation, in every region now has a decision to make. Either you are with us or you are with the terrorists. ... May God grant us wisdom, and may He watch over the United States of America. (Bush, 9/20/01)[77]

And with this divide we find the requisite demonizing of those on the outside:

> All of their equipment and gates and technology will not prevent, nor harm, except by God's will. The believers do not fear such things. The only ones that fear it are the allies of Satan, who are brothers of the devil. (Atta, 9/10/01)[78]

> My administration has a job to do and we are going to do it. We will rid the world of evil-doers. (Bush, 9/16/01)[79]

> We value life; the terrorists ruthlessly destroy it. (Bush, 11/08/01)[80]

And there is the escalation of the stakes:

> All these crimes and sins committed by Americans are a clear declaration of War on God. (Osama bin Laden, 2/23/98)[81]

> We wage a war to save civilization itself. (Bush, 11/08/01)[82]

The basic premise of evolutionary psychology is that the cognitive/emotional predispositions designed in the course of our species' evolution continue to shape the way we process our experiences today. The evolved psychology of our moral sense, wedded with the evolved predispositions that underlie religious thought, creates mental schema for interpreting and responding to the world. We found this exemplified in religious texts written thousands of years ago and we find it at work in the world today. Even in ostensibly secular situations, such as an American President responding to a security threat, the response assumes forms shaped by our evolved religious psychology. And this is not surprising, for these mechanisms evolved as adaptations to further group and individual security and survival. When that security is under fire, these mechanisms will be more easily tripped. We find further evidence of this in the dramatic increase in church attendance in the United States immediately after the attacks and the subsequent regress to the norm after the initial period of alarm passed.

While it is not surprising, it is of great import. Religion is supported by deep and ancient cognitive and emotional tools. These deeply ingrained, emotionally rich faculties give religion tremendous power to amplify moral predispositions – for better and for worse. If for no other reason this makes the study of religion essential: An understanding of the psychological bases of religion is literally a life and death issue.

We started this chapter with a quote from President Bush characterizing Islam as a religion of peace and we said this type of thinking represents an impoverished view of religion. Clearly, his strategy was to offset the equally impoverished, though more prevalent and dangerous view in the fall of 2001, that Islam is a religion of violence. But countering one intellectually dubious proposition with another does not help. Islam is a cultural expression of the same underlying evolved moral psychology that underlies Judaism and Christianity. It generates altruism and compassion for others, a willingness to care for the needy and to protect the weak, to sacrifice the immediate personal good for the larger social good that are essential for successful group living, and are among humankind's most precious attributes. This is as much a part of Islam as it is part of Judaism and Christianity. However, the evolved moral psychology that underlies Islam also generates a willingness to use violence and a readiness to disregard the suffering of the out-group that is just as much part of Islam as are the pro-social sentiments – and in this Islam is no different from Christianity or Judaism.

This is not to downplay the great danger that violence committed by certain adherents of Islam constitutes in the world today. It is, rather, to argue that to understand the nature of this particular threat we need to understand the conditions that obtain, the environmental pressures as it were, that trigger the dark side of religious psychology. Given the potential for good and ill implicit in religion, and the great power religion wields, the question that we are left with is, What can be done about religious violence? And this involves asking, What can be done about religion? Can those aspects of religion that lead to violence be teased out leaving only the pro-social, peaceful aspects of religion? And if not, then does religion pose a lethal threat to a multi-cultural world with the technological ability to self-destruct? Many critics of religion would answer in the affirmative and therefore argue for the marginalization, if not elimination, of religion. But is this possible? And if it were, would it be desirable? Without religion would we be able to generate the large-scale cooperation that societies need to survive without falling into despotism? These are some of the issues I would like to begin to address in the final chapter.

6 | RELIGION
EVOLVING

The material of our study of human nature is now spread before us; and in this parting hour, set free from the duty of description, we can draw our theoretical and practical conclusions. (William James)[1]

Setting the Task

We have now completed our analysis of our evolved religious psychology and, it is hoped, have provided sufficient evidence to support the thesis that religious moral traditions are cultural expressions of underlying evolved cognitive pre-dispositions. Of course, more can and should be done to explore and challenge this thesis, but that is work for other times.[2] Having made at least a plausible case, it is time to consider the implications of this thesis for religious ethics and for religious violence.

Monotheistic traditions, despite their different expressions, emphases, values, laws, and so on, are constructed upon a common moral psychological framework. Among the major elements of this complex framework are predispositions to favor kin and a genuine altruism toward those in the group, along with a deep concern with reciprocation; and a concomitant predisposition to fear or distrust those outside the group, along with a reduced moral sensitivity toward out-group members. These basic elements give rise to second-order concerns over signals of willingness to cooperate and signals of group membership. This framework provides the basic cognitive architecture of human moral psychology in general, not simply of religious morality. Different cultures and traditions develop different ways of triggering the various aspects of this moral framework, which results in the variety of moral systems we find in the world, both secular and religious.

However, to get a religious moral tradition this moral framework must be joined with a framework of religious cognition. This evolved religious cognition provides a schema for god-beliefs in which gods are minimally counter-intuitive (MCI) concepts, that is, beings that fit, though imperfectly, the ontological category of *persons*. This generates a series of intuitively compelling expectations about such beings, while violating in significant ways a minimum number of those categorical expectations, making such beings memorable and important. Since our dealings with other persons is so centered on moral and social concerns, it is a natural expectation of members of the ontological category of *persons* that they are morally motivated social beings, and so it is an easy, and intuitively natural, step to conceive of gods in this way. It is not necessary to think of gods in primarily moral terms, but the gods that are conceived in this fashion assume an added significance. This added significance comes from the peculiar nature of gods as MCI concepts: They violate the categorical expectations of *persons* in having access to socially relevant information denied the typical person, and they have a power to reward and punish that demands our attention.

Once the cognitive framework for god-beliefs is connected with the cognitive framework for morality, god-beliefs are colored by our moral pre-dispositions. The rhetoric of kin-selection, the centrality of reciprocation, the special relationship between certain gods and certain communities all become part of our intuitive expectations about God's nature. Signals of commitment to the group assume a religious expression as signals of commitment to a god or to a religious tradition. This is of utmost significance, as the cognitive and emotional pre-dispositions that make up our moral framework are some of the deepest and most important cognitive tools. They possess tremendous power to motivate us to act. The integration of our religious cognitive framework with our moral cognitive framework imbues religious belief with this power.

However, the impact is not one-sided. Our basic moral psychology is enhanced by being connected to an MCI being. Belief in a moral god who oversees the bonds of the group provides a public mechanism for evaluating commitment to the group and makes the promise of reciprocation more secure and the temptation to defect less alluring.

The synergy created by the integration of our religious cognitive framework and our moral cognitive framework sets the conditions for the rise of cultural institutions – that is, religions – with a potential to shape human affairs unsurpassed by any other force in history. Given this, it is not surprising that cultures throughout history, and across the globe, have developed ways of tapping into this psychology that fit their own particular circumstances. And as we have seen, the moral traditions of Judaism, Christianity, and Islam are examples of cultural moral systems built upon the shared cognitive frameworks of evolved morality and god-beliefs. The particulars of these traditions are the results of the different social, historical, and environmental conditions that obtained during the developmental periods of their history. Whether it is the Mosaic Code, the Gospels, or Sharia Law, all fit within the contours of our evolved psychology. Our goal now is to consider the import of this theory.

Varieties of Religious Expressions

As I connect here for a second time with William James it is only fair to acknowledge the intellectual debt this work owes to James's groundbreaking classic. James set out to explore what science could, and could not, tell us about religion, using the cutting-edge theories of late nineteenth-century psychology. He believed experience was the primal level of religiosity upon which individuals and cultures built their religions as a way of articulating, understanding, and sharing those experiences. Having catalogued the variety of religious experiences he found by looking at religions across the globe, James concluded that beneath the dizzying variety of religious expressions lies a universal template for religious experience, a "common nucleus."[3] James's recognition of a shared psychological grounding beneath the variety of religious experiences makes him an intellectual forefather to this present work.

Of course, I have departed from James by focusing on religious texts rather than experiences. This is not to prioritize belief over experience but to recognize the continuing importance of beliefs as part of our religious experience, and the formative role texts continue to play in the shaping of belief. The authority of religious texts, particularly in moral matters, remains an important force, even if not as decisive as it once was. While religion is more than beliefs, using texts such as the Bible and the Qur'an as authoritative moral sources remains a decisive and intuitively compelling move for millions – and such moves often play a significant role in politics and public morals. Given this, an evaluation of the nature of the moral authority of these texts is a task with practical as well as theoretical import.[4]

I believe that the decisive moral authority accorded to one or another religious text is decisively undermined by the findings of this book. If all religious moral traditions are expressions of the same basic moral logic, then no one religious tradition can rightfully claim a privileged position. It may be argued that the general moral system shared by these texts retains normative significance, and we will consider this position, but it cannot be claimed that any particular expression of that moral schema – whether

Judaic, Christian, or Islamic – has any compelling moral weight, and we need to understand why.

Whether we are talking about Judaism, Christianity, or Islam, the moral systems of those traditions take on the specific character they do because a common moral psychology is being shaped by different social and historical conditions. One function of a moral system is to provide a social code that allows individual members of a community to work together to create a social environment in which they can pursue their inclusive fitness. Judaism, Christianity, and Islam developed different strategies for doing this – different laws and regulations, different signals of commitment – that were impressively successful in fulfilling this function, *in their own particular historical and social contexts*. How then may one argue, on objective grounds, for a privileged position for any one particular religious moral tradition?

Adherents of a particular religion, of course, might argue for a privileged position on the grounds that their tradition is a truer revelation of God's will – but this is just how a believer would argue. For the system to work for them, as a religious system, it must be seen as God's will. It is part of the design of religious moral traditions that they present themselves, and are perceived to be, the will of God – that is what makes them effective as moral systems. However, the deeply held convictions of believers that God's will is communicated through their religion's texts and traditions is no argument for the truth of that particular revelation because the very devotion that they feel, that sense of certitude and truth, is itself a function of our evolved religious psychology. A Christian who has believed from childhood, with all her heart, that salvation comes only through Jesus Christ, holds that belief as a result of being exposed to a Christian system that effectively tapped into deep, emotionally colored intuitions that are part of our common human psychology. Had that same person been exposed from childhood to a Judaic or Islamic system – both of which, like Christianity, have been honed for centuries to tap into our evolved intuitions – that person would have equally certain, equally sincere beliefs in very different propositions.

The deep sense of a religion's truth or realness, which for many is such a compelling ground for belief, is a function of an individual's developmental history (which is not simply individual, but includes layers of family and cultural history) shaping evolved psychological tools. And while this deep feeling has personal significance, whatever its origin, it cannot be used as evidence of a tradition's moral authority for anyone who does not share that experience.

This raises the question of the social authority a religious tradition may have for its adherents. It can be argued that religious moral traditions persist because they have proved their fitness in enhancing community building, while promoting inclusive fitness for its members, and that this speaks to their continuing value – at least for those particular communities. There is merit to this point. We still face the challenges of building cohesive communities that allow individuals to successfully pursue their inclusive fitness. Religions have been battle-tested for millennia; they have adapted to changing environments and are proven survivors. Does that not, even from an evolutionary perspective, earn them privileged status as moral systems? Even if no single religious tradition can claim superiority, cannot religious morality, per se, claim an important role in the modern world? Perhaps, but this needs to be explored. A more detailed exploration must wait till the final section of this chapter, but a few preliminary comments are in order.

Judaic, Christian, and Islamic moral traditions were shaped to serve the needs of particular communities as those communities sought their own identity and their own good in a world dominated by an opposing out-group. Christianity and Islam, through various missionary activities, were able to extend the boundaries of their in-group, which then became dominant in their social environments. Judaism adapted to the loss of political independence by fostering a strong sense of group identity in a landscape dominated by hostile out-groups.

The world we live in today provides vastly different environments. We live in an increasingly globalized world, with porous group boundaries and a flexibility of identity formation and reformation unimaginable even a century ago. This has serious consequences for the group-identity formation function of religion. This is a key aspect of religious morality, and it often brings with it a moral devaluation of out-group members. While this is just part of the moral psychology of religion, it is a part that poses great danger in a world littered with nuclear and bio-chemical weapons. And it's not simply the damage that can be done by dramatic acts of terrorism that poses a danger, it is also the smaller scale, but more personal harm, caused by an in-group moral mentality: the constant devaluation of the other, the moral insensitivity that is tolerated, the social divisiveness that follows, the intimate humiliations imposed on fellow human beings for the crime of falling on the wrong side of the moral wall. Religious moral systems bring much of value but all this follows in its wake. The question is, Can we any longer afford to take the bad with the good?

In identifying the psychological frameworks upon which religious beliefs and moral systems are built we have uncovered a common nucleus to religious ethics. This is a finding that some believers might happily embrace. Perhaps the way to understand the world's religions is to see them as different attempts to discern God's moral will, and each religion as an attempt to articulate that moral truth. A particular religion might want to claim that it alone has *the Truth*, but more liberal religionists have long treated that claim as unacceptable ethnocentricity, incompatible with a Universal God. In this sense perhaps what this investigation into religious morality has done is to help uncover that sacred truth each religion struggles to express in its own idiom. James found such a view perfectly compatible with his own understanding of religion, referring to each variety of religious expression as "a syllable in human nature's total message."[5]

This suggests a counter-point to the naturalistic reading I am giving here. It may still be possible to see the hand of God behind all of this. It may be that God, creator of the universe, and designer of the laws of nature, designed the laws of evolution so as to give rise to minds capable of perceiving His presence, and a moral psychology sensitive to the moral truth, as He designed it. In this scenario it might be that each religion is an expression of God's divine will and that what we need to do is to cull from the chaos of moral diversity a core moral framework representing God's true will. Indeed, attempts to reconcile the cognitive study of religion and faith along these lines are being developed.[6]

In assessing this counter-interpretation we need to keep in mind that we have traced the origin of the mental frameworks that constitute this common nucleus to our evolutionary history. We have proposed evolutionary paths for the moral elements that come to be expressed as the *word of God*; we have exposed the evolutionary strategies behind the various laws and commands that religions present as the *will of God*. Not only that, we have seen that many of these expressions issue in practices that are xenophobic, racist, or misogynistic, at one extreme, and simply mundane and uninspiring at the other. This is just what one would expect of moral systems that developed to promote within-group cohesion in the ultimate service of reproductive fitness. It does not fit easily with the image of a supremely good and supremely wise God, cherished and promoted by so many religious believers.[7]

When Darwin introduced his theory it immediately smacked up against an influential view of the world as having been designed by God. The complexity and design apparent throughout nature cried out for a Divine Designer, a Cosmic Watchmaker, who ordered the chaos of the material world. Darwin's theory of natural selection offered a different explanation, one with a far more powerful explanatory schema, supported by a wealth of empirical evidence. An important aspect of Darwin's victory over design was that the wastefulness of extinction, the brutality of the struggle for survival, the inelegance and inefficiency of design found throughout nature all fit better with a world resulting from natural selection than a world created by an omnipotent Designer.

I believe a similar situation applies here: The moral systems found in the texts of Judaism, Christianity, and Islam fit better with a moral psychology designed by evolution than one designed to express divine truth. The violence and bigotry found throughout sacred texts have long proved difficult to reconcile with nobler expectations of religion, and many have tried to dissociate the pro-social, inspiring messages contained in these texts from the darker material. However, such a move is not warranted from a psychological perspective. The same moral schema that gives rise to religion's moral beauty also gives rise to its moral horrors – and that moral schema is more consistent with an evolutionary source than with a divine source. I believe a conclusion of the theory set out here is that not only can no individual religion claim a privileged position for its moral system, but religious morality itself can claim no privileged position vis-à-vis non-religious moral systems, for they cannot justify the claim that they derive from a higher source of moral truth.

It does not follow from this that religious moral traditions are insignificant or that they have value only for the faithful. What we find in the various religious texts are accounts of different human cultures struggling to deal with shared human problems. They are records of humanity's efforts at moral world-making, and as such they have great value to any student of human nature or human history. Indeed, they are much more than this: They are examples of social/moral "experiments in living," to borrow John Stuart Mill's phrase. These systems not only met the needs of their people, in their times, but did so in a way that had staying power. They may provide valuable insight into questions of social justice, personal responsibility, and ethical relations that humans will always struggle to address. The Bible, the Qur'an, and other sacred writings have enduring value to the human community – not as divine texts revealing a higher truth but as textbooks containing the results of some of the most significant social experiments in human history, whose failures we can learn from, as well as their successes.

Admittedly, this is not a conclusion that some religious believers are hoping comes from the cognitive science of religion, and a more developed engagement with their arguments to the contrary is certainly warranted. Here, however, we must limit such an engagement to the issue of morality and the sufficiency of an evolutionary account of ethics. As we continue to explore of the value of religious ethical traditions it is worthwhile to consider in greater detail the relationship between morality and religion, and the impact of evolution on this relationship.

If There Were No God ...

In Dostoyevsky's *The Brothers Karamazov*, which contains some of the more profound meditations on religion to be found in Western literature,

Ivan Karamazov suggests that if there were no God, all would be permitted. This captures what seems to be a fairly popular sentiment about the relationship between religion and morality – that if there is no God to legislate and/or to enforce moral codes, then in some sense there can be no moral limit to what is permitted. If you do not believe in God, then how can you be trusted? Theologian John Haught presents a more nuanced understanding of the religion/morality nexus, admitting that "there is no point in denying that people can be very moral without believing in God"[8] but concluding that without an "eternal ground" moral values cannot be anything but "arbitrary, conventional, historically limited human concoctions."[9] Our evolutionary analysis allows us both to understand and to assess this supposedly necessary link between morality and religion.

Given the deep emotional pull of our evolved moral mechanisms, and the amplification of these responses by their integration with religion, an assault on one may well feel like an assault on both: Moral deviance is not simply defection from the social contract but is an offense against God, and to criticize God or, worse, to deny his existence, is to unsettle the moral order. If God functions as the overseer and enforcer of the moral bonds of society, then if there is no God, those bonds are cast asunder. A society without a functioning moral code is no society at all. In such a world, with no secure grounds for trusting in reciprocation, social cooperation and trust become dangerous flights of idealism – we are on a Hobbesian precipice. Because of the psychological connections between moral and religious frameworks, a simple act, such as swearing on a Bible, takes on real significance for it signals a commitment to the God that oversees the community's moral bonds. From a strictly rational perspective we recognize, of course, that placing one's hand on a Bible does nothing to guarantee moral conduct in office. But this is not an act with rational justification; it is an act that triggers the mechanisms for signaling commitment to the group's moral code by signaling commitment to its moral Lord.

This may shed some light on the unreasonably contentious issues that pop up regularly in American politics, such as prayer in school or pledging allegiance to "one nation under God." Those who critique such practices see them as unconstitutional intrusions of religion into the public sphere – but that is a rational analysis, and something deeper is going on here. Advocates of school prayer, and of keeping God in the pledge, see these acts for what they are (even if they are not conscious of this): signals of commitment to a moral code that unites us into one community. How can we be a community if we do not have a moral communion, and means for signaling commitment to that communion? Opponents for their part can also be understood as responding to the psychological significance of these ritual acts, even if they want to argue for a purely rational or legal motivation. Signaling allegiance to God does signal allegiance to a moral order.

But in America "God" is not some neutral concept – it comes loaded with specifically Judeo-Christian interpretations – and so pledging allegiance to God can imply allegiance to a particular religious moral tradition, and that rightfully provokes resistance in an increasingly pluralistic culture.

The cognitive/evolutionary understanding of religious moral traditions provides a way to understand these social conflicts over religion that is more effective than a simple rational analysis, but what does it say about the supposedly necessary connection between religion and morality?

When we consider the relationship between morality and religion, the issue is not really about conventional codes of conduct that allow particular societies to function. These, it may be granted, are not dependent upon God, and may in fact have been necessary precursors to a fully developed morality. What morality lacks without God, it is said, is an *ultimate* justification: something that makes sense of our moral obligations and duties, our sense of right and wrong, which is not grounded in the merely contingent. This, it is held, cannot be provided by a purely naturalistic account of morality.

This is one of the more serious criticisms of evolution from a religious perspective. Religious criticism of evolution is common currency in the United States, where debates over evolution and creationism – or in a slight variation on that theme, evolution versus intelligent design – make their way with dismaying regularity into the papers, school board meetings, and the courts. These debates raise serious challenges to evolution, but only as social and political issues, as they impede the teaching of evolution that is an essential part of any educated person's training. They are not, however, serious theoretical or intellectual challenges. On intellectual grounds they are simply silly, and as such deserve no serious engagement. Unfortunately, given the political climate in the United States (and now, increasingly, in other parts of the world), creationism cannot receive the dismissal it deserves, but nor does every discussion of religion and evolution need to rehearse the arguments undermining creationist's arguments. These are well documented, and the interested reader can consult those works.[10]

Here I wish to focus on this moral critique of evolutionary thinking. This is a more serious challenge to an evolutionary worldview because this critique, in its best expressions, works with a professional understanding of evolutionary theory, and fully accepts that theory for what it is: the best theory ever developed to explain the history, diversity, and relationship of all life on earth. The criticism instead focuses on what is said to be an unjustified extension of evolutionary thinking into realms inappropriate for empirical investigation, for example, the moral realm. This position strikes at the heart of this book's implicit premise that morality is an appropriate subject for empirical investigation, and so we need to pay attention to it.

John Haught, one of the more prolific and respected writers on the relationship between evolution and theology, makes a strong case for this position. Haught has a deep respect for evolution's explanatory power. He recognizes that evolution conflicts in decisive ways with literalist readings of religious texts, and that this requires an abandonment of such a reading of the Bible, but without requiring an abandonment of religion. Haught argues forcefully that a reading of the Bible, such as that proffered by proponents of creationism and intelligent design, is a superficial approach to the texts and leads not only to bad science, but to bad theology.[11] A more theologically sophisticated understanding of religion not only fails to conflict with evolutionary thinking but is enhanced by it, as it allows a deeper understanding of the nature of material existence and of God's nature.[12]

All of this makes Haught's understanding of the relationship between religion and evolution an important theological reading for anyone interested in these issues, but it is particularly germane to this book. For although Haught works with a grasp of evolution and theology superior to most of those engaged in the public debates, I take issue with his claim that we need for a theological perspective to make full sense of the basis of morality. I believe that Haught has a limited view of just how far-reaching is the impact of evolutionary theory, embedded in the new cognitive science paradigm, and how this challenges theology, particularly as it relates to morality.[13]

Haught contends that an evolutionary account of morality is insufficient for making sense of our moral lives. He writes, "I am inclined to suspect that over the course of generations human moral aspiration would eventually wither and die unless it were sustained by a trust that the whole of being, including the physical universe, is the embodiment of transcendent meaning."[14] Not only does our species' moral future require a religious grounding, it has always been so: "[A]t least until the age of science, the main stimulus to ethical commitment was religious belief in a meaningful universe."[15] Even recognizing the fact of religious violence, Haught maintains a firm conviction. He asserts that as "barbarous as our religious traditions may sometimes have been, I am persuaded that only their conviction that the universe itself in some way ultimately makes sense has been able to nourish, throughout a succession of epochs, the human longing for goodness."[16]

Haught makes two major assumptions. One is that the morality of individuals, past and present, is motivated by a sense of the universe's "transcendent meaning." But how can anyone know this? The world's wisdom literature, both religious and secular, certainly provides evidence that the "longing for goodness" has often sought refuge in an enduring reality that transcends the finite world, but there is also literature that grounds that moral goal in the here and now. More critical is that this wisdom literature, even if it does display a predominant concern for the transcendent, is the work of the more literate, educated, and intellectually gifted portion of humanity, those who by their training and inclination seek to go beyond the surface and look for deeper connections. On what grounds can we extrapolate the longings of this group to the greater portion of humankind? I would not deny that a longing for something more lasting, a sense that there is something higher than mundane existence, may be a very common human trait. But to go from that admittedly speculative position to assert that this longing is necessary to sustain morality is a much greater leap, and one that seems ill-suited to support such grand conclusions as Haught draws from it.

The second assumption, more significant for our present discussion, is that without this sense of cosmic purposefulness the moral aspirations of humankind will wither and die. As mentioned, Haught concedes that without religion people can still be moral. He accepts that even without a sense of cosmic purpose we may be able to find "precarious havens of human warmth ... as we huddle in the cold of the cosmos," but insists that this would never amount to what "most humans have taken to be a mean-ingful life."[17] Suppressing the urge to cry out, "How do you know what 'most humans have taken to be a meaningful life'?" we must continue to see just why an evolved morality is so lacking.[18]

In discussing Richard Dawkins's account of evolutionary ethics Haught writes, "Evolutionary insights into the story of how morality emerged in natural history may not be wrong as far as they go, but they do not work well if taken as adequate or final explanations." Why not? Because "a blind, indifferent, and amoral natural process, which is how Dawkins has always characterized evolution, can hardly explain why justice, love, and the pursuit of truth are now unconditionally binding virtues."[19] This raises some key meta-ethical questions about the justification of ethics, as well as begging the question of whether there are any "unconditionally binding" moral rules, which I will not go into here.[20] Haught's argument, however, is based not simply on philosophical concerns but on psychological ones, and these touch on our themes.

Haught makes his point by considering the critiques of the "new atheists" – Dawkins, Sam Harris, Daniel Dennett, and Christopher Hitchens – charging them with inconsistency in their moral outrage at religion's abuses, which expresses a moral certitude incompatible, he claims, with an evolutionary understanding of our moral sense. Haught argues that "to know with such certitude that religion is evil [as Harris et al. suggest], one must first have already surrendered one's heart and mind to what is unconditionally good." And then he challenges them:

> What is the basis of your moral rectitude? How, in other words, if there is no eternal ground of values, can your own strict standards be anything other

than arbitrary, conventional, historically limited human concoctions? ... [I]f you, your tribe, or mindless Mother Nature are the ultimate ground of your values, why does your sense of rightness function with such assuredness in your moral indictment of all people of faith?[21]

This is a challenge that must be met: If our values are the results of our evolved psychology interacting with our social environments, as I argue, then, since our evolutionary history is contingent and our social environments are dynamic, can moral values be anything but "arbitrary, conventional, historically limited human concoctions"? And if this is so, and we are aware that this is so, how can we feel such certitude about our moral judgments? Why would we accept them as binding?

I believe that from the evolutionary perspective set out in this book we can argue that moral values are neither arbitrary nor conventional nor historically limited concoctions, but neither are they unconditionally binding, eternal verities. It is not an either/or option, and this is often lost in discussions about naturalistic ethics.

The moral values that have developed over our history are the product of a contingent evolutionary process. Evolution could have led to very different sorts of rational creatures; the history of hominids could have taken different paths, and conceivably could have led to a very different moral psychology. Had that happened we would likely be facing different moral challenges. But the key fact is that our evolutionary history unfolded the way it did, and led to the kind of creatures we are, with the moral psychology we have. This moral psychology, in interaction with dynamic social environments, is the ultimate source of our moral values, but that does not make those values arbitrary. We have the sort of moral psychology we have for very good reasons. It developed the way it did because this enabled us to respond effectively to the individual and social challenges that we actually had to meet. This resulted in a moral grammar common to all humans, which finds diverse expression in diverse environments. This is not an arbitrary result, any more than the fact that humans are bipedal is an arbitrary result. Of course, it was not necessary that hominid evolution produced bipeds, but it did, and for reasons that make good evolutionary sense.

Given that our evolved moral grammar finds diverse expressions in response to differing social environments, it can be said that there is something conventional about those expressions. All cultures need to find a way to establish reliable systems of reciprocation and of discouraging defection and cheating, but how this is done is an expression of that culture's history, and this may be said to be conventional – on one level. However, what lies beneath that conventional system is a shared moral grammar that allows for the possibility of real communication and understanding of moral differences. We gain insight into the moral conventions of another culture by recognizing that, ultimately, that culture's moral system is trying to do something very similar to our moral system – and those deeper moral goals are not mere conventions or human concoctions.

Haught seems to be concerned that if moral systems are merely conventional then we have no good reason to be attached to them. But that is not necessarily so. I can recognize that my moral values are conventional expressions of a deeper moral grammar but still be attached to them – not out of chauvinism but out of an appreciation of how successfully those conventions serve deeper moral goals. It also follows that my particular moral convention may not function well, or not as well as some other convention. An open-minded individual will have to accept that his or her moral conventions may need revision. In this sense, a moral value will not be absolutely binding, on the level of conventional expression. But if we understand that morality, too, has a history, why would we expect any value to be absolutely binding? Still, "not absolutely binding" does not mean "arbitrary." An evolutionary account of morality leads to a view of morality that is always open to investigation and revision, not because morality is arbitrary but because the social environment in which those values function is dynamic. Morality, to fulfill its function of promoting social cohesion and individual striving, must be responsive to the particularities of its social environment. I want to return to this discussion, but let me say here that this does not lead to the moral relativism that Haught and others fear (and appropriately so) but rather to moral pragmatism.

What remains of Haught's critique is the question that, if moral values are the product of contingent, dynamic processes and do not deserve absolute commitment, then how can it be that so many individuals, even the skeptics, experience their moral convictions with such a sense of certitude? His answer is that this can be only because they tap into a "mode of being, a realm of rightness that does not owe its existence to human invention, Darwinian selection, or social construction."[22] This is an unjustified inference: Since evolution is contingent and yet I experience something absolute, its source cannot be evolution; hence, there must be a realm of being beyond the workings of evolution. This does not follow – a sense of absolute certitude may simply be unjustified. Just because I experience something does not mean that that experience is an accurate reflection of reality. This is supported by numerous common experiences of any reflective person. For example, one may be so in love that he or she feels – with certitude – that he or she will always feel this way, but we know this is not always true; the one who is so hurt by lost love that he or she feels – with certitude – that he or she will never love again is, fortunately, often mistaken.

In each of these cases a person judges something to be absolutely true because that person *feels* that certitude in a very powerful way. The judgments stem from affective states – and these affective states are products of our evolved psychology. We saw in Chapter 1 that emotions play important roles in commitment situations. It is vital that we can signal our commitments in a way that is convincing to others, and one of the best ways to convince others is to be convinced ourselves. Complete confidence in what we believe is often a valuable component of successful action. That humans so often feel unjustified certitude does not challenge an evolutionary understanding of psychology; it follows from it.

This is all the more obvious in terms of moral psychology. Morality touches on such crucial human needs, and taps into such ancient cognitive/ emotional tools, that moral judgments possess great power to convince us of their truth – they must if they are to be effective. It is not moral certitude that needs explaining, but moral skepticism. That is the phenomenon that strains against our evolutionary heritage: the willingness to consider, in a real way, that I might be wrong. Moral doubt requires me to step back from my moral intuitions and reflect on them, to develop a rational justification that may conflict with my emotional reactions, but moral intuitions lead to quick and decisive judgments, to a sense of certitude.

An evolutionary account of morality can explain why we have the moral grammar that we do, and it can justify that moral grammar as a nonarbitrary response to the challenges of human existence. It can also give an account of why moral judgments are pronounced with such certitude and felt to be so binding. An evolutionary account of morality does not require an eternal grounding in order to justify moral judgments, and does not need a religious worldview in order to make sense of them. On the other hand, an evolutionary account does not allow us to treat our moral values as absolute truths, nor does it allow us to see our particular moral system as absolutely binding. This raises the specter of moral relativism and the fear that without God, all is permitted, but this does not follow necessarily from an evolutionary account. In fact, an evolutionary account of morality, while it does deny us the comfort of moral certitude, actually allows us an insight into morality that may open the door to true moral progress.

We now can turn to the practical implications of this study of evolved morality and consider what an evolutionary interpretation of religion says about the continuing role of religion in moral issues.

Religion, Ethics, and Violence: An Assessment

The bond between religion and morality that is so readily asserted, or implicitly endorsed, receives confirmation by the evolutionary analysis presented in this book, but the nature of this bond is not what many take it to be. There is an interaction between our evolved cognitive moral frameworks and our evolved cognitive religious frameworks that makes this connection intuitively compelling, but this connection is not a necessary one. Our moral intuitions do not stem from nor are they dependent upon religion for their justification or their motivation, and the moral overtones so associated with religious beliefs need not have a divine source.

Furthermore, the connection between religion and violence, which so many seek to deny or minimize, is also confirmed by an evolutionary analysis. The apologetic move of characterizing violence done in the name of religion as an abuse of intrinsically peaceful belief systems is undermined by an evolutionary understanding of the moral psychology embedded in religion that gives rise to both pro-social moral behavior and violence against those identified as out-group members or defectors from the religious in-group.

It is time to reflect on these findings and consider what they may tell us about the continuing role of religion, in terms of morality and violence.

In the previous section I argued that this evolutionary understanding of religious moral traditions rules out any religion justly claiming a privileged status for its moral teachings. The United States went through a phase recently (although I am afraid it was not just a phase) where it was suggested that the Ten Commandments be recognized as the foundation of its moral and legal system and that posting the commandments in courthouses was an important measure to promote justice in the land. Constitutional arguments aside (and ignoring the question of just which Ten Commandments constituted *the* Ten Commandments), from the analysis presented here we can see just how weak an argument this is. The Ten Commandments are the product of an ancient Jewish community's attempt to give expression to an underlying moral psychology, designed to promote group cohesion and individual strivings, in a way that fit the social environment of that community. Whatever continuing value the Ten Commandments have (other than being a record of a successful attempt at community building – one of many we have access to) depends on the degree to which their formulation of those more fundamental moral concerns continues to serve the functions of community building and personal striving.

As we saw, many of the Commandments – for example, you shall not kill; you shall not steal – express in very straightforward terms moral values that are found in cultures throughout the world, and there is nothing of particular value in their Biblical formulations. The Commandments that do express values more specific to that Biblical code – for example, I am the Lord, thy God, you shall have no other gods before me; remember the Sabbath – served as signals of commitment to that ancient Jewish community. These are inappropriate in a society such as the United States; not because there is anything intrinsically wrong with them – they served their purpose well – but because they no longer fit the social environment we live in today. In a pluralistic society such as ours, these signals of commitment are too particularistic to function effectively. Since the Ten Commandments possess no intrinsic superiority as a moral code, they can make no claim to a special status. The only basis on which one can claim the Ten Commandments deserve special moral status is that they continue to function as effective signals of commitment to bind together a moral community and that they provide distinctive moral guidelines to promote social cohesion and individual strivings in the social environment that exists today. And I would argue those claims fail.

This argument is not limited to an evaluation of the Ten Commandments but holds for all religious codes. Since no religious moral tradition can claim special status, the *only* basis for according a religious moral value any normative status in the public sphere is to argue that it continues to promote social cohesion and individual flourishing. This is what I meant by moral pragmatism, an approach captured by Jesus' saying, "By their fruits you will know them."

By advocating pragmatism as the appropriate method of moral judgment I recognize that I am wading into turbulent philosophical waters. I cannot, at this point and in this venue, hope to provide a defense of this move sufficient to the philosophical issues involved (although I have tested those waters before[23]), but I believe that some discussion is called for. In terms of developing a pragmatic moral method I find it best set out in the writings of the great American philosopher John Dewey.

Born in 1859, the year of Darwin's grand entrance onto the world scene, Dewey grew up in an intellectual world abuzz with debates and controversies surrounding the new evolutionary paradigm. He came to embrace Darwinism, recognizing its profound implications for philosophy and the study of human existence. Darwin's great contribution was to extend this fundamental scientific insight that we live in a dynamic universe to the living world: "[T]he influence of Darwin upon philosophy resides in his having conquered the phenomena of life for the principle of transition, and thereby freed the new logic for application to mind and morals and life."[24] Dewey recognized this opened up the way to a true science of the mind and a reformulation of morality – in effect, an evolutionary psychology and evolutionary ethics.

In terms of morality, the significance of the Darwinian revolution is that moral values can no longer be treated as eternal truths, existing somewhere beyond human experience, but rather are products of human strivings to create a worthwhile life as social beings in a natural world that provides both opportunities and dangers, and that is intrinsically dynamic. As the contours of the social environment change, these values may be challenged. New situations can create new dilemmas to which the traditional answers may no longer apply. If we understand morality as a response to the demands of social living, then we recognize that moral traditions are not expressions of eternal truths but records of past attempts to negotiate the needs of individuals and the needs of the group at particular points in our history. As I have pointed out, consistent with Dewey, this does not deny that these traditions have continuing worth as examples of successful negotiations (they must have had sufficient success to survive long enough to become a tradition). However, traditions are about the past, what has worked; moral judgments are about the future – how we will act, how we will structure our communities. Dewey captures this succinctly: "[T]he thing actually at stake in any serious deliberation is ... what kind of self is in the making, what kind of world is in the making."[25]

Such an understanding of morality has been criticized as an invitation to moral relativism or, worse moral chaos – "all is permitted." Dewey rejects this as a symptom of the anxiety produced by letting go of fixed answers, and the (false) security they provide. Humans resisted this move in relation to our knowledge of the physical world, but once we adapted ourselves to a dynamic universe and an empirical approach to knowledge of that world, we initiated a revolution in our understanding and control of nature. Dewey sees the same potential for progress in our understanding of human behavior and in our relations to each other, in steeling ourselves to let go of eternal, fixed morals and to embrace a more dynamic, pragmatic approach.[26]

Moral chaos will not follow because this method does not lead to a wholesale abandonment of moral tradition. Despite the dynamic nature of the universe, and the changing social environments we need to adapt to, these changes are not wholesale, and often not dramatic. Even when dramatic changes occur there are always constants. We will still need to negotiate the sometimes conflicting, but often complementary goals of individual good and social good. Moral traditions provide valuable resources for this task and will continue to exert an influence on our moral judgments. Dewey certainly believed this to be the case, even without the benefit of cognitive science's understanding of human psychology – which has revealed a conservative tendency built into human psychology (e.g., frequency-biased cultural transmission). The problem then is not one of moral chaos but of moral stagnation – which may explain why it is often only major shifts in the social environment that occasion the rise of novel moral systems, and even then there is continuity as well as innovation.

We saw evidence of this in our analysis of the development of Christianity out of its Judaic soil. Even with the rise of a new moral tradition, much of the older tradition was preserved. In both the Antitheses and in his reformulation of the Ten Commandments, Jesus did not so much reject the moral tradition of Judaism as rework it to fit the needs of a new community.

Even in periods of moral innovation there is a good deal of conservation of the past.

In fact, this example of Jesus' moral innovation can be seen as pragmatism at work. Jesus, or the early Christian communities that produced these stories, recognized the social world had changed (more accurately, that part of the social world most relevant to the early Christian communities) and that the old law – the Old Testament – no longer adequately served the community's needs. He developed a reconstructed moral system, to use Dewey's concept,[27] by dropping those rules and practices that no longer served their moral function but holding on to those that did, and represented them in a way more fitting to the new social realities. In fact, the case can be made that this is just what the early Hebrew community did as it struggled to thrive in a world where the older moral traditions no longer served, and it is what Mohammed, or the early Muslim communities that produced the texts of Islam, did in response to the changed social environments of seventh- and eighth-century Arabia.

In suggesting a pragmatic approach to religious moral traditions I am not proposing something radically new. Rather, I am advocating that we consciously adapt a procedure that has been at work throughout human history. Specifically, I am urging that we recognize that religious moral values have only contingent value, that their value stems directly and wholly from their positive contributions to self-making and world-making. Now, because of their record of success, the potential of religious values to contribute to these moral goals should not be underestimated, but they can no longer be granted normative force simply because they are embedded in a religious tradition or a "sacred" text. Supporting an argument by grounding it in the Torah, or Gospels, or Qur'an, can no longer carry decisive moral weight, in and of itself; these texts gain significance only as elements of a larger argument that a value will contribute to human flourishing.

We live in a time when the social environment is undergoing significant change. The "new world order" that was supposedly emerging after the fall of the Iron Curtain already seems an antiquated notion; information and communication technology has, in less than a generation, revolutionized the way we interact with each other and access information; the fear of nuclear war between the superpowers has morphed into a less predictable and perhaps more dangerous threat of nuclear terrorism, supplemented by fears of bio-chemical and cyber-terrorism. The globalization of our planet, which brings with it great opportunities, is creating such an integrated web that problems of social injustice, economic deprivation, and human rights abuses in distant parts of the world resonate at home, as well.

In other words, we are living in the midst of one of those periods of dramatic social change that strain the effectiveness of traditional responses. Dewey teaches us that we are, therefore, in the midst of moral reconstruction. The question before us is whether we will participate in this change in an intelligent way, making use of the best information available for understanding human behavior and morality, or whether we will trust our fortunes and our futures to the workings of forces we choose not to control (to the degree that they can be controlled, of course).

How to understand, much less respond to, the great challenges facing us goes far beyond the capability of any work or author. This much is obvious. An adequate response calls for the efforts of a much larger community and, clearly, not just a scholarly community. But we each must do what we can. Religion, for better or worse – or more accurately, for better *and* worse – plays a major role in the events facing us, and so one part of the response must be an evaluation of the role religion plays or can play in the problems and in the possible solutions.

Religious violence is a significant danger. From the analysis presented here we can see that "religious violence" really is about religion, even if not exclusively. Religion is almost always mixed with other factors, such as politics, economics, and social injustice, and it is not always possible to determine which factor or combination of factors is primary. But this does not mitigate the causal force of religious beliefs, for religion is intimately involved with all these other factors. The point of connecting religion with the violence done in its name is not to demonize religion or to minimize other factors, but to counter apologetic treatments that would marginalize religion in our assessment of these destructive acts. Such views can blind us to the full power of religious symbols and rhetoric to motivate human behavior.

Of course, there are those who clearly see the religious aspect of so much of the violence and hatred in the world, and thus are moved to take a stand against religion, per se. This is an attitude that animates the works of the "new atheists," who assert a moral urgency in the critique of religion. On this point I am in complete agreement with them: There is a moral urgency in our need to respond to religious violence (and, of course, to all violence) and a critical evaluation of religious claims is part of that work. However, we just as urgently need to avoid knee-jerk reactions and sloppy analysis. Countering extreme expressions of religious fervor with equally extreme expressions of secular fervor gets us nowhere, and in fact makes matters worse. When an influential author such as Christopher Hitchens subtitles his book "How Religion Poisons Everything," we have moved into the sphere of a secular fundamentalism that is no more justifiable than religious fundamentalism. Hitchens's work shows little concern with truly understanding religion, in all its complexity and diversity, and seems satisfied with over-generalizations that would not be accepted in an introductory logic class. This is not the way to promote reason and intellectual inquiry.

Sam Harris presents a more reasonable, though still extreme, approach, but also treats religion on a relatively superficial level. He writes, "Religious violence is still with us because our religions are *intrinsically* hostile to one another."[28] Which religions? one may ask. Is Buddhism *intrinsically* hostile to Christianity? And which variant of which religion? Are Unitarian Universalists *intrinsically* hostile to those of the Baha'i faith? And what does it mean to be *intrinsically* hostile? In once sense, what Harris seems to be getting at is the hostility that so often erupts between members of different religious sects springs from something inherent in those traditions and is not simply a corruption of those traditions. And in this, he is correct. But to go from "there is a source of violence inherent in religious psychology" to "religions are intrinsically hostile" is an unjustified leap in logic. And again, it does no good for the heralds of reason to reason poorly, and not simply for the sake of good reasoning. This kind of facile over-generalization does not allow us to formulate an effective response to what is a serious problem. What is it about religions that generate violence? It is not just that they are religions. Harris does provide a somewhat more specific answer. He says, "[I]f religious war is ever to become unthinkable for us ... it will be a matter of our having dispensed with the dogma of faith."[29]

So, the problem is not "religion" but "faith," which for Harris is the essence of religion.[30] For Harris "faith" indicates a certitude of belief inconsistent with the evidence for that belief. John Haught, however, denies this is what "faith" means. I am going to leave aside the problems with this formulation and the theological debates over just what "faith" means. However we define the word, the phenomenon Harris targets – belief on insufficient evidence – is a real phenomenon, not restricted to religious belief but common to religious belief – and I am in complete agreement with Harris that it is a serious social and moral concern. But what of Harris's suggestion that the way to address this concern is to "dispense" with religion, that to get rid of religious violence, we must get rid of religion? Well, clearly, if there were no religions, then by definition there could be no religious violence. However, that would be an improvement only if it leads to a decline in violence, rather than merely a re-categorizing of that violence. But would that be the case? This raises the question of the conditions that lead to both religious faith and religious violence, the central themes of this book.

In a sense, what Harris and others, and not just secular extremists, are pondering is whether we would be better off without religion This is an understandable response to the many problems that stem from religion in the modern world, but it is not a well-formed question. What would constitute a world without religion? Would a world without churches or temples suffice? No more organized traditions or sacred texts? But these, we must recognize, are expressions of a deeper religious impulse. We have seen that efforts to eliminate religion – think of Russia during its communist period – may prove temporarily effective, but once those efforts cease the religious impulse flourishes again – think of post-communist Russia. Eliminating the public, outward signs of religion is not the same thing as eliminating religion.

And furthermore, even if we could eliminate religion, would that be an unqualified good? A key position of this book is that religion has played an important role in sustaining social cohesion and answering personal needs. What would be the consequences of doing without it? If we consider a hypothetical situation in which the wildest dreams of the "new atheists" came true, that humans came to see the illusory promises of religion for the illusions they are, to recognize the weakness of its claims, and to turn away from all such systems, what would such a world look like? Would it be a better world, one that allowed humans, embracing reason instead of "faith," to fulfill their potential, while living in just and stable communities? (And if the desire to rid the world of religion is not meant to move us toward such a world, then what value does it have?) It is, of course, impossible to answer these questions with any degree of confidence. However, our evolutionary analysis of morality and religion does offer some insight into the issue.

The picture of the human mind emerging from the cognitive sciences is one in which cognitive and emotional predispositions are the source of most of our interpretations of, and responses to, the world. What we traditionally think of as rational thought comes into play when these cognitive/emotional intuitions clash (reason then works to resolve the conflict) or when these intuitions are challenged, either by others with differing intuitions or by our encountering novel aspects of the environment (reason then either provides justification of our intuitions or reworks those intuitions to accommodate the novel situation). But for the most part, it seems that what we refer to as rational thought is, as James put it, merely "rearranging our prejudices" – and this holds just as well for the most hard-headed atheist as it does for the most soft-hearted believer (to again borrow James's phrasing).

If we could somehow dispense with religion, even hypothetically, there is no reason to believe that we would then become more rational thinkers, because it is not religion that makes us so susceptible to belief without sufficient evidence – that is a consequence of having the kind of minds that we do. Returning again to our early history as a species, that environment favored those who could make quick, satisficing judgments about what to do, not those who would ponder all the available evidence, draw out the various possibilities, weigh the options carefully, and then decide. Quick, decisive action means making judgments even without sufficient evidence – and we must recognize that these decisions are often successful. We do not always have to wait for all the evidence to come in for us to know what to do, and this is as true today as it must have been throughout our evolutionary history. So, it is not religion that makes us susceptible to belief without sufficient evidence; it is our pre-disposition to believe without sufficient evidence that makes us susceptible to religion. Getting rid of religion would not change that (although it might eliminate a major source of such beliefs).

Nevertheless, our evolutionary environment did not always demand a quick response. The dynamic nature of that world also presented novel situations that required a more deliberate approach, and so we do have the faculties for critical judgment, as well. We have the potential to be more thoughtful, more reasoned, in our thinking. If we developed this faculty, would that not undermine the pull "faith" has, and perhaps create the conditions under which religious belief would "wither" away? At the beginning of the twentieth century there were many who thought that just such a process was not only possible but under way, that we were approaching the end of religious belief and the dawning of a more thorough secularization of society, at least in the West. At the dawn of the twenty-first century we can see just how mistaken those predictions were. Instead of withering away, religion has become more robust and taken a more prominent role on the world stage, often dramatically and, sadly, too often violently. Why were those predictions so wrong?

This is a complex question, and theorists from a variety of disciplines will have much to say, but I believe that part of the answer is a lack of understanding of our evolved religious psychology. Religion derives from cognitive tools that are important parts of the mind's strategy for interpreting and classifying the world. Furthermore, religious systems tap into deeply ingrained psychological and moral intuitions, and thus are subjectively experienced as compelling. These cognitive tools that underlie and nourish religion are part of our psychological makeup and cannot be argued away.

It is, of course, possible for individuals to develop a worldview that rejects religious belief. It is possible to create the conditions that forestall the development of religious interpretations of experience or that weaken the powerful emotional force religion so often generates.[31] One can live a purely secular life (which is not the same thing as a purely rational life, although deliberate reasoning will likely have to play a more significant role than it typically does). A non-religious life is an option for humans, and an option that brings with it all the possibilities for moral commitment and meaning others find in a religious existence. This is not in question. Rather, the question is one of scale, of extent. Can a secular life ever become the preferred alternative for humans on a large scale?

Given the ingrained mental and emotional pre-dispositions that are entwined with religion; given that religions have shaped, and been shaped by, the cultural landscape for thousands of years, becoming an integral, often implicit component of human culture; given the precarious, uncertain, and anxiety-provoking environment we continue to inhabit (just the sort of environment to prime those psychological mechanisms that underlie religious beliefs); and given the relative weakness of deliberate reasoning in comparison to emotionally laden, quick, intuitive judgments (which are responsive to systems, like religion, that are designed to trigger these judgments), it seems that religion, in some form or another, will continue to be a central part of life, for a great part of humanity.[32]

So, for better and worse, religion is here to stay. The issue then is not whether to dispense with religion or not. Instead, the question is, Given religion, is it possible to create conditions that trigger those individually rewarding, pro-social expressions, while minimizing the conditions that give rise to religion's more lethal side? For humanity's sake, we must hope so. And so we reach the final issue: What can our understanding of our evolved moral and religious psychology contribute to this project?[33]

Responding to Religion, Ethics, and Violence: Some Proposals

One aspect of religious psychology implicated in religious violence is the sense of certitude that accompanies belief. When that certitude extends to moral beliefs, disputes are readily perceived in black and white terms. From this perspective, moral ambiguity, which is part of a thoughtful analysis of human affairs, is washed away by the certitude imparted by being on God's side. John Collins argues that the Bible has "contributed to violence in the world precisely because it has been taken to confer a degree of certitude that transcends human discussion and argumentation."[34] This is the religious expression that so incenses Harris, and rightfully so. To "know" you are right is to cut off from the start any possibility of a reasonable resolution. The only "reasonable" response in the face of an obviously wrong and possibly evil position is to combat it – forcefully and relentlessly.

To counter the dangers of certitude we must stimulate critical thinking. Despite the secondary status of reason compared with emotionally colored intuitions, it can be an effective force in human affairs – but it needs to be fostered and nurtured. Working with Haidt's insights, we have identified two conditions that trigger a more reflective cognitive response: when our intuitions conflict and when we are called to justify them to others who do not share them. So, one strategy to counter the certitude of religious intuitions is to introduce competing intuitions, and there are at least two ways to do this.

One method is already in practice in many areas: Introduce people to alternative religious worldviews in a manner that treats all the alternatives as viable expressions of humanity's religious impulse. The more an individual comes to appreciate another religion as a legitimate option for decent human beings, rather than as some foreign system embraced by the "other," the less likely that person is to dismiss other viewpoints. Whether intended or not, this is the moral benefit of introducing children to world religions at an early age, before their religious tradition becomes for them the only legitimate worldview. By exposing children to diversity we provide them with the mental tools that work against certitude and prejudice.

Of course, some parents oppose such religious education on the very grounds that it can lead children to grow up thinking that all religions are equally valid. But we should be very wary of those who want children to grow up thinking that any one religion is the only true religion; such an attitude is a major ingredient in religious violence.

Another way to counter the certitude of religious belief is to subject those beliefs to critical examination. To foster a discussion of religion, not from a confessional perspective but from a critical perspective, is a step toward a more civil public discourse on religion and on issues important to religious traditions. This is where Harris et al. can play a valuable role. The impressive popular success of the "new atheists" is a telling sign that there is receptivity to a critical evaluation of religious claims. It is not clear how much of their audience was already disposed to hear a critique of religion or how much of their success is a "preaching to the choir" phenomenon. My sense is that this is certainly part of their success but that there is a sizable and growing portion of the population open to a more critical discussion of religion. While all the polls show Americans remain among the most religious people in the industrialized world, they also show that the way in which religion is lived is moving away from traditional forms. There is a greater openness to explore various religious expressions, and even secular alternatives to religion, such as humanist groups and ethical culture societies.

This indicates that the groundwork is there to establish a public, critical discussion of religion. This is a much needed antidote to the often extreme, unquestioning, and unquestioned stream of religious pronouncements that flow regularly from so many popular television and radio religious figures, and not a few political leaders. We need a critical context in which such pronouncements can be assessed and judged. This is a concern not only for the non-religious but for the vast number of religious believers who cannot relate to what passes as religious discourse in this country. This is where the work of the "new atheists" could have played a constructive social role, but I fear they have squandered much of that opportunity.

I do believe that the "new atheists" have made a contribution by putting religious criticism back on the public radar, and I am in sympathy with a great deal of what they have to say. Their criticism of some very influential and popular forms of religious traditions is well taken. Religion often plays a very negative role in the modern world: It can impede scientific and medical progress, and it can have an adverse impact on a wide range of social and political issues. I also agree with Richard Dawkins that religious belief and values are accorded an undeserved degree of respect in public discourse and that religious sensitivity to criticism is treated with excessive deference.[35] This is done in the name of religious tolerance, of course. However, in shutting down public criticism of religion we cut ourselves off from one of the sources available for engaging our rational faculties, and leave the field to ancient moral biases. The "new atheists" understand this point, and it is, I believe, what animates their work. This is a morally laudable goal and I am happy to join them in its pursuit.

My problem with their analysis – and this is where they squander their opportunity to make a real contribution to public discourse – is that the conception of religion they work with is too thin. They tend to take one version of religious expression, and a more extreme, inflexible version, and treat that as if it were "religion" itself. Their critiques lack the nuance and the critical study that the subject requires. As Jonathan Haidt puts it, "When I read the New Atheist books ... I see battlefields strewn with the corpses of straw men."[36] Now, the version of religion they target is a real phenomenon, and one that is the source of significant social challenges. It needs to be addressed. But the manner in which this is done, by its crude reduction of the religious impulse to this extreme version, becomes offensive to many religiously oriented individuals who do not practice such an extreme religious tradition. In fact, it becomes offensive to even those who are not religiously inclined. My experience in teaching and speaking on these issues has brought home to me that even those who might otherwise be receptive to the content of their arguments are turned off by the uncivil tone of their rhetoric. This uncivil tone may cause more damage than their critical arguments do good, and an understanding of our evolved psychology makes this evident.

One of the effects of the "new atheists" is to promote an in-group/out-group mentality. Their rhetoric is so divisive, their moral vision so clear, and the urgency of the problem so great that they threaten to re-create in secular terms the conditions that underlie religious violence. We can see this in Harris, for example. In the following passage he argues against religious moderates:

> I have written elsewhere about the problem I see with religious liberalism and religious moderation. Here, we need only observe that the issue is both simpler and more urgent than liberals and moderates generally admit. Either the Bible is just an ordinary book, written by mortals, or it isn't. ... If the Bible is an ordinary book, and Christ an ordinary man, the basic doctrine of Christianity is false. ... If the basic tenets of Christianity are true, then there

are some very grim surprises in store for nonbelievers like myself. ... So let us be honest with ourselves: in the fullness of time, one side is really going to win this argument, and one side is going to lose.[37]

We should be able to recognize in this passage the dichotomous thinking that we identified as a major aspect of our evolved moral psychology. This psychology underlies secular as well as religious worldviews, and here we see it in Harris. In the end, there are winners and losers. Either Jesus is divine and one side is right, or he is not and the other side is right. In extending his attack to moderates and liberals, Harris is denying that there is any middle position, or neutral side. You are on the side of reason or the side of religious fanaticism (by giving comfort to the enemy); you are either with us or against us. And just as we found when we looked at religious violence, the stakes of the battle have been raised to the highest levels: "religion poisons everything," "the end of faith and the future of reason."

The predisposition to divide the world into in- and out-groups is easily triggered. By explicitly dividing the world into the religious and non-religious, Harris et al. trigger this mechanism in their audience and force them to take sides. Am I on the side of reason or am I on the side of God? Given our understanding of how deeply embedded god-beliefs are within our moral psychology, to force this choice is to force one to choose between the relatively weak pull of rationality against the emotionally laden, deeply intuitive, morally colored beliefs associated with god. This will often be a losing battle. It need not be a losing battle, but by couching the terms of the issue in an either/or way, Harris moves the issue into an arena where the odds all favor religion. But there is no reason to make this move. It is not a battle between reason and superstition, between reality and delusion, between the religious and atheists. The world, and our psychology, is much more complicated than that, much richer than that.

The battle is between a reasoned, critical approach to the issues that face us as individuals and communities and an approach that leaves us prey to a psychology designed to function in a much different world. Granted, religious superstition and prejudice are serious social concerns – but this is not the whole of religion. Serious problems demand serious responses, and this means not giving in to the natural and emotionally satisfying tendency to give voice to our own moral prejudices. An effective critique of religion, and the development of an effective response to its dangerous expressions, must work with a more nuanced reading of religion, and a more empirically grounded understanding of the religious mind, that avoids an unjustified division of the world into opposing camps.

Clearly, this is what animates my evaluation of religion. My deepest hope for this book is that it will, to some small degree, move the critical evaluation of religion out of the arena of in-group/out-group rhetoric and provide some insight into the moral psychology that informs these issues and so allow for a more effective response. To develop this response we need to keep in mind how religion works, for better and worse.

On the pro-social side of the ledger, religious morality has functioned to extend the force of our moral sense to a larger and more complex society. It gives shape to our moral psychology and imbues that moral sense with a feeling of intuitive "rightness" that can make moral claims compelling. It has helped to sustain the conditions that allowed the development of a deep and powerful altruistic tendency in beings comprised of ultimately "selfish genes." It has nurtured our sense of belonging to a reality larger than ourselves and of a connection to our fellow beings that gives to our existence the possibility of meaning and purpose that are among life's most rewarding qualities. Now, none of these achievements requires religion, but religion has contributed significantly to these moral accomplishments, and continues to contribute to them.[38]

The tragic flaw in religious moral psychology begins with drawing a boundary around the group, setting it apart from the other. This creation of a boundary line was essential to creating a sense of communal identity and marking out the extent of moral obligation, but doing so also sets the limit of moral obligation – and it is this moral divide that creates the conditions for religious violence. Creating this divide is not unique to religion; it is a basic cognitive strategy for beings like ourselves who in order to succeed in evolutionary terms needed to discern clearly who to trust and who not to trust, who is in and who is out. It has its roots deep in our moral psychology, and in ways both large and small shapes our moral response to the world. Religion, however, serves as an amplification device for this mental tool. By connecting the in-group with a divine judge and enforcer, and by raising the stakes for being on the right side of that divide, religion – at least monotheistic religion – has imbued this divide with deadly power. These two aspects – setting a moral boundary around an in-group and raising the stakes – are recognized by scholars to be common to religious violence. To address religious violence we must devise ways to counter these.

In his important study, *Terror in the Mind of God*, Mark Juergensmeyer notes that in almost all of the incidents of religious violence he has studied, "the script of cosmic war is central."[39] A key element in elevating a conflict to cosmic levels comes from seeing it through a religious lens:

> When a struggle becomes sacralized, incidents that might previously have been considered minor skirmishes ... are elevated to monumental proportions. The use of violence becomes legitimized. ... What had been simple opponents become cosmic foes. ... the process of satanization can transform a worldly struggle into a contest between martyrs and demons.[40]

In cosmic war, you are either on the side of good or on the side of evil, and this clears the path for what Marc Shell calls the "barbarism of universalism"[41] – a means of negating the very humanity of those in the out-group. To counter the conditions that generate religious violence we need to understand what contributes to the escalation of conflict to such fervent levels.

Important work is being done on this topic by Scott Atran. We met Atran earlier as a key player in developing an evolutionary understanding of religion. He is also working to apply the insights provided by the behavioral sciences, including cognitive and evolutionary psychology, to the phenomenon of suicide terrorism. To defend ourselves against this particularly deadly manifestation of religious violence we need to understand the social and psychological conditions that support it – and this is a weak point in current responses to terrorism. Atran points out that some popular characterizations of suicide terrorists, shared by many in the U.S. government, as "evil" individuals, uneducated and impoverished, is not supported by the evidence.[42]

In fact, studies show that suicide bombers tend to be relatively educated and economically stable in comparison to the general population of their communities. Such individuals seem to be motivated by a sense of "relative deprivation," in which political and social conditions "produce diminishing opportunities relative to expectations, thus generating frustrations that radical organizations can exploit."[43] It is frustration with thwarted opportunities for social and personal movement, often the result of living in depressed environments or oppressive societies, that creates the conditions that lead individuals to be open to terrorist organizations.[44]

Atran argues that to understand how this frustration is turned into deadly action we need to attend to the institutional aspects of suicide terrorism, how it is that terrorist institutions convince stable, educated individuals to turn themselves into walking bombs, willing to kill not only themselves but scores of other humans. They accomplish this by tapping into our evolved psychology. The preparation for suicide missions often begins by forming recruits into small, closely knit groups, creating a "family of cellmates ... willing to sacrifice for one another as a parent for a child." This taps into the psychology of kinship to foster a willingness to give all for a "fictive brotherhood."[45]

We have considered ways in which groups motivate individuals to override their evolved instinct for self-preservation through various forms of indirect reciprocity, moving people to sacrifice for the good of the group in order to promote their inclusive fitness via benefits, direct or indirect, to their extended kin. These methods succeed in getting individuals to commit to socially necessary, although personally dangerous projects. The same psychological strategies that societies use to get individuals to become police officers, firefighters, and soldiers can be manipulated to get individuals to blow themselves up for the good of the community.

But despite this effective manipulation of our evolved moral psychology, Atran argues, "religion may also be needed."[46] Consistent with the view of religion set out in this book, Atran points out that with religious terrorism the sacred values embedded in all religions are "manipulated ... for the organization's benefit at the expense of the individual."[47] And by introducing a "sacred" aspect into a conflict, the terms of that conflict are altered.

A study by Atran and colleagues provides suggestive evidence that a conflict seen as involving sacred values, as opposed to secular ones, changes the reasoning used to assess the possible resolutions. In a secular conflict over land, for example, instrumental reasoning may lead one side to be willing to concede in exchange for financial compensation. But when that conflict is seen in sacred terms – as a conflict over "holy land" – instrumental attempts to resolve the dispute actually increase the intensity of the conflict. They tested this with a survey of those embroiled in the Israeli-Palestinian conflict, which many on both sides see in sacred terms. Their research supported the hypothesis that people "would react with outrage and support violent opposition to any attempt at compromise over sacred values for instrumental reasons."[48] And this should make sense to us now.

Something having "sacred" value taps into all the emotional and cognitive predispositions that constitute our religious moral psychology. These give support to the bonds of society and the sense of purpose we get from having our good intertwined with that of the group. Strong emotional reactions, such as moral outrage, signal our commitment to the group in which we seek our good, and serve to over-ride rational calculations of self-interest. The offer to give up what is sacred is an offer to defect from the moral bonds of society. Being perceived by others in my group as willing to break my commitment undermines my reputation and threatens to cast me into the out-group. We have seen how evolution has designed us to be very sensitive to such situations.

So, another lesson of an evolutionary study of religion and morality is that to treat religiously tinged issues as if they were mere disagreements over the terms of a deal to be settled by rational compromise is to completely misread what is going on, and may indeed instigate a violent response. In this regard it is significant to note that Atran et al. did find that compromise in sacred disputes is possible. While "instrumental benefits increased opposition to compromises over sacred values, we found that opposition decreased when the deal included the adversary making a symbolic compromise over one of their own sacred values."[49]

Compromise between adversaries makes sense only when each side feels it is receiving something of comparable value for its sacrifice or that their opponent's sacrifice is of comparable value. Mere material compensation cannot be comparable to something with sacred value, and to suggest as much is insulting. Insults to our reputation, as an individual or a group, are serious threats to our future well-being. They cannot be tolerated. But if the exchange is conducted on a sacred level by both sides, insult is avoided, as is the need to use violence to protect the integrity of one's reputation.

In considering the apparently intractable nature of the Israeli-Palestinian conflict, it has been suggested that this is a prime example of how religion contributes to violence and hatred – and I believe this is correct (without suggesting that religion is the sole or primary culprit). The religious coloring of this conflict changes the nature of the problem, and does indeed make resolution more difficult as it raises the stakes and taps into powerful, emotional dispositions not readily susceptible to rational arbitration. In an ideal world it would be wonderful to strip away the religious fervor of this conflict by getting those involved to see through the unfounded pretensions of their religion's claims. But we do not live in an ideal world. The world we live in is one in which we need to take into account the psychological mechanisms underlying religion if we hope to resolve such conflicts – or as Atran puts it, if we want to stop this deadly use of religious devotion, we need to study the "configurations of psychological and cultural relationships" that lure "mostly ordinary people into the terrorist organization's martyr-making web."[50]

The work of Scott Atran provides a valuable insight: If we want to combat religious violence we need to recognize the role religion plays in triggering deeply ingrained moral and emotional responses, the ways in which religion changes the very nature of a conflict.

Religious values are embedded in a moral psychology that was designed to contribute to our inclusive fitness. This is so central to evolutionary success that we have powerful emotional predispositions that serve to promote this goal. Threats to our religious values trigger these deep emotional reactions and contribute to the sense of urgency and inflexibility that characterize so much religious violence. We need to recognize just what is at stake psychologically in a religious dispute if we are to have any hope of a peaceful resolution. Regardless of our sympathy or antipathy toward religion, we ignore religion's significance at our own peril. And to respond to religion without a sound understanding of how it shapes our behavior and our perceptions is morally irresponsible – for after all, it is not merely our own peril we risk.

The other key element in the structure of religious violence is the bifurcation of human beings into in-groups and out-groups, with the consequent moral differential that comes with it. This pronounced tendency in human nature – often implicit, unconscious; though sometimes conscious but rationalized – to treat those we identify as "us," as part of "our group," with greater moral sensitivity and leniency, while being less morally sensitive and more morally critical of the "other," of those not "one of us," amplified by the certitude and cosmic urgency supplied by a religious perspective, is implicated in much of the violence and hatred that mars our world.[51] Combating this moral prejudice is not only part of a response to religious violence, it must be part of the task in responding to violence in general. How might we counter this?

It might appear that the obvious move is to do away with all boundaries between groups – if no divide between in-group/out-group, then no moral prejudice against the out-group. But this raises questions. It is one thing to propose such a move, even to rationally justify it, and quite another to implement it. What we are talking about is a quest for moral universalism or moral egalitarianism, in which all are part of the moral in-group, and all are equal. Such moral goals are admirable, but we have seen how difficult they are to actualize. When we examined the example of Christian universalism we discovered the insidious in-group/out-group divide lurking deep within that system; and Islam, which refused to cast Jews and Christians into a morally suspect out-group, nevertheless drew that moral boundary against all other faiths and non-faiths. In setting this boundary, however broadly it was drawn, both "universal" religions set conditions that allow the demonization and moral devaluation of the "other" – those outside the bounds of universal moral concern. This is not simply a criticism of those religions – although it is that – but it also demonstrates the difficulty of formulating a truly universal moral community.[52]

Philosophical systems of ethics have also attempted to erase this moral boundary. Immanuel Kant identified rationality as the necessary and sufficient condition for moral agency and argued in a very persuasive manner for the absolute equality of all moral agents, and all moral obligations.[53] The Utilitarian school set sentience as the condition for moral concern, thereby placing all sentient beings on the same moral plane in terms of evaluating our obligations.[54] These are admirable attempts to erase the limiting conditions on moral concern, and I believe they have contributed to expanding our moral awareness, but they too face problems: In demanding a rational and impartial evaluation of moral dilemmas these systems strain too mightily against our evolved psychology.[55]

Our morality is a function of our moral sense, much more than it is of moral reasoning.[56] Moral reasoning is important but it gains its efficacy by tapping into this evolved moral sense. It is our moral sense that creates our sense of moral significance and supplies the feeling of obligation and duty. A hypothetical purely rational being might be proficient at determining a cost/benefit analysis but could not determine what factors have the moral worth to be entered into that calculation. Such a being would not be a recognizable moral being (as countless science fiction scenarios attest). To propose a moral system that demands we subjugate our moral sense to some rationalized conception of morality is to propose we start down a path that, if successful, would undermine our moral nature itself. We can be grateful that evolution has produced a psychology well guarded against such a possibility.

To develop a practicable response to religious violence, and the moral prejudices that generate it, we need to work with the constraints imposed by our evolved psychology.

As we have seen, these constraints are not absolute – we can stretch the conditions of our moral imagination – but neither are they absolutely flexible. Recognizing this is not to surrender to fatalism or to determinism, nor is it to deny the possibility of moral innovation, but we must work with realistic expectations of what innovation may accomplish.

The reasoned conclusions that all humans possess moral worth; that we are all members of one extended family (a lesson that evolution teaches as effectively as any religious tradition); that we should judge people on the "content of their character," rather than on any signal of group affiliation, are major moral accomplishments and the basis of a truly universal ethics. However, these are the results of critical reflection. The challenge is to transform them into embedded moral intuitions. But how is this to be done given our deep predispositions to group thinking? If the in-group/out-group divide triggers our moral sensitivity to others, do we weaken our moral sense if we eliminate that divide? Moral universalism advocates we see all humans as part of our group, and this is an important move in expanding the circle of our moral community – but can there be an in-group without an out-group? Philosophical attempts may be successful on theoretical grounds, but that is not what moves people. Attempts to neutralize this predisposition to group-thinking may require we snap our biological leash. I believe a much more promising strategy is to develop ways to extend it.

Our study of religious moral traditions attests to this. The history of these traditions shows the possibility of redefining the in-group, of extending the boundaries of the group. As environmental conditions change, threats and challenges change. This has an impact on what constitutes the in-group, and we instinctively understand this. A perhaps facetious, though telling, bit of evidence can be gleamed from science-fiction works. In every sci-fi show that treats an invasion of Earth from extra-terrestrials, the entire globe joins together into one community to confront the danger. This makes perfect sense to the audience, on an intuitive level. The alien invaders have redefined the boundaries of "us" and "them." Since "them" are the non-earthly invaders, "us" includes everyone on earth, regardless of previous affiliations along national or ethnic lines.

The question then is, Barring such a fortuitous invasion, how do we redefine the boundaries of the group? While we are not facing the threat of space aliens, we are in fact facing threats of a global nature, requiring a global response. The threat to the planet's environment is just one, but an important one. Focusing on the worldwide dangers posed by global warming and climate change should redefine the boundaries of the group. It threatens us all and can be met only by a worldwide response. However, I fear that the threat of environmental disaster seems too distant, too vague a threat to extend our sense of in-group (this despite the fact that the threat is not distant or vague). I believe, though this is just speculation at this point, that the conditions that might truly enlarge our sense of moral community must be something that triggers more basic psychological needs.

In this regard, the threat of terrorism fits the bill. The insecurity that is engendered by the fear that even the most innocuous daily activity may place one in mortal danger clearly touches humans in a very powerful way. The fact that terrorism respects no national, ethnic, or religious boundaries actually makes those boundaries less significant. If a sense of in-group moral identity requires an out-group other, terrorists may serve.

The problem here is that the rhetoric of both terrorists and the opponents of terrorists appropriate the language of group identity. Take for example the constant reference to "Islamic terrorism," on the one hand, and, on the other, of terrorists warning of the evils of "the West" and the West's "war on Islam." Such rhetoric perpetuates the perception that this is a battle between competing groups, and triggers all the moral biases that follow in the wake of such a perception. This may, however, point to a strategy for expanding our moral sense. Instead of waiting for conditions to arise that will trigger a response that can redefine our sense of our in-group, perhaps we can recast our interpretation of current events so as to mute the perception of *us versus them*. Just such an approach is set out by Nobel laureate Amartya Sen.

In *Identity and Violence*, Sen focuses on the human propensity to divide the world into distinct categories – "those belonging to 'the Islamic world,' 'the Western world,' 'the Hindu world,' 'the Buddhist world'" – and he recognizes the moral peril that this entails: "a fostered sense of identity with one group of people can be made into a powerful weapon to brutalize another."[57]

Such classifications unjustifiably restrict our identity. Humans do not belong to one group only, nor do they simply identify with one group. A person may be religiously a Christian, ethnically Chinese, nationally an American, politically a Republican, professionally an electrician, personally a member of the ACLU, and so on. All of these affiliations may make important demands on an individual's sense of identity, and establish a sense of belonging and obligation to others, enmeshing the individual in numerous, perhaps over-lapping in-groups. To choose just one of these and make it *the* defining identity of an individual is a form of reductionism Sen calls "singular affiliation."[58] This ignores complexity of personal identity and narrows the field for finding a basis for commonality. Sen calls the failure to recognize this "identity disregard."[59]

This is a vitally important point. Our moral sense is triggered in a positive way and at a very intuitive level by identifying someone as a member of the in-group; identifying someone as the out-group has very different psychological consequences. While the noble aspiration to see all humans as part of my in-group has significant practical limitations, Sen alerts us to another option. Humans have diverse identities and belong to many in-groups. This richer sense of identity provides numerous points of possible connection between individuals that otherwise may be overlooked if people are classified by singular affiliation. The diverse nature of our identities provides a moral resource that can be tapped into to counter a simplistic in-group/out-group divide.

In one sense this is a fairly common strategy, to highlight what we share rather than what we do not. But as common-sense as this may seem, it needs to become a self-conscious move in order to counter the pervasive tendency to reduce people to singular affiliations. Sen points out the particularly pernicious role this plays in terms of religious violence – take, for example, the notion of "Islamic terrorists."

To speak of "Islamic terrorists" reduces the identity of the terrorists to a single affiliation, that is, Muslim. Of course, some terrorists actually are Muslims, but this label implies that it is being Muslim that makes them terrorists, when, in fact, these terrorists also have multiple identities. To identify them simply as Muslims reduces the complexity of the factors that contribute to making these particular Muslims violent, dangerous human beings. The problem is not that we do the terrorists a disservice; we are doing ourselves a disservice by limiting our ability to understand the conditions that lead to terrorism.[60] Now, one of the factors, perhaps an important factor, that leads an individual into terrorism may be Islam; religion does play a causal role in religious violence. But Islam is, as are all religions, a multifarious, complicated set of beliefs, practices, interpretations, and rituals that has no essence that can be said to lead people into terrorism, although there are elements of Islam that can contribute (just as there are within Christianity and Judaism).

Also, by reducing terrorists to a singular affiliation we facilitate the engagement of in-group/out-group moral discrimination. Constantly coupling "Islam" and "terrorism" can foster a psychological bond between those two concepts that (1) is unjustified, as most Muslims are not terrorists, and many terrorists are not Muslims; (2) reduces the moral regard we extend to all Muslims, regardless of their behavior, and disregards their other group affiliations, many of which over-lap significantly with those of non-Muslims; (3) enables terrorists to categorize the "war on terrorism" as a war of the West against Islam, which enhances the sense of us versus them and thereby reduces our moral status in the eyes of others. Sen sees this as particularly self-defeating:

> It is, of course, not surprising at all that the champions of Islamic fundamentalism would like to suppress all other identities of Muslims in favor of only being Islamic. But it is extremely odd that those who want to overcome the tensions and conflicts linked with Islamic fundamentalism also seem unable to see Muslim people in any other form than their being just Islamic.[61]

One of the lessons to be taken from this study of our moral psychology is that words matter, rhetoric matters. The way we speak about people and the language we use to identify them classifies them, and this classification triggers psychological mechanisms that engage our in-group/out-group mentality and our moral reactions. Some people refer in a derogatory manner to "political correctness," as if that were simply about not hurting people's feelings, but there is something else at stake in the language we use. How we talk about people affects how we intuitively categorize them, and this is a first step to how we morally evaluate them, and, in turn, how they categorize and evaluate us.

We can also impose a singular affiliation upon ourselves, cutting ourselves off from connections to a larger world and richer existence. Sen sees this limiting approach to identity inherent in many educational and child-rearing practices, particularly in faith-based schools. He is critical of a movement in the United Kingdom to extend the number of faith-based schools to include a broader array of religious traditions. This is done in the name of equity and diversity, but Sen sees it as counter-productive. Consistent with our understanding of the role of reason, Sen argues that the "opportunities for cultivating reason" are much greater in a mixed environment in which people (in this case, children) are confronted regularly with diverse views and practices. This is more likely to occur in "less sequestered places of learning" than in faith-based schools, where a sense of singular affiliation is more likely to develop. In a poignant and morally powerful conclusion, Sen writes: "In the schooling of children, it is necessary to make sure that *smallness* is not 'thrust upon' the young, whose lives lie ahead of them. Much is at stake here."[62]

There are dangers in classifying people in ways that reduce the complexity of identity, and learning this lesson may help us avoid fanning the flames of religious violence. A singular focus on religious identity is a "problematic way of trying to reduce the hold of religious sectarianism."[63] To deal more effectively with our in-group/out-group mentality as that relates to the problem of religious violence, Sen says,

The question we have to ask is not whether Islam (or Hinduism or Christianity) is a peace-loving religion or a combative one ... but how a religious Muslim (or Hindu or Christian) may combine his or her religious beliefs or practices with other features of personal identity and other commitments and values. To see one's religious ... affiliation as an all-engulfing identity would be a deeply problematic diagnosis.[64]

The advantage of such an approach is that it works with the human tendency, the human need, to identify with communities. Rather than striving to break the leash that leads us to divide the world into groups, we must recognize this is a widespread tendency that creates myriad groups that can command our allegiance as an in-group. The greater the emphasis we put on the diversity of groups that count as "in," the less over-riding significance any one group is accorded; the more conscious we become of the richness of human identity, the greater the opportunity to find the commonality that allows us to see the "other" as "us."[65] This is a much more promising path to enlarging the moral community than attempts to erase all boundaries in the name of some idealized universal solidarity.

This is not to disparage universal solidarity. Rather, it is a call for a more pragmatic approach to enlarging the sphere of our moral concern. I do believe there are conditions that unite us all into a moral community and that there is a basis for a universal moral system. However, I must admit, following the example of academic candor set by William James, that at this point I leave the bounds set by evidence and enter the realm of "over-beliefs."[66] Not that these views are without empirical grounding, nor are they inconsistent with our evolved psychology; they are but one way of pulling all this material together, one I trust I can argue for, but will not, at this time, for fear of imposing too much on the reader's good will and patience. However, in closing the chapter on this discussion, and thereby closing the book, I will venture to set out those conclusions I draw most readily from all that has come before.

Conclusions

Let me start by being blunt: I do not believe any belief is "sacred." Beliefs are the product of social and psychological processes. These are natural processes that result in conclusions that must be evaluated on the basis of the evidence for them, and the ends they produce. Beliefs are not sacred, only truth is sacred, and the only holy office is the enduring pursuit of it. This is a credo that would serve humans well, for the pursuit of truth – not the possession or protection of truth – is an open-ended, on-going process, and one that can be pursued only by a community of inquirers,[67] and it is one, by its very nature, that demands the engagement of our critical faculties.

The fundamental premise of this book is that evolution has endowed the human mind with a common set of mental tools to categorize, interpret, and respond to the challenges of our environments. This does not deny the real differences between human beings or human cultures, as this common evolved mind finds diverse expression in response to diverse and dynamic environments. Also, as we possess the ability to step back from our intuitions and reflect on them it is possible to mold those intuitions into novel configurations; add to this the mental tools that make culture a causal force in giving shape to human existence, and we can see that the evolutionary model of psychology and morality does not condemn us to biological determinism; but neither does it support the view of human nature as a blank slate nor countenance any version of cultural determinism.

Our evolved psychology provides a common ground from which we may address moral conflicts. The basic contours of this psychology create the possibility for true moral dialogue and understanding. Morality serves the evolutionary function of promoting inclusive fitness within a social environment, but that is its *ultimate* function; we live in the *proximate* world. On the level of our lived experiences, we can translate ultimate evolutionary goals into proximate terms and say that the function of morality is to promote a stable social environment that can support the individual flourishing of its members, and we can see that a stable social environment can be established and maintained only by the active contribution of its members to the common good.

How to define human flourishing, and how to organize a society conducive to flourishing individuals, is open to discussion and experimentation. There is no reason to think that there is only one way to achieve these goals. This conclusion supports moral and cultural diversity. It does not, however, support moral or cultural relativism. To the degree that a culture does not establish the conditions conducive to the flourishing of its members, that society is morally deficient – it is not fulfilling its moral function. And to the degree that an individual is not contributing to the achievement of society's moral function or, worse, is hindering that goal, that individual is morally blameworthy (although such contributions are only part of an individual's rightful moral concerns). This, of course, is another articulation of the moral pragmatism I introduced earlier. However, pragmatism is a moral method; here I am suggesting a value system – one that is consistent with moral pragmatism – and this is best termed *humanism*.

Humanism is a somewhat vague term, open to different interpretations and misreadings, so allow me to stipulate what I mean by the term: Humanism is a moral system in which the central value, in regards to which moral judgments are made and moral questions decided, is the well-being – physical, emotional, intellectual, social, spiritual – of human beings; given our social nature, this entails as an essential component of human flourishing living in stable, functioning societies that provide for its members opportunities to pursue the good. A practice, tradition, or law is good just to the degree that it serves these moral ends; it is bad to the degree that it works contrary to these ends.

Humanism does not deny the diverse sources of identity that constitute human beings, nor does it seek to minimize that diversity. In fact, humanism celebrates human diversity as a testament to the richness of human existence – but just to the degree that this diversity does not impede the central values of humanism. A humanistic value system would not eliminate moral disagreements and conflicts; nor would it result in a homogeneous moral code or social system. It would, however, work with a basic framework of what is a morally acceptable variant – only to the degree that a variant can be said to contribute to human flourishing and social justice can it claim moral worth.

In this system the basis for moral judgment is not, however, any particular identity or affiliation, but is the pragmatic method we have set out.

Interestingly, as I pointed out earlier, there was a moment within early Christian moral history that moved toward such a view. When Jesus rejected family and ethnic affiliation as the conditions of kinship with him, he substituted in their stead moral action: "[H]e who does the will of my Father is my mother, and brothers and sisters." I claimed that this move, also found in other ancient religious and philosophic moral traditions, was a high-water mark in human moral progress: To see others as part of my group not because of any incidental affiliation but because of their moral behavior opens up the possibility of a functional universalism. The group is open to all who act morally. I also pointed out that this achievement was quickly subordinated to faith in Jesus as the basis of membership, closing off that most promising path for moral progress.

It is not fair to blame Jesus or Paul for this. The idea that we can make moral behavior the sign of membership for the in-group makes sense only if we can agree on what constitutes acceptable moral behavior. Since evolution designed us to see acceptable moral behavior as that which my group designates as acceptable, breaking away from this mindset is very difficult, even today. But I do believe that today, with the advancements made in moral philosophy, and the more recent advances in moral psychology, we have the ability to set out a common framework for acceptable moral behavior that can resonate with humans, whatever group or groups they identify with – and humanism is that framework.

Humanism, however, is controversial, at least within the United States where it is often presented as the opponent of religion. So, how does humanism, as I am using it, relate to religion? Actually, based on the analysis we have made of moral psychology and its religious expression, we can see that humanism can relate quite well to religion. The argument I make for humanism is that it embodies, in proximate terms, the ultimate goals that an evolutionary morality supports but extends moral concern beyond narrowly defined in-groups. I have argued that the various religious moral traditions we have considered, for all their diversity, are really expressions of the same evolved moral psychology. Given that, these traditions also embody on some level the humanistic value of human flourishing within stable, just societies. Humanism can be promoted within a religious system; it need not be a strictly secular system.

This does not mean that religions are humanistic simply because they are expressions of our evolved moral psychology. Religious traditions developed to serve the goals of individuals and societies at the stage of human development when those systems arose. To the degree that these systems persisted they served those goals admirably. However, as social conditions change, moral systems must keep pace if they are to continue to promote human flourishing, but given the generally conservative nature of human culture and practices, this will not always happen. A moral system can outlive its usefulness but still continue to exert an influence due to the collective weight of its cultural and religious history. A religious tradition can come to serve its own interests as a tradition, rather than serving humanistic ends (and this is true of other systems, as well, both cultural and political). So, a religion is humanistic just to the extent that its values place human flourishing at the center of the moral world. With this definition, there are many religious expressions that are deeply humanistic, but clearly there are many that are not.[68] We must also point out that there are secular traditions that are not humanistic, either. So, in the end, the key designation is *humanism*; whether that humanism is expressed in religious terms or secular terms is morally irrelevant.

Support for this conclusion can be taken from the fact that one of the greatest philosophers of humanism, John Dewey, though himself clearly secular in his worldview, when he sought to express his moral hopes for humankind, expressed it in terms of a faith.[69] Dewey wrote,

> We who now live are parts of a humanity that extends into the remote past, a humanity that has interacted with nature. The things in civilization that we most prize are not of ourselves. They exist by the grace of the doings and the sufferings of the continuous human community in which we are a link. Ours is the responsibility of conserving, transmitting, rectifying and expanding the heritage of values we have received that those who come after us may receive it more solid and secure, more widely accessible and more generously shared than we have received it. Here are all the elements for a religious faith that

shall not be confined to sect, class, or race. Such a faith has always been the common faith of mankind.[70]

If we hope to counter the destructive impulses embedded in religious psychology, while continuing to avail ourselves of the sources of meaning and wonder that religion at its best inspires, then we need a religious expression "not confined to sect, class, or race." Humanism, expressed so beautifully in Dewey's passage, whether in its secular or religious garb, is that common faith that must be nurtured. Here I do not use faith as Sam Harris uses it – belief without evidence – for the humanism that Dewey and I advocate is the fruit of a deep engagement with the best science has to offer in terms of understanding the human condition. Instead, it is faith in the sense that Paul Tillich used the term: an ultimate concern,[71] a personal and deep commitment to a moral vision that can shape and sustain our strivings.

To the extent that the analysis of religion offered in this book is correct then it is only a humanistic religion, one that embraces a self-critical, pragmatic approach to its own moral traditions, that can lay claim to our moral allegiance in the modern world or can deserve a place in the public square. All others threaten to trap us into cultural constructs that perpetuate a moral outlook designed for a much smaller, and much crueler world. We can no longer afford, nor need we accept, ideologies that so painfully constrict our moral vision. A larger world, and a richer existence, are there for the making.

NOTES

Notes for Chapter 1

1   Nietzsche, 1892.
2   I should also note here that the paradigm of evolutionary psychology that I employ also comes in for more than its share of criticism and misreading. Of course, as a new discipline it has been prone to over-statements and unfounded pronouncements, and there is an appropriate critical evaluation of its premises. I address some of these issues throughout the book. It is not my aim here to defend evolutionary psychology but, given this paradigm, to see what it may tell us about religion.
3   Mayr, 1993.
4   Dennett, 1995, p. 50.
5   Dawkins, 1976, p. 36.
6   Ibid., p. 88.
7   Hobbes, 1688.
8   Nowak, 2006.
9   See, e.g., Axelrod, 2006, and Axelrod and Hamilton, 1981.
10   Fehr and Fischbacher, 2003, p. 786.
11   Ibid.
12   Henrich et al., 2006, p. 1769.
13   For a discussion of the differing conditions of cooperation and punishing, see O'Gorman et al., 2005.
14   Trivers, 1971, p. 35.
15   Dawkins, 1976, p. 36.
16   Fehr and Fischbacher, 2003, p. 786.
17   For discussions, see Price et al., 2002, and Fehr and Gachter, 2002.
18   Hauser, 2006 – although in Hauser the Hobbesian creature is not in the running as a metaphor of our moral minds.
19   In his work on the evolution of morality, Richard Joyce points out, correctly I believe, that while it may not be possible to compile a complete list of necessary and sufficient qualifications that can make sense of just what constitutes a moral judgment, an evolutionary account of morality must address

two aspects of moral judgments: (1) they target a "distinctive subject matter," i.e., interpersonal relations, and (2) they are a "particularly authoritative kind of evaluation," i.e., they have a normative force. Joyce, 2006b, pp. 260–263; see also Joyce, 2006a. These are the aspects of morality of particular concern here.

20 Hauser, 2006, pp. 14–15.
21 Ibid., pp. 24–25.
22 See Greene et al., 2001, 2004; Haidt, 2001, 2006; Greene and Haidt, 2002; Greene, 2003, 2005; Hauser, 2006.
23 Greene et al., 2004. Also see Greene et al., 2001; Greene and Haidt, 2002.
24 See Greene et al., 2001; Greene and Haidt, 2002; Greene et al., 2004.
25 Greene et al., 2001.
26 A later study by Greene further supported the interpretation that the lag time in reaction is due to conflicting brain systems rather than, as some suggested, simply a more involved cognitive analysis required in personal dilemmas. Greene et al., 2004.
27 Ibid., p. 397.
28 Ibid.
29 See Haidt, 2001; Greene and Haidt, 2002.
30 Greene and Haidt, 2002, p. 517.
31 Damasio, 1994.
32 See, e.g., Blair, 1995; Blair et al., 1997; Raine et al., 2000; Greene, 2005.
33 Hume, 1739.
34 I think that Hume might be much closer to the synthetic view than Hauser supposes, but this is not germane here.
35 Greene, 2005; see also Greene and Haidt, 2002.
36 Hauser, 2006, p. 42.
37 Ibid., p. 411.
38 Iibid., pp. 45–47.
39 Rawls, 1971, pp. 46–47, cited in Hauser, 2006, p. 43.
40 See Haidt, 2001; Greene and Haidt, 2002; Greene, 2005; Hauser, 2006.
41 Hamilton, 1964, pp. 1–2.
42 Note that I do not say that genes cause behavior. The relationship between particular genes and phenotypic traits is complex and often poorly understood – and this is even more so in terms of behavioral traits. However, it is fairly clear that there is a genetic component to a large range of human behaviors or behavioral predispositions. My somewhat vague formulation is intended to respect both the causal thread between genes and behavior and the uncertainty surrounding the actual pathways from genes to behavior.
43 Singer, 1981. Frans De Waal (1996), uses the metaphor of floating pyramids to express the structure of moral psychology.
44 Dennett, 1995, p. 504; see pp. 501–505 for a fuller discussion.
45 And even with children, it is only the woman who can be absolutely certain of her genetic relationship – a fact that has contributed to the evolution of human mating and sexual psychology. See Buss, 1994.
46 Lieberman, Tooby and Cosmides, 2003, p. 821.
47 Ibid., for experimental data supportive of co-habitation as a kin estimator.

48   Lisa M. Debruine and her colleagues have conducted a series of experiments that show perceived facial resemblance increases levels of trust, willingness to contribute to a common pool of resources, and ratings of attractiveness. See DeBruine, 2002, 2004, 2005; and Krupp, Debruine, Barclay, 2008.

49   See Jones, 2003, for a discussion of the possibilities and limitations for extending the concept of kin.

50   Trivers, 1971.

51   Ibid., p. 37.

52   Ridley, 1997, p. 63.

53   De Waal, 1996.

54   Trivers, 1971

55   See De Waal, 1996.

56   See Stevens and Hauser, 2004, for the argument that the cognitive complexity required for reciprocal altruism to function makes it difficult for non-human animals.

57   Studies of food sharing among modern hunter-gatherer societies such as the Hiwi and Ache provide support for the role, even if not an exclusive one, of reciprocal altruism in human communities. See Gurven et al., 2000; Gurven, 2004. Importantly, studies of Meriam and Maasai hunter-gathering societies show how culture can modify the role of reciprocal altruism. See Bird et al., 2002, and Cronk, 2007. See also Gurven, 2006.

58   See Axelrod and Hamilton, 1981; Panchanathan and Boyd, 2004.

59   See Nowak, 2006.

60   See, e.g., Boyd and Richerson, 1988; Henrich and Boyd, 2001. Also, Alencar, Siqueira and Yamamoto, 2008.

61   Gintis et al., 2003, p. 153; see also Gintis, 2000.

62   See, e.g., Traulsen and Nowak, 2006.

63   Alexander, 1987, p. 94

64   See Nowak, 2006. Nowak also cites nine studies that indicate that those "who are more helpful are more likely to receive help" (p. 1561).

65   Alexander, 1987, p. 100; see also Nowak and Sigmund, 1998, on image scoring.

66   Fehr and Fischbacher, 2003, p. 787.

67   Ellingsen and Johannesson, 2008.

68   Haley and Kessler, 2005, cited in Nowak and Sigmund, 2005.

69   Humans have a well-attested interest in the doings of other humans, even when not directly involved in those doings (reality TV is just one unfortunate manifestation of this universal human trait). Robin Dunbar (1997) has done fascinating work on the social importance of gossip, which rather than being a petty sharing of others' dirty laundry, actually originates as a crucial practice for sharing significant social information.

70   See Barkow et al., 1992.

71   Vanneste et al., 2007.

72   Verplaeste et al., 2007.

73   Whiten and Byrne, 1997.

74   A recent study evaluating risky behavior found that men were much more likely to engage in behaviors that entailed the risk of high losses/high gains

when they were in the presence of other men they perceived to be of similar social status than when there was a clear status distinction, whether higher or lower (no such effect was found for women). The authors theorize that cognitive systems for weighing risk are influenced by cues of dominance. Ermer et al., 2008.

75 Alexander (1987) makes an interesting case that it was the frequency of intergroup conflict that created the conditions for indirect reciprocity to become established.

76 One criticism sees it working solely in terms of reputation effects and then points out the perils and limitations of accurately evaluating reputations (e.g., Panchanathan and Boyd, 2004; Richerson and Boyd, 2005), although others have suggested ways to stabilize these dangers (e.g., Panchanathan and Boyd, 2003, 2004; Nowak and Sigmund, 1998, 2005; Traulsen and Nowak, 2007). Some of the criticism of IR may be muted by keeping in mind that, according to Alexander, the effects of IR are not limited to reputational effects but can also come in the form of a more secure social environment in which individual inclusive fitness is pursued.

77 Michael Shermer provides an accessible discussion of these issues in *The Science of Good and Evil*, see esp. pp. 31–42.

78 See Boyd and Richerson, 1992; Henrich and Boyd, 2001; Fehr and Gachter, 2002; Gintis et al., 2003; Fehr and Fischbacher, 2003, 2004; Nowak and Sigmund, 2005; Fehr and Gintis, 2007.

79 Boyd and Richerson, 1992.

80 Gintis, 2000.

81 Gintis et al., 2001.

82 For a discussion, see Barkow, 2005, and a review by Kurzban, 2002.

83 See De Waal, 1983, 1996, and for an important discussion of the significance of primate studies to an understanding of human morality, see 2006.

84 Richerson and Boyd, 2005, p. 5.

85 Ibid., pp. 7–8.

86 This is a consistent theme in Boyd and Richerson; for another discussion of this, see Teehan, 2002.

87 Boyd and Richerson, 2005, pp. 148–190.

88 My sense is that this is a position shared by Boyd and Richerson, although I may take a more conservative view of the relative power of culture.

89 Boyd and Richerson, 1985; Richerson and Boyd, 2005; also see Soltis et al., 1995.

90 See Boyd and Richerson, 2002; Richerson and Boyd, 2005; and Efferson et al., 2008.

91 Boyd and Richerson, 2002.

92 Soltis et al., 1995.

93 Richerson and Boyd, themselves, see IR as a theoretically plausible explanation for ultra-sociality but believe it does not match the explanatory power of cultural group selection. Although in support of IR, Boyd has conducted a study that shows that IR can overcome several of the limitations ascribed to it by its critics and stabilize cooperation in large-scale groups. However,

he points out that this works only in models in which collective action is already established. See Panchanathan and Boyd, 2004; see also Boyd and Richerson, 2002.

94   Frank, 1988, p. 47.

95   Nesse, 2001, pp. 16–17.

96   Ibid.

97   There is much more to this area than we can or need to cover here, so further investigation is highly recommended. In addition to Frank, 1988, and Nesse, 1990, 2001, see also the other works collected in Nesse, 2001, as well as Nesse and Williams, 1996.

98   Nesse, 1990, p. 268.

99   Ibid., pp. 270–271.

100   Ibid, pp.272–273.

101   Frank, 1988, p. 4.

102   Ibid., p. 51.

103   Ibid., p. 53. Frank's list is taken from the work of Adam Smith, 1759, who along with other eighteenth-century British philosophers, most notably David Hume, established a philosophical precursor to the Darwinian model being developed by Frank, Nesse, and others. This "moral sentiment" school of ethics was overshadowed by rational, rule-based approaches, such as Kant's, much to the detriment, in my opinion, of both philosophy and moral theory. This situation is being rectified both within and without philosophical circles. In addition to the evolutionary moralists discussed see also, e.g., the work of Gibbard, 1990; Flanagan, 1991; Rottschaefer, 1997; Lakoff and Johnson, 1999; Hinde, 2002; Casebeer, 2003.

104   Frank, 1988, pp. 12–13.

105   Ellingsen and Johannesson, 2008.

106   Ibid., p. 54.

107   Nesse, 1990, p. 277.

108   Trivers, 1971, p. 49.

109   Fehr and Gachter, 2002.

110   See Price, Cosmides and Tooby, 2002; Herbert Gintis (2000) proposes that a pronounced predisposition to punish cheaters may be the defining trait of strong reciprocators – i.e., those altruists whose level of cooperation cannot be explained in terms of self-interest or reciprocity. And he points out that the presence of even a few such individuals can stabilize a group and increase that group's chances of survival.

111   Nesse, 2001, p. 17.

112   Ibid., p. 18.

113   Frank, 1988, p. 35, claims that kin selection and reciprocal altruism are insufficient to account for the "more noble impulses." One needs an account of commitment and emotions to develop such an account. I certainly agree with both Frank and Nesse that recent work on the capacity for commitment has led to a much deeper and more complete understanding of the evolution of our moral nature. I would merely emphasize, and I believe they would agree, that these capacities are layered on and at times constrained by the more primitive systems underlying kin selection and reciprocal altruism.

114   O'Gorman et al., 2008.
115   In speaking of the layering of our moral psychology, we should not think that one layer supersedes another or that a more recent layer subordinates earlier layers. I believe it is more accurate to see these layers as integrated, with the more recent layers being influenced and shaped by the earlier ones, but at the same time channeling and even re-directing those more basic tendencies. A consequence of this is that it is not possible to erect a single all-encompassing moral system or to identify a single over-riding moral rule. Any attempt to do so will necessarily privilege one aspect of our moral experience at the expense of others.

Notes for Chapter 2

1   Diamond, 1999, pp. 265–292. It should be noted that Diamond is not suggesting a necessary course of social development but rather is categorizing general patterns discernible in the archeological and anthropological record. In this he is following the work of anthropologist Elman Service, who set out this schema in his 1962 book, *Primitive Social Organization: An Evolutionary Perspective.*
2   Ibid., pp. 268–269.
3   Ibid., p. 271.
4   Ibid., p. 273.
5   Ibid., pp. 273–276.
6   Ibid., pp. 277–278.
7   As Paul Bloom notes, "Heaven is a reassuring notion only insofar as people believe such a place exists; it is belief that an adequate theory of religion has to explain in the first place" (Bloom, 2005, p. 107).
8   Atran, 2002, p. 57.
9   See, e.g., Guthrie, 1993; Boyer, 2001; Atran, 2002; Atran and Norenzayan, 2004; Bulbulia, 2004; Sosis, 2006; Tremlin, 2006.
10   For a philosophical treatment of this notion, see Rorty, 1979.
11   Guthrie, 1993, p. 41.
12   Ibid., p. 43.
13   Ibid., p. 61.
14   Ibid., p. 46. Guthrie here sites Kahneman and Tversky, 1982, and Jackendoff, 1987.
15   Ibid., pp. 89–90.
16   E.g., Kelemen, 1999, 2004a, b; Kelemen and DiYanni, 2005.
17   Kelemen, 2004a, pp. 295–296.
18   Ibid., p. 295.
19   Even when the action has no empirical relation to the problem at hand, action can have an anxiety-reducing effect. This is at least part of the benefits that come with certain religious practices. See Sosis, 2007, 2008.
20   Guthrie, 1993, p. 61.
21   Quoted in ibid., p. 63.
22   See ibid., pp. 62–82, and Guthrie, 2007.

23   Guthrie, 1993, p. 64.
24   Ibid.
25   Ibid., p. 86; see also pp. 86–89.
26   Ibid., p. 89.
27   This is such an important strategy that it seems to be not limited to humans. For a discussion of non-human animals and anthropomorphizing. See Guthrie, 1993 and 2002.
28   Davis, 2009, refers to this as "caveman logic" and points out the power, and danger, of facing the modern world with mental equipment designed for very different environments.
29   Kelemen's studies on promiscuous teleology show the effect is stronger in younger children than older children, and lower in adults, indicating the ability of education to mitigate the response. But she also reports on studies that show that adults not educated in science show a level of promiscuous teleology similar to young children. Kelemen, 2004a, p. 300.
30   See the appropriate chapters in Guthrie, 1993.
31   Ibid., p. 178.
32   Guthrie, 2007, p. 37.
33   Guthrie, 1993, p. 96.
34   Guthrie, 2008, p. 243.
35   See. e.g., Boyer, 2001; Pyysiainen and Anttonen, 2002; Whitehouse, 2004.
36   Whitehouse, p. 32.
37   Guthrie, "Gods, Abominable Snowmen, and Chiquita Bananas: Why do we generate the humanlike beings of religion?" Presented at the International Conference on Minds and Gods: The Cognitive Science of Religion, Ann Arbor, Michigan, 2002, as cited in Whitehouse, 2004. Also, Guthrie 1980 and 1993.
38   Barrett, 2004, p. 31.
39   Ibid., p. 32.
40   See e.g., Boyer, 2001; Atran, 2002; Bulbulia, 2004; Kelemen, 2004; Bloom, 2004, 2005; Atran and Norenzayan, 2005; Tremlin, 2006.
41   Barrett, 2004, p. 4.
42   See, e.g., Boyer, 2001; Atran, 2002; Barrett, 2004 for a more detailed discussion.
43   Barrett, 2004, p. 4. He also notes disagreement over whether describers are separate tools from categorizers or whether categorizers complete both functions. Resolving this is not relevant to our present purposes. See p. 22, n. 6.
44   Boyer, 2001, p. 65.
45   Ibid.. p. 62.
46   Atran, 2002, p. 93.
47   Barrett, 2004, pp. 10–11. See also Barrett, 1999.
48   Slone, 2004.
49   Ibid., p. 93.
50   Ibid., p. 95.
51   Ibid., p. 93.
52   Tremlin, 2006, p. 96.
53   See Boyer, 2001; Atran, 2002.

54   See Atran, 2002, pp. 101–107; Boyer, 2001, pp. 80–81; Barrett and Nyhoff, 2001. Boyer refers to this balance as "a cognitive optimum position." This may be stating things too strongly, as per Alles, 2006.

55   Atran and Norenzayan, 2004, pp. 721–724.

56   Boyer, 2002, p. 72.

57   See esp. Guthrie, 2002, 2007. Alles, 2006, and Kelemen and DiYanni, 2005, have raised provocative challenges to this conceptualization, while Boyer, 2001; Atran, 2002; and Atran and Norenzayan, 2004 defend the notion.

58   Guthrie, 2007, p. 47

59   Bloom, 2004, p. 199.

60   Ibid., pp. 9–14.

61   Ibid., p. 16.

62   Ibid. pp. 15–16.

63   Bloom, 2005, p. 109.

64   See Kelemen, 2004a, 2004b, for a similar understanding. Also, Bering, 2002, 2006, and Bering et al., 2005, for empirical studies indicating that this de-coupling persists throughout life and may provide a natural foundation for belief in souls and an afterlife.

65   Even Bloom recognizes that gods are counter-intuitive concepts: "if a notion did not violate our commonsense understanding of reality, why would we think of it as supernatural in the first place?" (2004, p. 210).

66   See, e.g., Cohen et al., 2008; Wilson, 2002.

67   Boyer, 1994, p. 391. For a more developed discussion of the interaction of culture and cognition, see Boyer, 2001; Atran, 2002; Barrett, 2004; Lawson and McCauley, 1990; Sperber, 1996.

68   Atran, 2002, p.14

69   Bulbulia, 2008, p. 30. See also Atran, 2002; Pyysiainen and Anttonen, 2002; Bulbulia, 2009.

70   Keltner and Haidt, 2003; Cohen et al., 2004.

71   Rozin et al., 2000; Cohen et al., 2004.

72   Solomon et al., 1991; Atran and Norenzayan, 2004; Landau et al., 2004; Sosis, 2007; Boyer and Lienard, 2006.

73   Kirkpatrick, 2005; King, 2007.

74   Sosis and Alcorta, 2003, 2008; Alcorta and Sosis, 2005; Sosis, 2006.

75   Barrett, 2004, p. 87.

76   Ibid., p. 91. Barrett has also done some very interesting work with children showing that the formation of MCI and god-concepts arise in early develop-mental stages. See Barrett 2001 for a discussion; see also Barrett et al., 2001; Barrett and Richert, 2003.

77   Of course, this has been no more than a sketch of the theoretical work being done to substantiate the position that evolution has channeled "human expe-rience toward religious paths." Atran, 2002, p. 11. It is my hope that the reader will be motivated to go to the original sources to appreciate just how strong the evolutionary/cognitive approach to religion has become. The main point to be taken from these sections is that "the explanation for religious beliefs and behaviors is to be found in the way all human minds work," and the workings of the human mind bear the stamp of its evolutionary history. Boyer, 2001, p. 2.

78   Boyer, 2001, p. 144.
79   Tremlin, 2006, p. 101.
80   See ibid. and Boyer, 2001 for valuable discussions.
81   Boyer, 2001, p. 122; see also Whiten and Byrne, 1997.
82   This is of course the often disabling disadvantage suffered by individuals with autism. See Bloom, 2004, for a relevant discussion.
83   Boyer, 2001, p. 155.
84   Ibid., p. 158
85   Ibid., p. 160.
86   Barrett et al., 2001; also see Kelemen, 2004a, for a discussion.
87   Kelemen, 2004a, reports there is some cross-cultural evidence for this result; also see Bloom, 2004, for a discussion of the false-belief task and beliefs about God.
88   See also Bering and Johnson, 2005.
89   Boyer, 2001, p. 172.
90   Ibid., pp. 170–172.
91   Ibid., p.172.
92   Roes and Raymond, 2003; Johnson, 2005. The definition of "high gods" is taken, by Johnson, from Swanson, 1960.
93   See, e.g., Johnson and Kruger, 2004; Bering and Johnson, 2005; Bering et al., 2005; Johnson, 2005; Johnson and Bering, 2006; Shariff and Norenzayan, 2007; Norenzayan and Shariff, 2008.
94   Shariff and Norenzayan, 2007.
95   Bering, 2003; also discussed in Bering and Johnson, 2005.
96   Bering et al., 2005.
97   Johnson, 2005, p. 415.
98   Boyer, 2001, p. 167.
99   Irons, 2001, p. 298.
100   Irons, 1996 and 2001.
101   Irons, 2001, p. 293; see also Atran, 2002, p. 140.
102   Sosis, 2006, p. 63.
103   See Sosis, 2009, for a costly-signal explanation for why synagogue services are so long; or Sosis, 2006, for why certain Jewish sects require members to wear heavy, black clothing even in warm weather.
104   Sosis and Alcorta, 2003, p. 268; also Sosis, 2000, 2003; Sosis and Bressler, 2003; and Ruffle and Sosis, 2006; Sosis et al., 2007; see also Irons, 1996, 2001; and Zahavi and Zahavi, 1997.
105   See Finkel et al., 2009; Atran and Norenzayan, 2004; Deely, 2004; Sosis and Alcorta, 2004; Alcorta and Sosis, 2005; Bulbulia, 2009.
106   Irons, 2001, p. 307. Also, before moving on we should note that Scott Atran has pointed out a limitation of some commitment theories. He has charged them with being "mindblind" because they do not adequately recognize the influence of cognitive structures; while on the other hand he criticizes cognitive theories for being motiveless. He sets out, in his book, to reconcile the two approaches. The view I have sketched here represents, I believe, just such a reconciliation (influenced as it is by Atran's work, among others). Cognitive theories explain why it is that god-concepts are so particularly well suited to

assume a moral dimension, and commitment theory explains why people become so passionately involved with beliefs and rituals that attach to god-concepts.

107   Atran, 2002, p. 117.

108   Wilson's understanding of the group-level functioning of religion is, I believe, consistent with much of what I have presented here, although Wilson sees these functions as products of group selection. I would not deny that selection can take place at the level of the group. However, I believe that given the significance of the group to an individual's pursuit of inclusive fitness, and the necessity of individuals' contributions to group success, teasing out group-selected traits is a very difficult task. As my topic is the psychology of religion, focusing on individual-level selection seems more appropriate, and I believe is adequate to explain the range of processes under consideration. For a different take, see Wilson, 2002, and 2005.

109   Ruffle and Sosis, 2006.

110   For further discussions of religion and the in-group bias, see Atran and Norenzayan, 2004; Hansen and Norenzayan, 2006; Norenzayan and Shariff, 2008.

111   There is a vibrant debate within the field about just how to characterize the relationship between evolution and religion. Is religion a by-product, the accidental output of cognitive processes that evolved for other purposes? For adherents of the "by-product" view. see, e.g., Guthrie, 1993; Boyer, 2001; Atran, 2002; Atran and Norenzayan, 2004. Or is religion an adaptation that played an active role in human evolution? For the "adaptation" side, see Wilson, 2002; Bulbulia, 2004; Johnson and Kruger, 2004; Alcorta and Sosis, 2005; Johnson, 2005; Bering and Johnson, 2005; Bering, 2006. There is also a variation on the by-product theory that sees religion as a "meme" that exploits our cognitive architecture to replicate itself; see Dawkins, 2006; Dennett, 2006.

For the record, allow me to state my position. I do not see this as an either/or issue. It seems to me that religious beliefs, particularly god-beliefs, are the by-products of cognitive/emotional predispositions that evolved to serve other fitness needs. However, once such ideas are culturally available they can play a role in fostering pro-social behavior, which in turn can contribute to increased reproductive success. If this is so, then religion may be an adaptation built upon beliefs that themselves are by-products. (Several participants in this debate adopt a similar "mixed" take on the question. See Bering, 2006, and Johnson and Kruger, 2004; Bering and Shackelford, 2004; Alcorta and Sosis, 2005; Dow, 2006.) If god-beliefs can generate changes in behavior, and behavior has an impact on inclusive fitness, then "psychological processes enabling humans to interpret certain natural events ... as symbolic of supernatural intentions may have been subjected to selective pressures" (Bering and Shackelford, 2004, p. 733).

In terms of memes, while this view of religion has received a fair share of attention in popular works, it does not receive much attention in the research literature, and often the attention it gets is negative – and for good reason. I will not go into a discussion here, but I believe that, in general, meme theory has inherent flaws as a proposed mechanism for cultural evolution and, in terms of religion, cannot explain the particular contours of religious belief nor make the predictions about the effects of religious belief, offered by either by-product views or adaptationist views. For a wonderful discussion, see Bulbulia, 2008.

Notes for Chapter 3

1   Goldberg, 2009, presents a collection of essays exploring Judaism from a biological perspective that is very much in the spirit of this work. It is a worthwhile resource for those interested in the topic.
2   See Barton, 2002, p.78.
3   See, e.g., Finkelstein and Silberman, 2001
4   Rogerson et al., 1998, p. 49.
5   This is the approach adopted by, e.g., Brevard Childs, whose study of Exodus figures large in my work; also see Rogerson et al., 1998, pp. 105–109.
6   Berlinerblau, 2005, p. 22.
7   See Friedman, 1997, for a good introduction to the Documentary Hypothesis that set out this interpretation of Biblical texts. However, one needs to be aware that Biblical scholarship has moved beyond the comparatively neat model presented by that hypothesis.
8   See Slone, 2004, for a more developed discussion of this conflict between theology and belief.
9   Guthrie, 1993.
10 Segal, 2004, pp. 74–76.
11 There is of course debate about how to enumerate and distinguish the various commandments. I use the delineation of the RSV Bible, without implying any greater authenticity to this model. For my purposes the exact delineation is not crucial.
12 Joseph Blenkinsopp has suggested that connecting the promulgation of the law with stories of God's active presence in the life of the community may be a unique feature of the ancient Israelite legal tradition (2000, p. 225). This may be so, but connecting the law to the communal god as overseer is not unique – and Blenkinsopp does not deny this – but is a characteristic of legal codes throughout the Ancient Near East.
13 Childs, 1974, pp. 402–403.
14 The move away from this default position and toward monotheism seems to be prompted by certain sociological factors. For example, the development of philosophic monotheism in Greek thought was a response to socio-political changes occurring throughout the Mediterranean world during the process of Hellenization – one of history's most famous examples of globalization. As more local and direct forms of social life gave away to larger, impersonal forms, philosophers shifted their thoughts to questions of personal flourishing and/or salvation, and of the relation of the individual to the larger forces that seemed to control human destiny. The idea developed that behind the myriad forces of the universe was a supreme deity, a universal mind, or *Logos*, that controlled the cosmos. This trend toward a single su-

preme divine being or principle can also be found within the proliferating Mystery Cults, some of which held that their god was god, and all other divine beings were manifestations of this one true deity (see Tripolitis, 2001). The ancient Israelites were not exempt from the stresses and creative tensions brought on by the process of Hellenization, and Judaic monotheism may have been shaped during this same period. By this I do not mean to suggest that Jewish monotheism was a product of the Hellenistic age; it seems to have predated Hellenism and developed independently. Still, when and why monotheism became the definitive belief system of the Jewish faithful, and not just of the priests, is a fascinating issue.

15 Childs presents a worthwhile discussion of the issue, suggesting that the prohibition stems from God's chosen means of self-revelation – that is, through the spoken word – and that this sets the mode of appropriate worship, verbal not imagistic (1974, pp. 404–409).

16 See Buss, 1994.

17 Ezekiel 16 takes this even further and uses the metaphor of the unfaithful wife to develop an allegorical telling of Israel's history and its destruction. Thanks to Deena Grant for this reference.

18 See Fewell and Gunn, 1993, for a discussion of the role of gender and power in the Hebrew Bible.

19 See, e.g., Johnson and Kruger, 2004; Bering and Johnson, 2005; Bering et al., 2005; Johnson, 2005; Johnson and Bering, 2006; Shariff and Norenzayan, 2007; Norenzayan and Shariff, 2008.

20 Of course scholars recognize another interpretation of this story as arising from political concerns between the divided kingdoms of Israel and Judah. See, e.g., Freidman, 1997. I find this account quite plausible, but that the story was chosen to remain as the Jewish scriptures were canonized, centuries after the divisiveness between the two Jewish states, seems consistent with the fact that it can also play the role I assign it.

21 Davies, 1967, p. 164.

22 Childs, 1974, pp. 410–412.

23 Ibid., p. 415; see also Blekinsopp, 2000, p. 219.

24 See Childs, 1974, p. 416.

25 See, e.g., Barton, 2002, pp. 4–5. Barton also notes, "The Decalogue does not tell us anything about the moral rights or duties of women ... but only about those of the people who ran Isrealite society ... it is addressed to free men."

26 See "Law in Judaism of the NT Period," *Anchor Bible Dictionary* (Doubleday, 1992), p. 258.

27 Blenkinsopp, 2000, p. 219.

28 Ibid., pp. 217–220.

29 See Childs, 1974, pp. 417–418; and Magonet, 1996, p. 204.

30 Childs, 1974, pp. 417–419.

31 Magonet, 1996, p. 204.

32 See Daly and Wilson, 1988, and Buss, 2005, for evolutionary analyses of homicide.

33 One of the best literary portrayals of this is found in Aeschylus' *Oresteia*, a classic story of the obsessive power of blood revenge that continues across multiple generations. The deadly cycle is only ended with the intervention of

the goddess Athena, who establishes trial by a jury of peers to judge the murderer Orestes. In this profound work we see both the deeply embedded evolutionary concerns driving the action and the role of religion in solving the problem. This also suggests that the method being used to analyze religious texts may be used for other genres. In fact, evolutionary literary criticism is a developing field, and I see this as kin to my work; see, e.g., Carroll, 1995; Barash and Barash, 2005. Barash, 2009, applies this approach to intrafamily conflict in the Hebrew Bible to interesting effect.

34   See, e.g., Childs, 1974, p. 422; Magonet, 1996, pp. 196–197; and Pressler, 1994.

35   Magonet gives an interesting reading to explain the severity of this penalty. If marriage is, as Genesis 2:24 describes it, the joining of man and woman into one flesh, then "the act of adultery is not just an assault on a man's property, but a kind of physical assault upon his person...[and] belongs to the same area of physical crime against an individual as the act of murder" (1996, p. 197).

36   Pressler, 1994, p. 103.

37   Ibid., pp. 110–111.

38   See Fisher, 1994, and Buss, 1994, for more general discussions of evolution and sexuality.

39   See Childs, who credits Alt with being the first to recognize this (1974, p. 423); also see Magonet, 1996, p. 197.

40   Harris, 2006.

41   Childs, 1974, p. 424.

42   Ibid., pp. 424–425.

43   Ibid., p. 425.

44   See ibid., pp. 425–426; and Magonet, 1996, pp. 198–199, where he cites both Midrash and Maimonides on this interpretation.

Notes for Chapter 4

1   See, e.g., Pagels, 1979, 2003; Ehrman, 2003, 2005.

2   See Ehrman, 2006. We must also admit as distasteful as this may be, that the most successful work to bring an alternative understanding of Christian origins to a wider audience has been the novel *The Da Vinci Code*, by Dan Brown.

3   See, e.g., Cohen, 1987; Lieu, 2002.

4   Lieu, 2002, p. 46.

5   Ibid., p. 18.

6   Boyarin, 1999, p. 11.

7   Ibid., p. 6.

8   I will restrict my discussion to the authentic letters of Paul, at least those letters least contentiously attributed to Paul, i.e., 1 Thessalonians, 1 and 2 Corinthians, Galatians, Romans, Philemon, and Philippians.

9   I believe a fruitful and interesting analysis of which gospels were canonized and why, from an evolutionary perspective, may be made; it is just beyond

the goal of this book to attempt such an analysis here. For example, an explanation of the failure of various Gnostic traditions to gain ascendancy may be, in part, explained in evolutionary terms. Gnosticism, in its various forms, focused on the individual's grasping of secret knowledge to escape from the corrupted physical world. It was not primarily interested in group survival and therefore did not tap into the evolved psychological mechanisms that allow a group to form cohesively and reproduce itself. It was thus at a distinct disadvantage competing with groups that did tap into these mechanisms. However, the modern-day Mandeans in southern Iraq, a Gnostic group that can trace itself back to ancient Gnosticism, may provide a case study for testing these ideas, although such a study should be conducted soon given the devastating impact the Iraq war has had on this vulnerable population.

10   Lieu, 2002.

11   See, e.g., Rolston, 2004.

12   It is interesting that Lahti makes a similar claim, 2004, p. 146.

13   Judaism also represented a new development in religious experience and constituted a distinct divergence from the polytheistic environment in which it developed, without thereby offering a radically novel tradition, as there is much in Judaism that can be connected to its polytheistic roots. Indeed, this is true of any identifiable cultural or religious community. If it did not present something distinct and novel we would not recognize it as a separate tradition.

14   Almost all; docetists denied that Jesus was a material person. See Ehrman, 2003.

15   I will refer to the gospels, for simplicity's sake as Mark, Matthew, Luke, and John, recognizing that these gospels were written anonymously, most likely by individuals who were neither first-hand witnesses nor even contemporaries of Jesus.

16   The death of Jesus presented a real challenge to constructing an MCI identity for him. Despite his impressive powers, if he did not have the power to save himself from a humiliating death, and so hold out that possibility to his followers, he paled in comparison to some competing deities of his day, e.g., Isis, Osiris, Orpheus, Dionysios. However, in trying to account for the inconvenient fact of Jesus' death in constructing a divine conception of him, the early followers of Jesus had these models to work with in tackling this problem. The notion of a dying god was not unfamiliar in the ancient world, and Jewish tradition also contained the notion of a Messiah who would suffer and die. Claiming that the Jesus who died was God and has risen connects the Jesus story to a mythic tradition already well established across the ancient Mediterranean and so was readily acceptable to Christian audiences. It also presented a conception of Christ that followed the cognitive formula for gods, and so was intuitively satisfying.

17   See Williams, 2005, p. 142.

18   We also should point out that aside from an evaluation of the claim to universalism, any claim that Christianity introduced the notion of moral universalism is woefully ignorant of history, as we can find universal moral aspirations not only in Judaism itself but in Buddhism and Stoicism, to name a few. And all of these traditions predate Christianity by centuries.

19 Cohen, 1987, p. 143.
20 See North, 1992, p. 191; Lieu, 2002, p. 47.
21 North, 1992, p. 191.
22 Cohen, 1987, p. 52
23 Rajak, 1992, p. 17.
24 See Stambaugh and Balch, 1986, for a discussion of the dynamics of sectarianism.
25 See Lieu, 2002, for a discussion of the polemics of identifying Christianity as a third "race" in opposition to Jews and Gentiles, pp. 49–68.
26 See Rolston, 2004, and Williams, 2005. We will return to these discussions of the exceptional nature of the Good Samaritan when we turn to the issue of reciprocal altruism.
27 See Lieu, 2002, pp. 173–174, for a discussion.
28 There were questions in the early decades of the Christian movements about just what was a Christian's obligation concerning the food laws. There is a dispute between Paul and the leaders of the Jerusalem church over whether Gentile converts needed to obey these laws – implying that at least some Jewish Christians continued to observe them. See Galatians 2:1–14.
29 It is not insignificant that in these stories the antagonists are identified as Pharisees, who were themselves Jewish sectarians, though not nearly as radical as the Christians. During the early centuries of the Common Era we find sectarianism diminishing and the gradual emergence of two new traditions, Christianity and Rabbinic Judaism. While there is a scholarly debate over this, it is fair to say that Rabbinic Judaism has roots in the Pharisaic movement, if not a direct descendant of that sect (see S. Cohen). By setting up the Pharisees as the foils to Jesus, as happens repeatedly throughout the New Testament, these stories function to signal not only a break from the established tradition but a distinction between the two sects. It helps to create a boundary between Christianity and Judaism, whether in its more traditional forms or in its newer manifestations.
30 See Sanders, 1977, pp. 551–552.
31 Lahti, 2004.
32 Ibid., p. 141.
33 Ibid., p. 139.
34 Ibid
35 See Meeks, 1986, pp. 129–130; also see Stambaugh and Balch, who point out the tension caused by the fact that early Christian churches were inside houses (1986, p. 140).
36 North, p. 186.
37 Rolston, 2004, p. 250.
38 Ibid, p. 251.
39 Lahti, p. 144.
40 North, 1992, pp. 191–192.
41 Once these elements of Christianity become embedded in the culture they can become detached from the contexts in which they are adaptive. For example, one may question whether contemporary Christian evangelizing to Third

World countries functions in a way advantageous to the in-group. But as Boyd and Richerson have shown, the power of culture can work at odds with evolutionary adaptiveness. This does not argue against an evolutionary account of the origins of such practices as adaptations.

42 Meeks, 1986, p. 103.
43 Lahti, 2004, p. 143.
44 Lieu, 2002, p. 177.
45 Meeks, 1993, p. 32.
46 Ibid., pp. 32–33.
47 Ibid., 1993, p. 96.
48 See Meeks, 1993, p. 96, for a discussion of the status-upsetting nature of the Lord's Supper.
49 Ibid., p. 68.
50 Ibid., pp. 215–216.
51 Ibid., p. 84.
52 Stephen Pope writes of the power of religious rites to "widen and deepen the scope" of altruistic behavior and believes that this points to "a degree of plasticity and indeterminacy in human nature despite genetic and evolutionary constraints." Religious practices and rhetoric can and do extend the mechanisms of evolved strategies such as kin selection and reciprocal altruism. In fact, I believe this is one of their main functions. Pope, 1994, p. 333.
53 "You shall love the Lord your God with all your heart, and with all your soul, and with all your might." (Deut. 6:5); "You shall love your neighbor as yourself" (Lev. 19:18).
54 Williams, 2005, p. 133.
55 Ibid., p. 140.
56 Ibid., p. 142.
57 Chapman, 2004, p. 112. He cites Williams, 2001, as a source for this assessment.
58 Rolston, 2004, p. 252.
59 Rolnick, 2004, p. 315.
60 In support of this analysis, of the 105 moral claims Lahti finds in Matthew's version of the Sermon, half "include a mention of consequences" and "in all of them adherence to the guidelines produces benefits for the individual so adhering, and failing to adhere produces long term costs." Lahti, 2004, p. 145.
61 *Summa Theologica*, Supplement to the Third Part. There is some question of whether this is actually Aquinas' teaching as this part of his work was completed by an aide after Aquinas passed away, leaving it incomplete. Authorship aside, it is part of Christian theology in keeping with the teaching of Paul.

Notes for Chapter 5

1 Moss, 2006, p. 29
2 Kimball, 2002, p. 7.

3   Stern, 2003, p. xv.
4   Lincoln, 2003, p. 73.
5   Talal Asad, 1993, provides a seminal discussion of this topic, tying the issue to the larger problem of trying to establish a transhistorical and transcultural definition of "religion" (pp. 27–54).
6   Juergensmeyer, 2001, p. 6.
7   Niditch, 1993, p. 29. Niditch provides a very useful analysis of the various roles of the term *herem* found throughout the Hebrew Scriptures that go beyond the examples being discussed here. All involve situations in which persons or things are seen as properly God's due and so are "devoted" to him. See also Ludeman, 1997; Collins, 2004a; and an early classic discussion in von Rad, 1958.
8   See Ludeman, 1997, p. 44; also p. 54 for a rejection of a relativistic defense of these stories.
9   See Kugel, 2007, for a discussion; also Finkelstein and Silberman, 2001, is a good entrance into this important and controversial field of study.
10 Collins, 2004a, b.
11 A study by Elizabeth Cashdan, 2001, suggests that out-group hostility is not a necessary correlate to in-group loyalty. However, under conditions of social stress, such as war, out-group hostility can rise. This is an interesting study as it suggests the possibility for positive inter-group relations – which we will explore in the final chapter. It also points to the particular power of embedding moral lessons in war narratives.
12 Hartung, 1995.
13 Niditch, 1993, p. 65.
14 See Rozin et al., 2000; and Cohen et al., 2004.
15 See Pinker, 1997; also Boyer, 2001; Haidt, 2001.
16 Haidt, 2001.
17 Kugel, 2007, p. 382.
18 Ibid., pp. 381–383.
19 See also Niditch for a discussion of the Ban as sacrifice and its contribution to drawing in-group/out-group distinctions (pp. 28–55).
20 Ibid., p. 50; see also Collins 2004b for a discussion of the Ban as sacrifice.
21 Niditch, 1993, p. 51.
22 Ibid., p. 50, cites Herbert Hendin and Ann P. Hass, *Wounds of War: The Psychological Aftermath of Combat in Vietnam* (New York: Basic Books, 1984).
23 Smith, 2007.
24 See ibid., p. 72; also De Waal, 1983, 1996.
25 Buss, 2005, p. 39.
26 Ibid., pp. 39–41.
27 See also Daly and Wilson, 1988.
28 Smith, 2007, esp. pp. 147–182.
29 Ibid., p. 183.
30 Ibid., pp. 187–196.
31 Ibid., p. 192.
32 Ibid., p. 199.

33 Ibid., p. 207.
34 Niditch, 1993, p. 50.
35 Collins, 2004a, p. 7.
36 Ibid., pp. 6–7.
37 Smith, 2007, p. 91.
38 Genghis Khan proclaims that "happiness lies in conquering your enemies …
    in taking their property … in raping their wives and daughters." And if a
    recent study is to be trusted, this was no idle boast – DNA analysis has linked
    some 16 million men living in Asia today to a single ancestor living sometime
    in the thirteenth century, with Genghis Khan being the prime suspect. Hillary
    Mayell, "Genghis Khan a Prolific Lover, DNA Data Implies," National Geo-
    graphic News, February 14, 2003; see also Buss, pp. 234–235.
39 Buss, 2005, relates a story of the Yanomamo people living in the Brazilian
    rainforest. During a raid against a neighboring village a young girl is about
    to be killed when someone shouts out, "No! No! No! Don't kill her. Can't
    you see she is healthy? She will bear us many children. … Only kill the babies
    and the wounded … we have to keep the healthy girls" (pp. 232–233).
40 See Collins, 2001a, b, for discussions of the import of this story, particularly
    its function in promoting cooperation within the group. See also Burlein,
    2002, for an account of how this story continues to resonate with those seek-
    ing to establish a group identity that is divinely policed, in this case that of
    the white-supremacist Christian Identity Movement.
41 Johnson and Kruger, 2004.
42 In terms of the Supernatural Punishment Hypothesis, God need not actually
    impose punishment. Studies show that the threat of punishment itself can
    have an impact on discouraging cheating and promoting cooperation and that
    such behavior can be effectively primed by god-beliefs. See Johnson and
    Kruger, 2004; Bering and Johnson, 2005; Bering and Shackelford, 2004;
    Johnson, 2005; Johnson and Bering, 2006; Shariff and Norenzayan, 2007.
43 Schwartz, 1997, p. 3.
44 Johnson and Kruger, 2004, also suggest that this approach to god-beliefs of-
    fers a way to understand variations between religions as "adaptive solutions
    to local cooperation problems" (p. 172).
45 Pagels, 1995, p. 84.
46 Spinoza, 1670, pp. 91–92; also see Marc Shell, 1991, for a discussion of this
    issue.
47 Pagels, 1995, p. 164.
48 Rubenstein, 1999, pp. 196–197.
49 Ibid., pp. 1–3.
50 Ibid., p. 2.
51 Athanasius, 1892, sec. 69.
52 Ibid., sec. 82.
53 Gibbon, 1781, p. 787.
54 Ibid., pp. 776–777.
55 Ibid., p. 777.
56 Augustine, 1887.
57 Luther, *Against the Murderous*, Thieving Hordes of Peasants.

58 Luther, *Jews and Their Lies*.

59 This is a position subject to debate within various contemporary Christian sects. The Unitarian Universalist Church makes the rejection of this view a foundational position. A prominent example from a more traditional sect comes out of post–Vatican II Catholicism. While the documents that came out of that council did not repudiate the tradition of "no salvation outside the church," it did seem to open the door of salvation to non-Catholics, even non-Christians. It did so, however, by raising the issue of just what it means to be part of the church (*Lumen gentium*, sec. 14, 1964). Following on this document, the *Catechism of the Catholic Church* (1992) also affirms that there is "no salvation outside the church" but leaves open the possibility of salvation to those "who, through no fault of their own, do not know Christ and his Church" (paragraphs 845–847). These debates are important, as they are engaging the issue of extending the moral boundary of Christianity. However, in terms of Scripture, and Christian history, I believe there is less room for debate. Thanks to Steve Clarke for raising this point.

60 Shell, 1991, p. 307.

61 Ibid., p. 306.

62 But even this may be questioned, as the doctrine of predestination, whether in Augustine or Calvin, in effect precludes membership to a portion – in some cases a significant portion – of humankind.

63 Shell, 1991, pp. 306–316.

64 Boyarin and Boyarin, 1993.

65 Epicurus, 1994.

66 Pope Benedict, The Seer of Patmos, Address to the General Audience, August 23, 2006. http://www.vatican.va/holy_father/benedict_xvi/audiences/2006/documents/hf_ben-xvi_aud_20060823_en.html. (accessed 10/13/09).

67 Ibid.

68 Martyrdom becomes an important part of the early Christian history, both as an actual experience that some Christians not only accept but welcome and as another rhetorical device to encourage in-group loyalty. See Boyarin, 1999; and Cobb, 2008.

69 Juergensmeyer also talks about an "internal logic" to religious terrorism (2001, p. 123). This focuses more on the logic at work in the violent act, while I am focusing on the underlying psychology that leads to conceiving violence as a religiously appropriate or acceptable response. I do not suggest that these are always distinct logics; indeed, there is overlap between the two. Nor is there a necessary priority of the one over the other. As Juergensmeyer points out, religion can lead to violence and violence can call for a religious justification, whatever its actual genesis (p. 161).

70 Ibid., pp. 161–162 for a discussion of how these aspects play out in religious terrorism.

71 Juergensmeyer provides some support for this view as he points out the theme of "us vs. them" that is found throughout "mythic themes of warfare" in numerous religious traditions. Ibid., pp. 157–160.

72 Shell, 1991, pp. 306–309.

73 Lincoln, 2003, p. 16.

74 Quoted in ibid., p. 94.
75 http://www.historyplace.com/speeches/gw-bush-9-11.htm (accessed 10/13/09).
76 Quoted in Lincoln, 2003., p. 103.
77 http://www.historyplace.com/speeches/gw-bush-9-11.htm (accessed 10/13/09).
78 Quoted in Lincoln, 2003, p. 95.
79 Quoted in http://archives.cnn.com/2001/US/09/16/gen.bush.terrorism/ (accessed 10/13/09).
80 http://archives.cnn.com/2001/US/11/08/rec.bush.transcript/ (accessed 10/13/09).
81 http://www.mideastweb.org/osamabinladen2.htm (accessed 10/13/09).
82 http://archives.cnn.com/2001/US/11/08/rec.bush.transcript/ (accessed 10/13/09).

Notes for Chapter 6

1   James, 1902, p. 485.
2   And there is a healthy debate ongoing – see Schloss and Murray, 2009, for a recent collection of valuable contributions to this debate.
3   Ibid., pp. 507–508.
4   For a very interesting, empirically grounded study of the role of the Bible in the evangelical community, see Malley, 2004.
5   James, 1902, p. 487.
6   See Barrett, 2004, 2009; also see Miller, 1999; Murray and Goldberg, 2009. It is interesting to point out that these authors develop their reconciliation in a less ecumenical way than I suggest here. Each is more particularly concerned with bringing Christianity in line with CSR.
7   This is not to imply that efforts have not been made to effect such a fit. This is a staple of theological and philosophical efforts to resolve the Problem of Evil. Delving into this issue will take us too far afield, but in brief I find such efforts less convincing than the evolutionary solution suggested here.
8   Haught, 2008, p. 72.
9   Ibid., pp. 25–26.
10 See, e.g., see Miller, 1999; Pennock, 2000; Shanks, 2007.
11 See Haught, 2000, 2003, and 2008. Haught is hardly alone in this understanding of evolution and religion; see also Zycinski, 2006, and Kung, 2007, for further theological support; and, e.g., Collins, 2007, and Miller, 1999, for support from scientists; and Ruse, 2001, for a philosophical treatment.
12 He is just as emphatic in taking to task those who would use evolution to reject religion. Recently, he has taken aim at the so-called new atheists – Richard Dawkins, Sam Harris, Daniel Dennett, and Christopher Hitchens – whom he charges, correctly I believe, with taking as their target a version of religion as superficial as that used by creationists. Haught, 2008.
13 I must admit that I have deep disagreement with much of the theology Haught develops. These questions deserve a more comprehensive treatment than can

be offered here, except as they relate to morality. For a more recent development of his critique of the sufficiency of evolution, see Haught, 2009.

14 Haught, 2000, p. 122.

15 Ibid., p. 123.

16 Ibid.

17 Ibid., p. 122.

18 See Provine, 1989, for a developed critique of just this point. For Haught's rebuttal, see Haught, 2000, pp. 121–122.

19 Haught, 2008, p. 71.

20 There is a wealth of philosophical literature on these issues. For discussions in line with an evolutionary approach, see, e.g., Rottschaefer, 1997; Hinde, 2002; Teehan, 2002; Teehan and DiCarlo, 2004.

21 Haught, 2008, pp. 25–26.

22 Ibid., p. 26.

23 See Teehan, 1994, 1996.

24 Dewey, 1909, pp. 8–9.

25 Dewey, 1922, p. 150.

26 See Dewey, 1922, 1929, and 1932 for his development of the view I am presenting here.

27 Dewey, 1920.

28 Harris, 2004, p. 225.

29 Ibid.

30 This is a major point of contention for Haught; see Haught, 2008.

31 See Barrett, 2004, for a fascinating treatment of conditions conducive to atheism.

32 A study by Shariff et al., 2008, suggests religiousness may be a more flexible, fluid trait than I suggest here. Their experiment showed that exposing subjects to secular arguments, such as those of Richard Dawkins, can lower self-reports of religiosity. Whether such an effect persists in the face of conditions that trigger religious cognition outside the lab is the question that needs to be explored in terms of rebutting my contention that religion is here to stay. However, this work demonstrates the need for continued empirical research into these questions. Also see Hinde, 1999, for a relevant discussion.

33 Loyal Rue, 2006, who develops an analysis of religion from an evolutionary perspective, offers a discussion of the moral/social lessons we may take from such an analysis that is in the spirit of this work.

34 Collins, 2004a, pp. 32–33.

35 Dawkins, 2006, pp. 20–27.

36 Haidt, 2009, p. 286.

37 Harris, 2006, p. 5.

38 Hansen and Norenzayan, 2006, make a distinction between "devotional" religiosity, which they find can function to expand an individual's moral worldview beyond the limits of group mentality, and "coalitional" religiosity, which "simply upgrades individual selfishness to group selfishness" (p. 26). This kind of nuanced, critical examination of religion is much more useful in approaching religion than that proposed by so many vocal critics of religion.

39 Juergensmeyer, 2001, p. 149.

40 Ibid., p. 163.
41 Shell, 1991, p. 332.
42 Atran, 2004, p. 73.
43 Ibid., p. 78.
44 Ibid.
45 Ibid., pp. 79–80.
46 Ibid., p. 76.
47 Ibid., pp. 82–83.
48 Ginges et al., 2007.
49 Ibid., p. 7359.
50 Atran, 2003, p. 1538.
51 Work by Susan Fiske, 2002, supports our concern with the consequences of the in-group/out-group bias but suggests that the more dangerous expressions of this bias come from a minority of more extreme in-group members. She did find the bias active even among those she categorized as "well intentioned moderates" who tended to express this bias by showing preferential treatment to in-group members, but not necessarily imposing punishment on out-group members.
52 I have suggested that my focus on monotheism was not intended to imply that this paradigm does not apply to other religious traditions. My sense is that this argument will apply just as well to other religious traditions, although the details of the analysis will differ. I can do no more at this point than suggest this and recognize that further study may prove me wrong in this. In fact, I must admit that elements of Buddhist ethics may provide an exception to the rule. However, even Buddhism, which as a moral system presents what may be a truly universal moral community in theoretical terms, has, in its implementation, given expression to our evolved moral psychology. See Juergensmeyer, 2001, pp. 112–116, for a discussion of violence and Buddhism.
53 Kant, 1785.
54 See Bentham, 1789, and Mill, 1863, for the classic statements of this position.
55 Kant's system demands a rational ability inconsistent with the best available data on how our evolved mind works. It places too great a demand on impartiality in our reasoning abilities, which we now recognize are inextricably bound up with affective elements of our mental toolbox – something which, for Kant, negates the moral quality of a judgment. Also, reason's role in providing post hoc rationalizations of our moral intuitions, along with our tendency toward self-deception, make it nearly impossible to assess the impartiality of our moral decisions (see Greene, 2003, 2007; Teehan, 2003; Hauser, 2006). Utilitarianism sought to correct Kant's heavy emphasis on reason to the detriment of emotion by bringing sentiment into the equation, but it too demands impartiality inconsistent with the demands of our evolved psychology.
56 Greene, 2007, argues that deontological systems, such as Kant's, actually are grounded in moral emotions that are given rationalized expressions.
57 Ibid, p. xv.
58 Ibid, p. 20.

59 Ibid.
60 Ibid., pp. 59–83.
61 Ibid., pp. 14–15.
62 Ibid., pp. 118–119.
63 Ibid., p. 79.
64 Ibid., pp. 66–67.
65 A moral system that works with a similar appreciation for human diversity as a path to a larger moral community is set out by Kwame Anthony Appiah, in his *Cosmopolitanism: Ethics in a World of Strangers*.
66 James, 1902, uses this term to set apart those beliefs that go beyond what strictly follows from the evidence but that appear the best conclusions consistent with one's moral/intellectual outlook. It also requires openness to revision as more evidence becomes available.
67 I borrow this from C.S. Peirce, 1877.
68 Erich Fromm, 1959, draws a distinction between "authoritarian" and "humanistic" that is in line with this argument.
69 For a recent, valuable discussion of Dewey's ideas on religion, see Rogers, 2009.
70 Dewey, 1934, pp. 57–58.
71 Tillich, 1957.

BIBLIOGRAPHY

Alcorta, Candace, and Sosis, Richard. 2005. Ritual, emotion, and sacred symbols: the evolution of religion as an adaptive complex. *Human Nature* 16, no. 4 (Winter): 323–359.

Alencar, Anuska Irene, Siqueira, José de Oliveira, and Yamamoto, Maria Emilia. 2008. Does group size matter? Cheating and cooperation in Brazilian school children. *Evolution and Human Behavior* 29, no. 1: 42–48.

Alexander, Richard. 1987. *The Biology of Moral Systems: Foundations of Human Behavior*. New York: Aldine de Gruyter.

Alles, Gregory. 2006. The so-called cognitive optimum and the cost of religious concepts. *Method and Theory in the Study of Religion* 18: 235–350.

Appiah, Kwame Anthony. 2006. *Cosmopolitanism: Ethics in a World of Strangers*. New York: W. W. Norton.

Aquinas, Thomas. 1981. *The Summa Theologica of St. Thomas Aquinas*. Christian Classics.

Asad, Talal. 1993. *Genealogies of Religion: Discipline and Reasons of Power in Christianity and Islam*. Baltimore, MD: Johns Hopkins University Press.

Asad, Talal. 2007. *On Suicide Bombing*. New York: Columbia University Press.

Athanasius. 1892. Life of St. Anthony. In *Nicene and Post-Nicene Fathers*, Second Series, Vol. 4. Alexander Roberts, James Donaldson, Philip Schaff, and Henry Wace, eds. Peabody, MA: Hendrickson Publishing, 1994.

Atran, Scott. 2002. *In Gods We Trust: The Evolutionary Landscape of Religion*. New York: Oxford University Press.

Atran, Scott. 2003. Genesis of suicide terrorism. *Science* 299 (March 7): 1534–1539.

Atran, Scott. 2004. Mishandling suicide terrorism. *Washington Quarterly* 27, no. 3: 67–90.

Atran, Scott, and Norenzayan, Ara. 2004. Religion's evolutionary landscape: counterintuition, commitment, compassion, communion. *Behavioral and Brain Sciences* 27: 713–730.

Augustine. 1887. Correction of the Donatists. In *Nicene and Post-Nicene Fathers, First Series*, Vol. 4. Alexander Roberts, James Donaldson, Philip Schaff, and Henry Wace, eds. Peabody, MA: Hendrickson Publishing, 1994.

Axelrod, Robert. 2006. *The Evolution of Cooperation*, revised ed. New York: Basic Books.

Axelrod, Robert, and Hamilton, W.D. 1981. The evolution of cooperation. *Science* 211: 1390–1396.

Barash, David. 2009. Intrafamily conflict in the Bible and biological theory. In Goldberg, ed., *Judaism in Biological Perspective*, pp. 62–83.

Barash, David, and Barash, Nanelle. 2005. *Madame Bovary's Ovaries: A Darwinian Look at Literature*. New York: Delacorte Press.

Barkow, Jerome. 2005. *Missing the Revolution: Darwinism for Social Scientists*. New York: Oxford University Press.

Barkow, Jerome, Cosmides, Leda, and Tooby, John. 1992. *The Adapted Mind: Evolutionary Psychology and the Generation of Culture*. New York: Oxford University Press.

Barrett, Justin. 1999. Theological correctness: cognitive constraint and the study of religion. *Method and Theory in the Study of Religion* 11: 325–339.

Barrett, Justin. 2004. *Why Would Anyone Believe in God?* Walnut Creek, CA: AltaMira Press.

Barrett, Justin. 2009. Cognitive science, religion, and theology. In Schloss and Murray, eds., *The Believing Primate*.

Barrett, Justin, and Nyhoff, M. A. 2001. Spreading non-natural concepts: The role of intuitive conceptual structures in memory and transmission of cultural materials. *Journal of Cognition and Culture* 1: 69–100.

Barrett, Justin, and Richert, R. 2003. Anthropomorphism or preparedness? Exploring children's concept of God. *Review of Religious Research* 44: 300–312.

Barrett, Justin, Richert, R. and Driesenga, A. 2001. God's beliefs versus mother's: the development of non-human agent concepts. *Child Development* 72: 50–65.

Barton, John. 2002. *Ethics and the Old Testament*, 2nd ed. London: SCM Press.

Benedict XVI. 2006. The seer of Patmos: address to the general audience, 23 August. http://www.vatican.va/holy_father/benedict_xvi/audiences/2006/documents/hf_ben-xvi_aud_20060823_en.html (accessed 10/13/09).

Bentham, Jeremy. 1789 (1988). *The Principles of Morals and Legislation*. Amherst, NY: Prometheus.

Bering, Jesse. 2002. Intuitive conceptions of dead agents' minds: the natural foundations of afterlife beliefs as phenomenological boundary. *Journal of Cognition and Culture* 2, no. 4: 263–308.

Bering, Jesse. 2003. On reading symbolic random events: children's causal reasoning about unexpected occurrences. Paper presented at the Psychological and Cognitive Foundations of Religiosity Conference, Atlanta, GA.

Bering, Jesse. 2006. The folk psychology of souls. *Behavioral and Brain Sciences* 29: 453–462.

Bering, Jesse, and Johnson, Dominic. 2005. "O Lord … you perceive my thoughts from afar": recursiveness and the evolution of supernatural agency. *Journal of Cognition and Culture* 5, nos. 1–2: 118–142.

Bering, Jesse, and Shackelford, Todd. 2004. Supernatural agents may have provided adaptive social information. *Behavioral and Brain Sciences*, 27, no. 6: 732–733.

Bering, Jesse, McLeod, Katrina, and Shackelford, Todd. 2005. Reasoning about dead agents reveals possible adaptive trends. *Human Nature* 16, no. 4 (Winter): 360–381.

Berlinerblau, Jacques. 2005. *The Secular Bible: Why Nonbelievers Must Take Religion Seriously*. New York: Cambridge University Press.

Bible. Revised Standard Version. Ignatius Press, 1994.

Bird, Rebecca Bliege, Bird, D. W., Smith, E. A., and Kushnick, G. C. 2002. Risk and reciprocity in Meriam food sharing. *Evolution and Human Behavior* 23: 297–321.

Blair, Richard. 1995. A cognitive developmental approach to morality: investigating the psychopath. *Cognition* 571: 1–29.

Blair, R., Jones, L., Clark, F., and Smith, M. 1997. The psychopathic individual: a lack of responsiveness to distress cues? *Psychophysiology* 34: 192–198.

Blenkinsopp, Joseph. 2000. *The Pentateuch: An Introduction to the First Five Books of the Bible*. Yale University Press.

Bloom, Paul. 2004. *Descartes' Baby: How the Science of Child Development Explains What Makes Us Human*. New York: Basic Books.

Bloom, Paul. 2005. Is God an accident? *Atlantic Monthly* (December): 105–112.

Boehm, Christopher. 1999. *Hierarchy in the Forest: The Evolution of Egalitarian Behavior*. Cambridge, MA: Harvard University Press.

Boyarin, Daniel. 1999. *Dying for God: Martyrdom and the Making of Christianity and Judaism*. Stanford, CA: Stanford University Press.

Boyarin, Daniel, and Boyarin, Jonathan. 1993. Diaspora: generation and the ground of Jewish identity. *Critical Inquiry* 19: 693–725.

Boyd, Robert, and Richerson, Peter J. 1985. *Culture and the Evolutionary Process*. Chicago: University of Chicago Press.

Boyd, Robert, and Richerson, Peter J. 1988. The evolution of reciprocity in sizable groups. *Journal of Theoretical Biology* 132: 337–356.

Boyd, Robert, and Richerson, Peter J. 1992. Punishment allows the evolution of cooperation (or anything else) in sizable groups. *Ethology and Sociobiology* 13: 171–195.

Boyd, Robert, and Richerson, Peter J. 2002. Group beneficial norms spread rapidly in a structured population. *Journal of Theoretical Biology* 215: 287–296.

Boyd, Robert, and Richerson, Peter J., eds. 2005. *The Origin and Evolution of Cultures*. New York: Oxford University Press.

Boyd, Robert, Gintis, Herbert, Bowles, Samuel, and Richerson, Peter J. 2003. The evolution of altruistic punishment. *Proceedings of the National Academy of Sciences* 100: 3531–3535.

Boyer, Pascal. 2001. *Religion Explained: The Evolutionary Origins of Religious Thought*. New York: Basic Books.

Boyer, Pascal, and Lienard, Pierre. 2006. Why ritualized behavior? Precaution systems and action parsing in developmental, pathological and cultural rituals. *Behavioral and Brain Sciences* 29: 595–613.

Bulbulia, Joseph. 2004. The cognitive and evolutionary psychology of religion. *Biology and Philosophy* 19: 655–686.

Bulbulia, Joseph. 2008. Meme infection or religious niche construction? An adaptationist alternative to the cultural maladaptationist hypothesis. *Method and Theory in the Study of Religion* 20: 1–42.

Bulbulia, Joseph. 2009. Religiosity as mental time-travel: cognitive adaptations for religious behavior. In Schloss and Murray, eds., *The Believing Primate*, pp. 44–75.

Bulbulia, Joseph, Sosis, R., Harris, E., Genet, R., Genet, C., and Wyman, K., eds. 2008. *The Evolution of Religion: Studies, Theories, and Critiques*. Santa Margarita, CA: Collins Foundation Press.

Burlein, Ann. 2002. *Lift High the Cross: Where White Supremacy and the Christian Right Converge*. Durham, NC, and London: Duke University Press.

Buss, David. 1994. *The Evolution of Desire: Strategies of Human Mating*. New York: Basic Books.

Buss, David. 2005. *The Murderer Next Door: Why the Mind Is Designed to Kill*. New York: Penguin Books.

Carroll, Joseph. 1995. Evolution and literary theory. *Human Nature* 6, no. 2: 119–134.

Casebeer, William D. 2003. *Natural Ethical Facts: Evolution, Connectionism, and Moral Cognition*. Cambridge, MA: MIT Press.

Cashdan, Elizabeth. 2001. Ethnocentrism and xenophobia: a cross-cultural study. *Current Anthropology* 42, no. 5: 760–765.

Chapman, Michael. 2004. Hominid failings: An evolutionary basis for sins in individuals and corporations. In Clayton and Schloss, eds., *Evolution and Ethics*.

Childs, Brevard S. 1974. *The Book of Exodus: A Critical Theological Commentary*. Louisville, KY: Westminster John Knox Press.

Clayton, Philip, and Schloss, Jeffrey, eds. 2004. *Evolution and Ethics: Human Morality in Biological and Religious Perspective*. Grand Rapids, MI: Wm. B. Eerdmans.

Cobb, L. Stephanie. 2008. *Dying to Be Men: Gender and Language in Early Christian Martyr Texts*. New York: Columbia University Press.

Cohen, Adam, Rozin, Paul, and Keltner, Dacher. 2004. Different religions, different emotions. *Behavioral and Brain Sciences* 27, no. 6: 734–735.

Cohen, Adam, Hill, Peter, Shariff, Azim, and Rozin, Paul. 2008. Furthering the evolution of discussion on religion: multi-method study, universality, and cultural variation. In Bulbulia et al., eds., *Evolution of Religion*, pp. 311–317.

Cohen, Shaye. 1987. *From the Maccabees to the Mishnah*. Louisville, KY: Westminster Press.

Collins, Francis. 2007. *The Language of God: A Scientist Presents Evidence for Belief*. New York: Free Press.

Collins, John J. 2004a. *Does the Bible Justify Violence?* Minneapolis, MN: Fortress Press.

Collins, John J. 2004b. The zeal of Phinehas, the Bible, and the legitimation of violence. In *The Destructive Power of Religion: Violence in Judaism, Christianity, and Islam*, vol. 1, J. Harold Ellens, ed. Westport, CT: Praeger.

Corballis, M., and Lea, S., eds. 1999. *The Descent of Mind: Psychological Perspectives on Hominid Evolution*. New York: Oxford University Press.

Cronk, Lee. 2007. The influence of cultural framing on play in the trust game: a Maasai example. *Evolution and Human Behavior* 28: 352–358.

Daly, Martin, and Wilson, Margo. 1988. *Homicide*. New York: Aldine de Gruyter.

Daly, Martin, and Wilson, Margo. 1999. *The Truth about Cinderella: A Darwinian View of Parental Love*. Yale University Press.

Damasio, Antonio. 1994. *Descartes' Error: Emotion, Reason, and the Human Brain*. New York: G. P. Putnam.

Darwin, Charles. 1859 (2001). *On the Origin of Species*. Cambridge, MA: Harvard University Press.

Davies, G. Henton Davies. 1967. *Exodus: Introduction and Commentary*. London: SCM Press.

Davis, Hank. 2009. *Caveman Logic: The Persistence of Primitive Thinking in a Modern World*. Amherst, NY: Prometheus Books.

Dawkins, Richard. 1976. *The Selfish Gene*. Oxford: Oxford University Press.

Dawkins, Richard. 2006. *The God Delusion*. New York: Houghton Mifflin.

DeBruine, Lisa. 2002. Facial resemblance enhances trust. *Proceedings of the Royal Society of London B* 269, no. 1498: 1307–1312.

DeBruine, Lisa. 2004. Facial resemblance increases the attractiveness of same-sex faces more than other-sex faces. *Proceedings of the Royal Society of London B* 271, no. 1552: 2085–2090.

DeBruine, Lisa. 2005. Trustworthy but not lust-worthy: Context-specific effects of facial resemblance. *Proceedings of the Royal Society of London B* 272: 919–922.

Deeley, Peter. 2004. The religious brain: turning ideas into convictions. *Anthropology and Medicine* 11, no. 3: 245–267.

Dennett, Daniel. 1995. *Darwin's Dangerous Idea*. New York: Simon and Schuster.

Dennett, Daniel. 2006. *Breaking the Spell: Religion as a Natural Phenomenon*. New York: Viking.

DeWaal, Frans. 1983. *Chimpanzee Politics: Power and Sex among Apes*. New York: HarperCollins.

DeWaal, Frans. 1996. *Good Natured: The Origins of Right and Wrong in Humans and Other Animals*. Cambridge, MA: Harvard University Press.

DeWaal, Frans. 2006. *Primates and Philosophers: How Morality Evolved*. Princeton, NJ: Princeton University Press.

Dewey, John. 1909. *The Influence of Darwin on Philosophy*. Gloucester, MA: Peter Smith.

Dewey, John. 1920. *Reconstruction in Philosophy: The Collected Works of John Dewey, the Middle Works, 1899–1924*. Jo Ann Boydston, ed. Carbondale: Southern Illinois University Press.

Dewey, John. 1922. *Human Nature and Conduct: The Collected Works of John Dewey, the Middle Works, 1899–1924*. Jo Ann Boydston, ed. Carbondale: Southern Illinois University Press.

Dewey, John. 1929. *The Quest for Certainty: The Collected Works of John Dewey, the Later Works, 1925–1953*. Jo Ann Boydston, ed. Carbondale: Southern Illinois University Press.

Dewey, John. 1932. *Ethics: The Collected Works of John Dewey, the Later Works, 1925–1953*. Jo Ann Boydston, ed. Southern Illinois University Press.

Dewey, John. 1934. *A Common Faith: The Collected Works of John Dewey, the Later Works, 1925–1953.* Jo Ann Boydston, ed. Carbondale: Southern Illinois University Press.

Diamond, Jared. 1999. *Guns, Germs, and Steel: The Fates of Human Societies.* New York: W. W. Norton.

Dow, James. 2006. The evolution of religion: three anthropological approaches. *Method and Theory in the Study of Religion* 18: 67–91.

Dunbar, Robin. 1997. *Grooming, Gossip and the Evolution of Language.* Cambridge, MA: Harvard University Press.

Efferson, Charles, Lalive, Rafeal, Richerson, Peter, McElreath, Richard, and Lubell, Mark. 2008. Conformists and mavericks: the empirics of frequency-dependent cultural transmission. *Evolution and Human Behavior* 29: 56–64.

Ehrman, Bart. 2003. *Lost Christianities: The Battles for Scripture and the Faiths We Never Knew.* New York: Oxford University Press.

Ehrman, Bart. 2005. *Misquoting Jesus: The Story Behind Who Changed the Bible and Why.* New York: HarperOne.

Ehrman, Bart. 2006. *The Lost Gospel of Judas Iscariot: A New Look at Betrayer and Betrayed.* New York: Oxford University Press.

Ellingsen, Tore, and Johannesson, Magnus. 2008. Anticipated verbal feedback induces altruistic behavior. *Evolution and Human Behavior* 29: 100–105.

Epicurus. 1994. *The Epicurus Reader: Selected Writings and Testimonia.* Brad Inwood and Lloyd Gerson, eds. Indianapolis, IN: Hackett Publishing.

Ermer, Elsa, Cosmides, Leda, and Tooby, John. 2008. Relative status regulates risky decision making about resources in men: evidence for the co-evolution of motivation and cognition. *Evolution and Human Behavior* 29: 106–118.

Fehr, Ernst, and Fischbacher, Urs. 2003. The nature of human altruism. *Nature* 425 (Oct.): 785–791.

Fehr, Ernst, and Fischbacher, Urs. 2004. Social norms and human cooperation. *Trends in Cognitive Sciences* 8, no. 4 (April): 185–190.

Fehr, Ernst, and Gachter, Simon. 2002. Altruistic punishment in humans. *Nature* 415 (Jan.): 137–140.

Fehr, Ernst, and Gintis, Herbert. 2007. Human motivation and social cooperation: experimental and analytical foundations. *Annual Review of Sociology* 33, no. 3: 1–22.

Fewell, Danna Nolan, and Gunn, David. 1993. *Gender, Power, and Promise: The Subject of the Bible's First Story.* Nashville, TN: Abingdon.

Finkel, Daniel, Swartwout, Paul, and Sosis, Richard. 2009. The socio-religious brain: a developmental model. *Proceedings of the British Academy* 158: 287–312.

Finkelstein, Israel, and Silberman, Neil Asher. 2001. *The Bible Unearthed: Archaeology's New Vision of Ancient Israel and the Origin of Its Sacred Texts.* New York: Free Press.

Fisher, Helen. 1994. *Anatomy of Love: A Natural History of Mating, Marriage, and Why We Stray.* New York: Ballantine Books.

Fiske, Susan. 2002. What we know about bias and intergroup conflict. The problem of the century. *Current Directions in Psychological Science* 11, no. 4: 123–128.

Flanagan, Owen. 1991. *Identity, Character, and Morality: Essays in Moral Psychology.* Cambridge, MA: Bradford Books.

Foot, Phillipa. 1978 (2003). The problem of abortion and the doctrine of double effect. In *Virtues and Vices and other Essays in Moral Philosophy*. Oxford: Oxford University Press.

Frank, Robert. 1988. *Passions within Reasons*. New York: W. W. Norton.

Friedman, Richard. 1997. *Who Wrote the Bible?* New York: HarperOne.

Fromm, Erich. 1959. *Psychoanalysis and Religion*. Yale University Press.

Gibbard, Allen. 1990. *Wise Choices, Apt Feelings: A Theory of Normative Judgment*. Cambridge, MA: Harvard University Press.

Gibbon, Edward. 1781 (1994). *The Decline and Fall of the Roman Empire*, vol. 2. David Womersley, ed. Allen Lane: London: Penguin Press.

Ginges, Jeremy, Atran, Scott, Medin, Douglas, and Shikaki, Khalil. 2007. Sacred bounds on rational resolution of violent political conflict. *Proceedings of the National Academy of Science* 104, no. 18: 7357–7360.

Gintis, Herbert. 2000. Strong reciprocity and human sociality. *Journal of Theoretical Biology* 206: 169–179.

Gintis, Herbert, Smith, Eric, and Bowles, Samuel. 2001. Costly signaling and cooperation. *Journal of Theoretical Biology* 213: 103–119.

Gintis, Herbert, Bowles, Samuel, Boyd, Robert, and Fehr, Ernst. 2003. Explaining altruistic behavior in humans. *Evolution and Human Behavior* 24: 153–172.

Goldberg, Rick, ed. 2009. *Judaism in Biological Perspective: Biblical Lore and Judaic Practices*. Boulder, CO: Paradigm.

Greenberg, Jeff, Pyszczynski, T., Solomon, S., Rosenblatt, A., Veeder, M., Kirkland, S., and Lyon, D. 1990. Evidence of terror management theory II: the effects of mortality salience on reactions to those who threaten or bolster the cultural worldview. *Journal of Personality and Social Psychology* 58, no. 2: 308–318.

Greene, Joshua. 2003. From neural "is" to moral "ought": What are the moral implications of neuroscientific moral psychology? *Nature Reviews/Neuroscience* 4 (Oct.): 847–850.

Greene, Joshua. 2005. Cognitive neuroscience and the structure of the moral mind. In Carruthers, P., Laurence, S., and Stich, S., eds., *The Innate Mind: Structure and Contents*. New York: Oxford University Press, pp. 338–352.

Greene, Joshua. 2007. The secret joke of Kant's soul. In W. Sinnott-Armstrong, ed., *Moral Psychology*, vol. 3: *The Neuroscience of Morality: Emotion, Disease, and Development*. Cambridge, MA: MIT Press.

Greene, Joshua, and Haidt, Jonathan. 2002. How (and where) does moral judgment work? *Trends in Cognitive Sciences* 6, no. 12 (Dec.): 517–523.

Greene, Joshua, Sommerville, R. B., Nystrom, L. E., Darley, J. M., and Cohen, J. D. 2001. An fMRI investigation of emotional engagement in moral judgment. *Science* 293: 2105–2108.

Greene, Joshua, Nystrom, L. E., Engell, A. D., Darley, J. M., and Cohen, J. D. 2004. The neural bases of cognitive conflict and control in moral judgment. *Neuron* 44 (Oct.): 389–400.

Gurven, Michael. 2004. Reciprocal altruism and food sharing decisions among Hiwi and Ache hunter-gatherers. *Behavioral Ecological Sociobiology* 56: 366–380.

Gurven Michael. 2006. The evolution of contingent cooperation. *Current Anthropology* 47, no. 1: 185–192.

Gurven, Michael, Allen-Arave, Wesly, Hill, Kim, and Hurtado, Magdalena. 2000. "It's a Wonderful Life": signaling generosity among the Ache of Paraguay. *Evolution and Human Behavior* 21: 263–282.

Guthrie, Stewart. 1980. A cognitive theory of religion. *Current Anthropology* 21, no. 2: 181–194.

Guthrie, Stewart. 1993. *Faces in the Clouds: A New Theory of Religion*. Oxford: Oxford University Press.

Guthrie, Stewart. 2002. Animal animism: evolutionary roots of religious cognition. In Pyysiainen and Anttonen, eds., *Current Approaches in the Cognitive Science of Religion*, pp. 38–67.

Guthrie, Stewart. 2007. Anthropology and anthropomorphism in religion. In Whitehouse and Laidlaw, eds., *Religion, Anthropology, and Cognitive Science*, pp. 37–62

Guthrie, Stewart. 2008. Spiritual beings: a Darwinian, cognitive account. In Bulbulia et al., eds., *Evolution of Religion*, pp. 239–245.

Haidt, Jonathan. 2001. The emotional dog and its rational tail: a social intuitionist approach to moral judgment. *Psychological Review* 108, no. 4: 814–834.

Haidt, Jonathan. 2006. *The Happiness Hypothesis: Finding Modern Truth in Ancient Wisdom*. New York: Basic Books.

Haidt, Jonathan. 2009. Moral psychology and the misunderstanding of religion. In Schloss and Murray, eds., *The Believing Primate*.

Haley, K. J., and Kessler, D. M. T. 2005. Nobody is watching? Subtle cues affect generosity in an anonymous economic game. *Evolution and Human Behavior* 26: 245–256.

Hamilton, William D. 1964. Genetic evolution of social behavior, I and II. *Journal of Theoretical Biology* 7: 1–52.

Hansen, Ian, and Norenzayan, Ara. 2006. Yang and yin and heaven and hell: untangling the complex relationship between religion and intolerance. In McNamara, ed., *Where God and Science Meet*.

Harris, Sam. 2004. *The End of Faith: Religion, Terror, and the Future of Reason*. New York: W. W. Norton.

Harris, Sam. 2006. *Letter to a Christian Nation*. New York: Alfred A. Knopf.

Hartung, John. 1995. Love thy neighbor: the evolution of in-group morality. *Skeptic* 3, no. 4: 86–99.

Haught, John. 2000. *God after Darwin: A Theology of Evolution*. Boulder, CO: Westview Press.

Haught, John. 2003. *Deeper Than Darwin: The Prospect for Religion in the Age of Evolution*. Boulder, CO: Westview Press.

Haught, John. 2008. *God and the New Atheism: A Critical Response to Dawkins, Harris and Hitchens*. Louisville, KY: Westminster John Knox Press.

Haught, John. 2009. Theology and evolution: how much can biology explain? In Schloss and Murray, eds., *The Believing Primate*.

Hauser, Marc D. 2006. *Moral Minds: How Nature Designed Our Universal Sense of Right and Wrong*. New York: HarperCollins.

Henrich, Joseph, and Boyd, Robert. 2001. Why people punish defectors: weak conformist transmission can stabilize costly enforcement of norms in cooperative dilemmas. *Journal of Theoretical Biology* 208: 78–89.

Henrich, Joseph, McElreath, R., Barr, A., Ensminger, J., Barrett, C., Bolyanatz, A., Cardenas, J.C., Gurven, M., Gwako, E., Henrich, N., Lesorogol, C., Marlowe, F., Tracer, D., and Ziker, J. 2006. Costly punishment across human societies. *Science* 312 (June): 1767–1770.

Hinde, Robert. 1999. *Why Gods Persist: A Scientific Approach to Religion*. London and New York: Routledge.

Hinde, Robert. 2002. *Why Good Is Good: The Sources of Morality*. London and New York: Routledge.

Hitchens, Christopher. 2007. *God Is Not Great: How Religion Poisons Everything*. New York: Twelve, Hachette Book Group.

Hobbes, Thomas. 1688 (1996). *Leviathan*. Cambridge: Cambridge University Press.

Hume, David. 1739 (2000). *A Treatise of Human Nature*. New York: Oxford University Press.

Hume, David. 1757 (2003). *Principal Writings on Religion Including Dialogues Concerning Natural Religion and the Natural History of Religion*. Oxford World's Classics. J. C. A. Gaskin, ed. Oxford: Oxford University Press.

Imhof, Lorens A., Fudenberg, Drew, and Nowak, Martin A. 2005. Evolutionary cycles of cooperation and defection. *Proceedings of the National Academy of Sciences* 102, no. 31 (Aug.): 10797–10800.

Irons, William. 1996. In our own self image: the evolution of morality, deception, and religion. *Skeptic* 4, no. 2: 50–61.

Irons, William. 2001. Religion as a hard-to-fake sign of commitment. In Nesse, ed., *Evolution and the Capacity for Commitment*.

Jackendoff, R. S. 1987. *Consciousness and the Computational Mind*. Cambridge, MA: MIT/Bradford Books.

James, William. 1902. *The Varieties of Religious Experience*. Martin E. Marty, ed. New York: Penguin.

Johnson, Dominic. 2005. God's punishment and public goods: a test of the supernatural punishment hypothesis in 186 world cultures. *Human Nature* 16, no. 4 (Winter): 410–446.

Johnson, Dominic, and Bering, Jesse. 2006. Hand of God, mind of man: punishment and cognition in the evolution of cooperation. *Evolutionary Psychology* 4: 219–233.

Johnson, Dominic, and Kruger, Oliver. 2004. The good of wrath: supernatural punishment and the evolution of cooperation. *Political Theology* 5, no. 2: 159–176.

Jones, Doug. 2003a. The generative psychology of kinship. Part 1. Cognitive universals and evolutionary psychology. *Evolution and Human Behavior* 24: 303–319.

Jones, Doug. 2003b. The generative psychology of kinship. Part 2. Generating variation from universal building blocks with Optimality Theory. *Evolution and Human Behavior* 24: 320–350.

Joyce, Richard. 2006a. Is human morality innate? In Carruthers, P., Laurence, S., and Stich, S., eds., *The Innate Mind: Culture and Cognition*. New York: Oxford University Press, pp. 257–279.

Joyce, Richard. 2006b. *The Evolution of Morality*. Cambridge, MA: MIT Press.

Juergensmeyer, Mark. 1993. *The New Cold War: Religious Nationalism Confronts the Secular State.* Berkeley and Los Angeles: University of California Press.

Juergensmeyer, Mark. 2001. *Terror in the Mind of God: The Global Rise of Religious Violence.* Berkeley and Los Angeles: University of California Press.

Kahneman, Daniel, and Tversky, Amos. 1982. Variants of uncertainty. In Kahneman, D., Slovic, P., and Tversky, A., eds., *Judgement under Uncertainty: Heuristics and Biases.* Cambridge: Cambridge University Press.

Kant, Immanuel. 1785 (1988). *Groundwork of the Metaphysics of Morals.* Mary Gregor, ed. Cambridge: Cambridge University Press.

Kelemen, Deborah. 1999. Beliefs about purpose: on the origin of teleological thought. In Corballis and Lea, eds., *The Descent of Mind*, pp. 278–294.

Kelemen, Deborah. 2004a. Are children "intuitive theists"? Reasoning about purpose and design in nature. *Psychological Science* 15, no. 5: 295–301.

Kelemen, Deborah. 2004b. Counterintuition, existential anxiety, and religion as a by-product of the designing mind. *Behavioral and Brain Sciences* 27, no. 6: 739–740.

Kelemen, Deborah, and DiYanni, Cara. 2005. Intuitions about origins: purpose and intelligent design in children's reasoning about nature. *Journal of Cognition and Development* 6, no. 1: 3–31.

Keltner, Dacher, and Haidt, Jonathan. 2003. Approaching awe, a moral, spiritual, and aesthetic emotion. *Cognition and Emotion* 17, no. 2: pp. 297–314.

Kimball, Charles. 2002. *When Religion Becomes Evil.* New York: Harper Collins.

King, Barbara. 2007. *Evolving God.* New York: Doubleday.

Kirkpatrick, Lee. 2005. *Attachment, Evolution, and the Psychology of Religion.* New York: Guilford Press.

Krupp, Daniel, DeBruine, Lisa, and Barclay, Pat. 2008. A cue of kinship promotes cooperation for the public good. *Evolution and Human Behavior* 29, no. 1: 49–55.

Kugel, James L. 2007. *How to Read the Bible: A Guide to Scripture, Then and Now.* New York: Free Press.

Kung, Hans. 2007. *The Beginning of All Things: Science and Religion.* Grand Rapids, MI: Wm. B. Eerdmans.

Kurzban, Robert. 2002. Alas poor evolutionary psychology: Unfairly accused, unjustly condemned. *Human Nature Review* 2 (March): 99–109.

La Cerra, Peggy, and Bingham, Roger. 1998. The adaptive nature of the human neurocognitive architecture: an alternative model. *Proceedings of the National Academy of Sciences* 95 (Sept.): 11290–11294.

Lahti, David. 2004. "You have heard ... but I tell you ...": a test of the adaptive significance of moral evolution. In Clayton and Schloss, eds., *Evolution and Ethics.*

Lakoff, George, and Johnson, Mark. 1999. *Philosophy in the Flesh: The Embodied Mind and Its Challenge to Western Thought.* New York: Basic Books.

Landau, Mark Jordan, Greenberg, Jeff, and Solomon, Sheldon. 2004. The motivational underpinnings of religion. *Behavioral and Brain Sciences* 27, no. 6: 743–744.

Lawson, E. Thomas, and McCauley, Robert. 1990. *Rethinking Religion: Connecting Cognition and Culture.* Cambridge: Cambridge University Press.

Lieberman, D., Tooby, J., and Cosmides, L. 2003. Does morality have a biological basis? An empirical test of the factors governing moral sentiments regarding incest. *Proceedings of the Royal Society, London B* 270: 819–826.

Lieu, Judith. 2002. *Neither Jew nor Greek? Constructing Early Christianity.* Edinburgh: T&T Clark Press.

Lieu, Judith, North, John, and Rajak, Tessa, eds. 1994. *The Jews among Pagans and Christians in the Roman Empire.* London and New York: Routledge.

Lincoln, Bruce. 2003. *Holy Terrors: Thinking about Religion after September 11.* Chicago: University of Chicago Press.

Ludeman, Gerd. 1997. *The Unholy in Holy Scripture: The Dark Side of the Bible.* Louisville, KY: Westminster John Knox Press.

Luther, Martin. *Against the Murderous, Thieving Hordes of Peasants.* http://www.historyguide.org/earlymod/peasants1525.html (accessed 10/13/09).

Luther, Martin. *The Jews and Their Lies.* http://www.jewishvirtuallibrary.org/jsource/anti-semitism/Luther_on_Jews.html (accessed 10/13/09).

Magonet, Jonathan. 1996. *A Rabbi Reads the Bible.* London: SCM Press.

Malley, Brian. 2004. *How the Bible Works: An Anthropological Study of Evangelical Biblicism.* Walnut Creek, CA: AltaMira Press.

Mayr, Ernst. 1993. *One Long Argument: Charles Darwin and the Genesis of Modern Evolutionary Thought.* Cambridge, MA: Harvard University Press.

McCauley, Robert, and E. Thomas Lawson. 2002. *Bringing Ritual to Mind: Psychological Foundations of Cultural Forms.* Cambridge: Cambridge University Press.

McNamara, Patrick, ed. 2006. *Where God and Science Meet: How Brain and Evolutionary Studies Alter Our Understanding of Religion.* Westport, CT: Praeger.

Meeks, Wayne. 1986. *The Moral World of the First Christians.* Philadelphia: Westminster Press.

Meeks, Wayne. 1993. *The Origins of Christian Morality: The First Two Centuries.* Yale University Press.

Mill, John Stuart. 1863 (2002). *Utilitarianism.* George Sher, ed. Indianapolis, IN: Hackett Publishing.

Miller, Kenneth. 1999. *Finding Darwin's God: A Scientist's Search for the Common Ground Between God and Evolution.* New York: Cliff Street Books/HarperCollins.

Moss, Stanley. 2006. The good shepherd. In *New and Selected Poems.* New York: Seven Stories Press.

Murray, Michael, and Goldberg, Andrew. 2009. Evolutionary accounts of religion: explaining and explaining away. In Schloss and Murray, eds., *The Believing Primate.*

Nesse, Randolph. 1990. Evolutionary explanations of emotions. *Human Nature* 1, no. 3: 261–289.

Nesse, Randolph, ed. 2001. *Evolution and the Capacity for Commitment.* New York: Russell Sage Foundation.

Nesse, Randolph, and Williams, George. 1996. *Why We Get Sick: The New Science of Darwinian Medicine.* New York: Vintage.

Newberg, Anthony, D'Aquili, Eugene, Ruse, Vincent, 2001. *Why God Won't Go Away: Brain Science and the Biology of Belief.* New York: Ballantine Press.

Niditch, Susan. 1993. *War in the Hebrew Bible: A Study in the Ethics of Violence.* New York: Oxford University Press.

Nietzsche, Friedrich. 1892 (1978). *Thus Spoke Zarathustra.* New York: Penguin.

Norenzayan, Ara, and Shariff, Azim. 2008. The origin and evolution of religious prosociality. *Science* 322 (Oct. 3): 58–62.

North, John. 1992. The development of religious pluralism. In Lieu et al., eds., *Jews among Pagans.*

Nowak, Martin A. 2006. Five rules for the evolution of cooperation. *Science* 314: 1560–1563.

Nowak, Martin A., and Sigmund, Karl. 1998. Evolution of indirect reciprocity by image scoring. *Nature* 393: 573–577.

Nowak, Martin A., and Sigmund, Karl. 2005. Evolution of indirect reciprocity. *Nature* 437: 1291–1298.

O'Gorman, Rick, Wilson, David Sloan, and Miller, Ralph R. 2005. Altruistic punishing and helping differ in sensitivity to relatedness, friendship, and future interactions. *Evolution and Human Behavior* 26: 375–387.

O'Gorman, Rick, Wilson, David Sloan, and Miller, Ralph R. 2008. An evolved cognitive bias for social norms. *Evolution and Human Behavior* 29: 71–78.

Pacheco, Jorge M., Traulsen, Arne, and Nowak, Martin A. 2006. Active linking in evolutionary games. *Journal of Theoretical Biology* 243: 437–443.

Pagels, Elaine. 1979. *The Gnostic Gospels.* New York: Random House.

Pagels, Elaine. 1995. *The Origin of Satan.* New York: Vintage Books.

Pagels, Elaine. 2003. *Beyond Belief: The Secret Gospel of Thomas.* New York: Random House.

Panchanathan, Karthik, and Boyd, Robert. 2003. A tale of two defectors: the importance of standing for evolution of indirect reciprocity. *Journal of Theoretical Biology* 224: 115–126.

Panchanathan, Karthik, and Boyd, Robert. 2004. Indirect reciprocity can stabilize cooperation without the second-order free rider problem. *Nature* 432: 499–502.

Peirce, Charles Sanders. 1877. The fixation of belief. *Popular Science Monthly* 12: 1–15.

Pennock, Robert. 2000. *Tower of Babel: The Evidence against the New Creationism.* Cambridge, MA: MIT Press.

Pinker, Steven. 1997. *How the Mind Works.* New York: Norton.

Pope, Stephen. 1994. *The Evolution of Altruism and the Ordering of Love.* Washington, DC: Georgetown University Press.

Pressler, Carolyn. 1994. Sexual violence and Deuteronomic law. In Brenner, A., ed., *The Feminist Companion to Exodus to Deuteronomy.* London: Sheffield Academic Press.

Price, Michael E., Cosmides, Leda, and Tooby, John. 2002. Punitive sentiment as an anti-free rider psychological device. *Evolution and Human Behavior* 23: 203–231.

Provine, William. 1989, Evolution and the foundation of ethics. In Goodman, Steven L., ed., *Science, Technology, and Social Progress.* Cranbury, NJ: Lehigh University Press, p. 261.

Pyysiainen, Ilkka, and Anttonen, Veikko, eds. 2002. *Current Approaches in the Cognitive Science of Religion*. London: Continuum Press.

Qur'an. M. H. Shakir, trans. Elmhurst, NY: Tahrike Tarsile Qur'an.

Raine, Adrian, Lencz, T., Bihrle, S., LaCasse, L., and Colletti, P. 2000. Reduced prefrontal gray matter volume and reduced autonomic activity in antisocial personality disorder. *Archives of General Psychiatry* 57: 119–127.

Rajak, Tessa. 1992. The Jewish community and its boundaries. In Lieu et al., eds., *Jews among Pagans*.

Rawls, John. 1971. *A Theory of Justice*. Cambridge, MA: Harvard University Press.

Richerson, Peter, and Boyd, Robert. 2005. *Not by Genes Alone: How Culture Transformed Human Evolution*. Chicago: University of Chicago Press.

Richerson, Peter, Boyd, Robert, and Henrich, Joseph. 2003. The cultural evolution of human cooperation. In Boyd and Richerson, eds., *Origin and Evolution of Cultures*.

Ridley, Matt. 1997. *The Origins of Virtue: Human Instincts and the Evolution of Cooperation*. New York: Viking Press.

Roes, Frans, and Raymond, Michel. 2003. Belief in moralizing gods. *Evolution and Human Behavior* 24, no. 2: 126–135.

Rogers, Melvin. 2009. *The Undiscovered Dewey: Religion, Morality, and the Ethos of Democracy*. New York: Columbia University Press.

Rogerson, John, Barton, John, Clines, David, and Joyce, Paul. 1998. *Beginning Old Testament Study*. Chalice Press.

Rolnick, Philip. 2004. Darwin's problems, neo-Darwinian solutions, and Jesus' love commands. In Clayton and Schloss, eds., *Evolution and Ethics*.

Rolston, Holmes III. 2004. The good Samaritan and his genes. In Clayton and Schloss, eds., *Evolution and Ethics*.

Rorty, Richard. 1979. *Philosophy and the Mirror of Nature*. Princeton, NJ: Princeton University Press.

Rottschaefer, William. 1997. *The Biology and Psychology of Moral Agency*. New York: Cambridge University Press.

Rozin, Paul, Haidt, Jonathan, and McCauley, Clark. 2000. Disgust. In Lewis, M., and Haviland-Jones, J. M., eds., *Handbook of Emotions*, 2nd ed. New York: Guilford Press, pp. 637–653.

Rubenstein, Richard E. 1999. *When Jesus Became God: The Epic Fight over Christ's Divinity in the Last Days of Rome*. Harcourt Brace.

Rue, Loyal. 2006. *Religion Is Not about God: How Spiritual Traditions Nurture Our Biological Nature and What to Expect When They Fail*. New Brunswick, NJ: Rutgers University Press.

Ruffle, Bradley, and Sosis, Richard. 2006. Cooperation and the in-group-out-group bias: a field test on Israeli kibbutz members and city residents. *Journal of Economic Behavior and Organization* 60: 147–163.

Ruse, Michael. 2001. *Can a Darwinian Be a Christian? The Relationship between Science and Religion*. Cambridge: Cambridge University Press.

Sagarin, R., and Taylor, T., eds. *Natural Security: A Darwinian Approach to a Dangerous World*. Berkeley and Los Angeles: University of California Press.

Sanders, E. P. 1977. *Paul and Palestinian Judaism*. Philadelphia: Fortress Press.

Schloss, Jeffrey, and Murray, Michael, eds. 2009. *The Believing Primate: Scientific, Philosophical, and Theological Reflections on the Origin of Religion*. New York: Oxford University Press.

Schwartz, Regina. 1997. *The Curse of Cain: The Violent Legacy of Monotheism*. Chicago: University of Chicago Press.

Segal, Alan. 2004. *Life after Death: A History of the Afterlife in Western Religion*. New York: Doubleday.

Sen, Amartya. 2006. *Identity and Violence: The Illusion of Destiny*. New York: W. W. Norton.

Shanks, Niall. 2007. *God, the Devil, and Darwin: A Critique of Intelligent Design Theory*. New York: Oxford University Press.

Shariff, Azim, and Norenzayan, Ara. 2007. God is watching you: priming God concepts increase prosocial behavior in an anonymous economic game. *Psychological Science* 18, no. 9: 803–809.

Shariff, Azim, Cohen, Adam, and Norenzayan, Ara. 2008. The devil's advocate: secular arguments diminish both implicit and explicit religious belief. *Journal of Cognition and Culture* 8: 417–423.

Shell, Marc. 1991. Marranos (pigs), or from co-existence to toleration. *Critical Inquiry* 17: 306–335.

Shermer, Michael. 2004. *The Science of Good and Evil: Why People Cheat, Gossip, Care, Share, and Follow the Golden Rule*. New York: Henry Holt.

Singer, Peter. 1981. *The Expanding Circle: Ethics and Sociobiology*. New York: Farrar Straus & Giroux.

Slone, D. Jason. 2004. *Theological Incorrectness: Why People Believe What They Shouldn't*. New York: Oxford University Press.

Smith, Adam. 1759 (2000). *The Theory of Moral Sentiments*. Amherst, NY: Prometheus.

Smith, David Livingstone. 2007. *The Most Dangerous Animal: Human Nature and the Origins of War*. New York: St. Martin's Press.

Solomon, Sheldon, Greenberg, Jeff, and Pyszczynski, Tom. 1991. A terror management theory of social behavior: the psychological functions of self-esteem and cultural worldviews. *Advances in Experimental Social Psychology*, vol. 24. San Diego: Academic Press, pp. 93–159.

Soltis, Richard, Richerson, Peter, and Boyd, Robert. 1995. Can group functional behaviors evolve by cultural group selection? An empirical test. *Current Anthropology* 36: 473–494.

Sosis, Richard. 2000. Religion and intra-group cooperation: preliminary results of a comparative analysis of utopian communities. *Cross-Cultural Research* 34: 70–87.

Sosis, Richard. 2003. Why aren't we all Hutterites? Costly signaling theory and religious behavior. *Human Nature* 14: 91–127.

Sosis, Richard. 2006. Religious behaviors, badges, and bans: signaling theory and the evolution of religion. In McNamara, Patrick, ed., *Where God and Science Meet*.

Sosis, Richard. 2007. Psalms for safety: magico-religious responses to threats of terror. *Current Anthropology* 48: 903–911.

Sosis, Richard. 2008. Pigeons, foxholes, and the book of Psalms. In Bulbulia et al., eds., *Evolution of Religion*, pp. 103–109.

Sosis, Richard. 2009. Why are synagogue services so long? An evolutionary examination of Jewish ritual signals. In Goldberg, ed., *Judaism in Biological Perspective*, pp. 199–233.

Sosis, Richard, and Alcorta, Candace. 2003. Signaling, solidarity, and the sacred: the evolution of religious behavior. *Evolutionary Anthropology* 12: 264–274.

Sosis, Richard, and Alcorta, Candace. 2004. Is religion adaptive? *Behavioral and Brain Sciences*. 27, no. 6: 749–750.

Sosis, Richard, and Alcorta, Candace. 2008. Militants and martyrs: evolutionary perspectives on religion and terrorism. In Sagarin and Taylor, eds., *Natural Security*.

Sosis, Richard, and Bressler, E. 2003. Cooperation and commune longevity: a test of the costly-signaling theory of religion. *Cross-Cultural Research* 37: 211–239.

Sosis, Richard, Kress, Howard, and Boster, James. 2007. Scars for war: evaluating alternative signaling explanations for cross-cultural variance in ritual costs. *Evolution and Human Behavior* 28: 234–247.

Sperber, Dan. 1996. *Explaining Culture: A Naturalistic Approach*. Oxford: Blackwell.

Sperber, Dan. 2000. Metarepresentations in an evolutionary perspective. In *Metarepresentations: A Multidisciplinary Perspective*. Oxford: Oxford University Press, pp. 117–137.

Spinoza, Baruch. 1670 (1991). *Theological-Political Treatise*. Samuel Shirley, trans. Hackett Publishing.

Stambaugh, John, and Balch, David. 1986. *The New Testament in its Social Environment*. Philadelphia: Westminster Press.

Stark, Rodney. 1996. *The Rise of Christianity*. HarperSanFrancisco.

Stern, Jessica. 2003. *Terror in the Name of God: Why Religious Militants Kill*. New York: Ecco/Harper Collins.

Stevens, Jeffrey, and Hauser, Marc. 2004. Why be nice? Psychological constraints on the evolution of cooperation. *Trends in Cognitive Sciences* 8, no. 2: 60–65.

Swanson, G. E. 1960. *The Birth of the Gods*. University of Michigan Press.

Teehan, John. 1994. Character, integrity and Dewey's virtue ethics. *Transactions of the C. S. Peirce Society* 31, no. 4: 841–863.

Teehan, John. 1996. In defense of a naturalism. *Journal of Speculative Philosophy* 10, no. 2.

Teehan, John. 2002. Evolution and ethics: the Huxley/Dewey exchange. *Journal of Speculative Philosophy* 16, no. 3: 225–238.

Teehan, John. 2003. Kantian ethics: after Darwin. *Zygon: Journal of Religion and Science* 38, no. 1: 49–60.

Teehan, John. 2006. The evolutionary basis of religious ethics. *Zygon: Journal of Religion and Science* 41, no. 3: 747–774.

Teehan, John, and DiCarlo, Christopher. 2004. On the naturalistic fallacy: A conceptual basis for evolutionary ethics. *Evolutionary Psychology*, 2: 32–46

Teilhard de Chardin, Pierre. 1969. *Christianity and Evolution*. A Harvest Book. New York: Harcourt Brace Jovanovich.

Tillich, Paul. 1957. *Dynamics of Faith*. Perennial Classics/HarperCollins.

Theissen, Gerd. 1984 (1985). *Biblical Faith: An Evolutionary Approach*. Minneapolis, MN: Fortress Press.

Thomson, J. J. 1986. *Rights, Restitution, and Risk: Essays in Moral Theory*. Cambridge, MA: Harvard University Press.

Traulsen, Arne, and Nowak, Martin A. 2007. Chromodynamics of cooperation in finite populations. PLoS ONE 2(3): e270. doi:10.1371/journal.pone.0000270.

Traulsen, Arne, and Nowak, Martin A. 2006. Evolution of cooperation by multi-level selection. *Proceedings of the National Academy of Sciences* 103, no. 29 (July): 10952–10955.

Tremlin, Todd. 2006. *Minds and Gods: The Cognitive Foundations of Religion*. New York: Oxford University Press.

Tripolitis, Antonia. 2001. *Religions of the Hellenistic-Roman Age*. Grand Rapids, MI: Wm. B. Eerdmans.

Trivers, Robert. 1971. The evolution of reciprocal altruism. *Quarterly Review of Biology* 46: 35–57.

Vanneste, Sven, Verplaetse, Jan, Van Hiel, Alain, and Braeckman, Johan. 2007. Attention bias toward noncooperative people. A dot probe classification study in cheating detection. *Evolution and Human Behavior* 28, no. 4: 272–276.

Verplaetse, Jan, Vanneste, Sven, and Braeckman, Johan. 2007. You can judge a book by its cover: the sequel. A kernel of truth in predictive cheating detection. *Evolution and Human Behavior* 28, no. 4: 260–271.

Von Rad, Gerhard. 1958 (1991). *Holy War in Ancient Israel*. Grand Rapids. MI: William B. Eerdmans.

Whitehouse, Harvey. 2004. *Modes of Religiosity: A Cognitive Theory of Religious Transmission*. Walnut Creek, CA: AltaMira Press.

Whitehouse, Harvey, and Laidlaw, James, eds. 2007. *Religion, Anthropology, and Cognitive Science*. Durham, NC: Carolina Academic Press.

Whiten, Andrew, and Byrne, Richard. 1997. *Machiavellian Intelligence: Extensions and Evaluations*. Cambridge: Cambridge University Press.

Williams, Patricia. 2001. *Doing without Adam and Eve: Sociobiology and Original Sin*. Minneapolis, MN: Fortress Press.

Williams, Patricia. 2005. The fifth R: Jesus as evolutionary psychologist. *Theology and Science* 3, no. 2: 133–143.

Wilson, David Sloan. 2002. *Darwin's Cathedral: Evolution, Religion, and the Nature of Society*. Chicago: Chicago University Press.

Wilson, David Sloan. 2005.Testing major evolutionary hypotheses about religion with a random sample. *Human Nature* 16, no. 4 (Winter): 382–409.

Wilson, E. O. 1999. *Consilience: The Unity of Knowledge*. New York: Vintage.

Zahavi, A., and Zahavi, A. 1997. *The Handicap Principle: A Missing Piece of Darwin's Puzzle*. Oxford: Oxford University Press.

Zycinski, Jozef. 2006. *God and Evolution: Fundamental Questions of Christian Evolutionism*. Washington, DC: Catholic University of America Press.

INDEX